OXFORD THEOLOGICAL MONOGRAPHS

Editorial Committee

Oxford Theological Monographs

CANONS OF THE COUNCIL OF SARDICA
A.D. 343
A Landmark in the Early Development of Canon Law

By HAMILTON HESS. 1958

THE LAW
AND THE GOSPEL
IN LUTHER

A Study of Martin Luther's
Confessional Writings

BY

THOMAS M. McDONOUGH, O.P.

OXFORD UNIVERSITY PRESS

1963

Oxford University Press, Amen House, London E.C.4

GLASGOW   NEW YORK   TORONTO   MELBOURNE   WELLINGTON
BOMBAY   CALCUTTA   MADRAS   KARACHI   LAHORE   DACCA
CAPE TOWN   SALISBURY   NAIROBI   IBADAN   ACCRA
KUALA LUMPUR   HONG KONG

© *Oxford University Press 1963*

PRINTED IN GREAT BRITAIN
AT THE UNIVERSITY PRESS, OXFORD
BY VIVIAN RIDLER
PRINTER TO THE UNIVERSITY

ACKNOWLEDGEMENTS

THIS volume began as a requirement for a degree in theology from the Dominican College of La Sarte, Huy, in Belgium. Subsequently it was completed at the University of Oxford, and accepted as a B.Litt. thesis.

My thanks are due to Father Humbert Cornelis, O.P., of Belgium, who first supervised my work on the subject and gave me new insights into the theology of Luther's basic writings; also to the Revd. Dr. Thomas M. Parker, Chaplain of University College, Oxford, who supervised the development of the thesis into this present book and taught me how to handle my material prudently and objectively; also to the Revd. Dr. E. Gordon Rupp, who advised me to publish the manuscript, and the Revd. Dr. G. V. Bennett, Dean of Divinity at New College, Oxford, who pointed out passages that needed correction.

Doctors Brian Monahan, O.P., of Blackfriars, Oxford, Mathieu de Durand, O.P., of Toulouse, France, Adrien Brunet, O.P., and Richard Mignault, O.P., of the Dominican Province in Canada, and John Schmieder, Pastor of Saint Mathew's Lutheran Church, Kitchener, Canada, read and criticized the manuscript. Without their assistance and encouragement, I do not think the manuscript would ever have appeared in print.

I am also grateful to my friend Robert Geisler and my father, who helped, in part, to subsidize the printing of this volume.

T. McD.

Saint Dominic's Priory
Port Credit, Ontario
January 1962

CONTENTS

ABBREVIATIONS

W.A.	*D. Martin Luthers Werke*, Weimar Gesamtausgabe* 1883–.
WAB	*Briefwechsel*, in Weimar, ,, ,,
T.R.	*Tischreden*, in Weimar, ,, ,,
D.B.	*Deutsche Bibel*, in Weimar, ,, ,,
Dok.	Otto Scheel, *Dokumente zu Luthers Entwicklung*, Tübingen, 1929.
Bek.	*Die Bekenntnisschriften der evangelisch-lutherischen Kirche*, Göttingen, 1952.
B.C.	*Book of Concord*, English translation of the Lutheran Confessional Writings, Saint Louis, 1957.
L.S.	*Les Livres symboliques de l'église luthérienne*, French translation, Paris, 1947.
D.K.	*Der deutsche Katechismus*, in *Bek*.
S.A.	*Die Schmalkaldische Artikel*, in *Bek*.
C.G.	*A Commentary on Saint Paul's Epistle to the Galatians*, prepared by P. Watson, London, 1956.
D.T.C.	*Dictionnaire de théologie catholique*. 15 vols., Paris, 1903–1950.
R.H.E.	*Revue d'histoire ecclésiastique*, Louvain, 1900 ff.
C.T.	*Catechism of the Council of Trent*.
Denz.	Denzinger's *Enchiridion Symbolorum*.
M.P.L.	Migne, *Patrologiae Series Latina*, Paris, 1844–64.
A.	*Luther's Works*, American edition in fifty-five volumes (still in progress), Philadelphia, 1957–.
Ph.	Philadelphia edition of Martin Luther's Works, in 6 volumes, 1943.
S.Th.	*Summa Theologiae* of Thomas Aquinas, ed. Piana, Ottawa, 1941.
Q.J.	*Quaestiones de Justificatione*, extract from Biels *Collectorium circa quattuor libros sententiarum*, published in fascicule form by Feckes, Aschendorff, 1929.

* When we quote from the Weimar edition of Luther's Works, we retain the spelling of the Latin and German text. Similarly in quotations from the *Bekenntnisschriften* the original spelling is retained, which often means that the umlaut is omitted where contemporary German would print it.

INTRODUCTION

IN recent Lutheran research, we feel, not enough care has been taken by theologians to determine what is basic and essential to Luther's religious teachings; to isolate fundamental doctrine from a mass of details and secondary considerations. For this reason, we wish, in this present study, to deal with what we think is most basic and fundamental; namely, Luther's Law-Gospel[1] doctrine of salvation, which entails a despair-faith experience of sin and grace.

What we mean here by a Law-Gospel doctrine, entailing a despair-faith pattern of experience, is best described as follows:

The Word of God, which Luther defends and believes in, is twofold: Decalogue precepts and promises and Gospel precepts and promises; or more simply, the Word as Law and the Word as grace. Together they produce in sinful man the dynamic dualistic struggle of self-righteousness against God's righteousness which, in so far as God moves and graces man, terminates in a personal experience of despairing utterly in self and believing absolutely in Christ.

The Law and the Gospel are, as it were, paradoxically and antithetically related to each other through the Christian's act of faith in the totality of God's Word and work. The Decalogue precepts command the Christian, under threat of eternal damnation, to do what he is powerless to do because of his morally corrupt nature; in this way, the exigencies of the Law reveal to him the depth and extent of his sinfulness; in falling short of the mark set by God, in failing to keep the Ten Commandments, he becomes aware of his moral impotence and of the fact that he is hopelessly damned by God's justice. This causes in him black sorrow and frustration of soul; he despairs totally in self, even to the point of blasphemy; but at this very point of absolute

---

[1] The compound adjectives 'Law-Gospel' and 'despair-faith', we have coined to describe Luther's doctrine and experience. We use these adjectives repeatedly throughout our thesis because we can find no synonym to express as adequately or as succinctly the same meaning. From the point of view of style this might be thought cumbersome or repetitious; but we see no serious reason why, in a theological study, precision of expression should be sacrificed for prettiness of style.

despair, the sinner is ripe for salvation; the Gospel paradoxically appears meaningful to him; it tells him that God alone creates him, redeems him, and sanctifies him; that Christ alone is victor and warrior, who alone fulfils the Law and conquers sin, the world, and the devil; the sinner then experiences the reassurances and consolations of a saving faith by which he surrenders himself to Christ and embraces all his Gospel precepts and promises. He now knows that the avenging God of justice no longer imputes sin to him or condemns his moral impotence; his sins are blotted out, covered over by the cloak of Christ's merits. In other words, the Law which condemns and the Gospel which saves are so related one to the other that the theologian may speak of them as two sides of the one coin— man's justification before and by God. In this relation, we shall see presently, Luther leaves no room for self-reliance, personal merit, or dependence on works as means to salvation. The Word of God alone, and faith in the Word, both as Law and as Gospel, render the sinner righteous before God and effect in him the dualistic dramatic experience of despair and faith. In this respect, we can say that Luther's doctrine is not just an 'evangelical' doctrine but more properly a 'Law-Gospel' doctrine.

To be sure, this doctrine is well known; it is impossible to read Luther's basic writings without encountering it. It is already implicit in the early Lectures on Psalms (1513–15), on Romans (1515–16), and on Galatians (1519); it is explicitly and eloquently formulated in his treatise *On the Freedom of a Christian Man* (1520) and the essay *On Good Works* (1520); and afterwards, reaffirmed again and again in numerous sermons[1] and other important writings, such as the *Bondage of the Will* (1524), the Catechisms (1529), the *Smalcald Articles* (1537), the later commentary on Galatians (1531), and most significantly in his autobiographical fragment of 1545, a year before his death.

We are, therefore, not implying, by any means, that we are the first to single it out for study. Others, before us, have dealt with the problem of the Law and the Gospel in Luther's theology. But, we think, in most instances, the problem is treated as a mere aspect of his theology, or as a recurring theme, or again

[1] See Gerhard Heintze, *Luthers Predigt von Gesetz und Evangelium*, Munich, 1958.

as another of the many telling paradoxes of his evangelical teaching. It is not clearly stated and explained that the Law-Gospel doctrine constitutes the very heart and core of his basic convictions; and that the various parts of his theology, on the Bible, faith, sin and grace, on justification, redemption and sanctification, on the Church, the Sacraments, prayer and good works, are intimately bound up with this doctrine and unintelligible apart from the personal experience which the Word, as Law and Gospel, is supposed to effect in the daily life of the Christian.[1]

On reading Luther's *De libertate christiana*, we have detected three essential aspects or 'elements'[2] of this doctrine which, we think, are indispensable to an understanding of the Law-Gospel relation, in man's justification by faith. These elements are:

[1] Melanchthon, in the *Apologia Confessionis Augustanae*, argues that the doctrine of justification by faith alone is the 'chief article' of Christianity: '. . . damnant nos [Catholic theologians] quod docemus, homines non propter sua merita, sed gratis propter Christum consequi remissionem peccatorum fide in Christum. Utrumque enim damnant et quod negamus homines propter sua merita consequi remissionem peccatorum, et quod affirmamus homines fide consequi remissionem peccatorum et fide in Christum justificari. Cum autem in hac controversia praecipuus locus [we translate: 'chief article'] doctrinae christianae agitetur. . .' (see *Bek.*, article IV, 'de justificatione', paragraphs 1 and 2, p. 158). In the German texts it reads: 'Dieweil aber solcher Zank ist über dem höchsten fürnehmsten Artikel der ganzen Christlichen Lehre. . .' (ibid.). Luther, himself, in the *Smalcald Articles*, exclaims that all is lost if the doctrine of justification is abandoned: 'Von diesem Artikel kann man nichts weichen oder nachgeben es falle Himmel und Erden oder was nicht bleiben will; denn es ist kein ander Name (Jesus) dadurch wir konnen selig werden, spricht Petrus Act. 4. . . .'

'Und auf diesem Artikel stehet alles, das wir wider den Bapst, Teufel und Welt lehren und leben. Darum mussen wir des gar gewiß sein und nicht zweifeln. Sonst ist's alles verlorn, und behält Bapst und Teufel und alles wider uns den Sieg und Recht' (in *Bek.*, 'Das ander Teil', pp. 415–16 20–22, 1–6). And the Formula of Concord, years later, quotes Melanchthon to this effect, and adds these words of Luther: 'Lutherus suo etiam testimonio confirmavit cum inquit: Si unicus hic articulus sincerus permanserit, etiam Christiana Ecclesia sincera, concors et sine omnibus sectis permanet; sin vero corrumpitur, impossibile est, ut uni errori aut fanatico spiritui recte obviam iri possit' (*Bek.*, 'Solida Declaratio', article III, 'de justicia Fidei coram Deo', paragraph 6, p. 916).

Here, we are not, in any sense, denying that the 'chief article' of faith, for Luther, is the doctrine of justification. On the contrary, we intend to show how this very article must be described and understood as a Law-Gospel doctrine of salvation, inseparable from a Law-Gospel experience of sin and grace, such as we have just outlined above. This is what we mean when we say that Luther's Law-Gospel doctrine is most basic and fundamental. If we fail to see his doctrine in this light, we run the risk of reducing it to an abstract theorem, unrelated to the living dynamic realities of his description of faith and reconciliation.

[2] See below, Chapter I, p. 9, n. 2.

man's enduring sinfulness before the judgement of God's Law, his passive role in the justifying work of faith, and the external or imputative character of his resulting righteousness.

We propose, in the First Part of our study, to disengage and discuss these elements, relying on other key writings of the Reformer to enlighten us on their meaning. Chapter I considers Luther's personal background, explaining how the elements of his doctrine are profoundly related to and best understood within the context of a Law-Gospel experience—an *erlebnismäßig* crisis of despair followed by the consoling reassurances of faith. The second chapter describes each element in more detail and attempts to grasp their significance for Luther's theology of the Word.

Next, in the Second Part, we select and analyse two basic writings of the Reformer—his *Large Catechism* and the *Smalcald Articles*. These writings, for Luther himself, are a true exposition of the pure Word of God;[1] they are confessions of faith teaching what every man must know in order to be saved and to be a Christian; their confessional character, aimed at preserving unity and instructing the faithful, forces the author to dwell on fundamentals—God's Word and the Sacraments, sinful man and his destiny—and not on secondary issues. One finds them comparatively free of polemical and negative outbursts; they present, with much clarity and simplicity, the positive side of the Revolt.

Besides, these writings are included in the *Corpus doctrinae* of the Lutheran Church— in the *Bekenntnisschriften*. They belong, therefore, to an important phase in the growth and development of Protestantism, and form a major part of the efforts of the early Lutheran divines to consolidate themselves doctrinally into a distinctive Church body set off from the hierarchical control of Rome, from emergent Calvinism and from extreme and factious elements. They remain today, if not a common

[1] Johannes Meyer, in his *Kommentar*, says: 'A scientific Luther-research dare not neglect Luther's catechism-ideas, for they are really understandable as being in the background of his theological ideas' (*Historischer Kommentar zu Luthers Kleinem Katechismus*, Gütersloh, 1929, p. 1; see also W. D. Allbeck, *Lutheran Confessions*, Philadelphia, 1952, p. 219). We wish to show that the 'catechism-ideas' are more than a background to his theology, but the very heart and soul of his religious thinking. We shall see, in the fifth chapter, that this is also true for the basic ideas of his *Smalcald Articles*.

doctrinal basis,[1] at least a recognized starting-point for Lutheran studies and debate.[2]

In these two confessional writings, we are able to observe clearly Luther's Law-Gospel perspective and doctrine. Indeed, we can see that, for him, what is truly basic and primary in the Christian faith is the dual work of the Word, as Law and Gospel, producing in sinful man the vital spiritual tension of despair and faith. This perspective and doctrine we can trace and analyse, in the light of our preliminary findings, and show how it underlies, orders, and determines every cardinal point of the Reformer's religious convictions.

With this in mind, we plan the Second Part of our study in four subsequent chapters. The third chapter places the *Large Catechism* in its historical setting and determines the genre and scope of the work. The fourth and fifth chapters then deal respectively with what we have labelled the Decalogue and Gospel

---

[1] We realize that Luther's confessional writings have not the same force of authority in Lutheran circles today as in the sixteenth century; also that Lutherans are divided on the evangelical content of all their confessional writings, and consequently on their official status as creeds. It is relevant to point out that the Lutheran World Assembly of 1947 formulates the doctrinal basis of its constitution in broad loose terms so as to render it acceptable to the various member Churches. Article II reads as follows: 'The Lutheran World Federation acknowledges the Holy Scriptures of the Old and New Testaments as the only source and the infallible norm of all Church doctrine and practice, and sees in the Confessions of the Lutheran Church, especially in the unaltered Augsburg Confession and Luther's Catechism (*Small Catechism*), a pure exposition of the Word of God' (*Proceedings of the Lutheran World Federation Assembly*, Lund, 1947).

The phrase 'sees in the Lutheran Confessions . . .' leaves plenty of room for private or group interpretation, since it does not specify what precisely is the 'pure exposition of the Word of God'. In addition, the adverb 'especially', used in connexion with the Augsburg Confession and the Catechisms, intimates, or perhaps admits of, a difference of faith among Lutherans concerning the evangelical content of the other creeds not expressly mentioned. Mr. Drummond, speaking of the Augsburg Confession, says that it appears in the twentieth century 'like a generous blanket to cover many diverse bodies that claim the name of Lutheran to-day, whether in Europe, America, or elsewhere' (A. Drummond, *German Protestantism since Luther*, London, 1951, p. 18).

[2] Though the Lutheran World Federation Assembly specifies the *Small Catechism* rather than the *Large Catechism*, in the above-quoted article, we have decided to deal with the latter in our thesis. Our reasons for this choice are twofold: firstly, Luther himself tells us that the *Large Catechism* is a fuller treatment of the *Small Catechism* and should be used by instructors to explain the contents of the latter. Secondly, this catechism insists more on the necessity of a despair-faith experience produced by the Word. In Chapter II we discuss, in more detail, the reasons why we have preferred to deal with the *Large Catechism* and why we think that it throws more light on Luther's Law-Gospel doctrine.

sections of the Catechism. The sixth chapter similarly studies the *Smalcald Articles*. On the Decalogue section, we outline Luther's ordering of the Ten Commandments, explaining how he centres everything on the First Commandment, or faith in God. Next we consider three salient points: the force of the Law, the function of the Law, and the fulfilment of the Law. These points are not actually separate divisions or isolated parts of the Catechism but rather dynamic properties of one and the same Law which the Reformer reiterates and reaffirms throughout the entire work. We study them separately and systematically for purposes of exposition.

The first point opens our eyes to the fact that the Law, for Luther, is sacrosanct, and every bit as important to the Christian's righteousness as the Gospel; the second point concerns, mainly, the role of the Law as a mirror of sin and a preparation to the advent of the Gospel promise of forgiveness; and also how it varies in effect, according as the subject of the Law is a believer or a non-believer. In this chapter, we only touch upon the question, postponing a fuller treatment to the final chapter. The third point belongs more properly to the fifth chapter on the Gospel section of the Catechism.

Here we consider what God has done for sinful man and the means He has provided for fulfilling the Law; namely the Gospel commandments—the Creed, the Lord's Prayer, and the Sacraments. They contrast diametrically with what men have tried and failed to do, and with their own inefficacious means to righteousness.

The final chapter analyses mainly the Third Part of the *Smalcald Articles*, inasmuch as it confirms the teachings of the Catechisms and sheds more light on the threefold function of the Law: The Law as a mirror of man's sinfulness, as a hammer crushing him into a state of despair, and as a mask, hiding the redemptive work of the Word in his heart, in preparation for justifying faith.

By adopting this plan for our study, and bearing in mind the importance of the three elements mentioned above, we can readily discern how Luther envisages God's Word as Law and Gospel, and how Old and New Testament Commandments (or precepts) are necessarily one in the Christian's act of faith, underlying and producing in him the daily experience of despair and consolation. Also, how this experience, itself, is in a sense the true sign that Christ is moving and causing the Christian man to struggle against sinful-self, the world, and the devil, and in such a way as to make him acknowledge that Christ alone is the real warrior and sole victor.

PART I

LUTHER'S LAW-GOSPEL EXPERIENCE AND DOCTRINE

I

BACKGROUND

MR. BAINTON, in his biography of Martin Luther, *Here I Stand*, has rightly pointed out that the Reformer's fundamental break with the Catholic Church 'was over the nature and destiny of man, and much more over the destiny than the nature'.[1] Nowhere is this more evident than in Luther's Law-Gospel doctrine of salvation. Here we find a description of man and God, of faith and redemption, which is basically Protestant, and which sets the theme of Luther's Catechisms and Smalcald Articles. Our reading of these confessional writings will be very superficial unless we first of all investigate certain elements of this doctrine. We are thinking of three elements or principles in particular: man's moral impotence before the Law, the transforming effects of faith on his sinful person, and the imputative character of his Christian righteousness. (See Chapter II).

These elements,[2] we believe, underlie the broader Lutheran

---

[1] Roland H. Bainton, *Here I Stand*, London, 1951, p. 253. In the *De servo arbitrio*, Luther replies to Erasmus: 'Deinde et hoc in te vehementer laudo et praedico, quod solus prae omnibus rem ipsam es aggressus, hoc est summam caussae, nec me fatigaris alienis illis caussis de Papatu, purgatorio, indulgentiis ac similibus nugis potius quam caussis, in quibus me hactenus omnes fere venati sunt frustra. Unus tu et solus cardinem rerum [i.e. the freedom of the will with respect to God's grace] vidisti et ipsum iugulum petisti, pro quo ex animo tibi gratias ago. . .' (*W.A.* xviii, 786. 26–31).

[2] By 'elements' or 'principles', we do not mean moral precepts or metaphysical abstractions; the words are used for convenience sake to designate correlated aspects of Luther's description of God's justification of the sinner; see below, section C.

principles often expressed in the Latin words: 'sola scriptura, sola fide, sola gratia'. *Sola scriptura* signifying that the sole source of divine revelation is the Bible; *sola fide* that the sole means of receiving and enjoying the fruits of this revelation is evangelical faith in Christ crucified and resurrected; and *sola gratia* that the sole cause of our salvation—our possession of the Word, our faith and holiness—is the Blessed Trinity, creating, redeeming, and sanctifying us. Now we say that the three elements with which we are concerned underlie these broader better-known principles because, fundamentally, they explain why, and in what sense, Luther acknowledges them as the basis of his religious convictions.

A. *Preliminary difficulties*

We realize, of course, that our attempt to limit our initial view to these three elements is a hazardous undertaking; firstly, because it inclines us to systematize what, for the Wittenberg monk, was not a system[1] but the outpourings of a soul deeply afflicted with the sense of its own sinfulness, overwhelmed by its own peculiar and personal experience of God, and firmly convinced of the fundamental Christian truth: God alone pardons man of his sins and saves him from eternal damnation. Secondly, because we are trying to give a certain clarity and precision to what, in fact, is imprecise and obscure; namely, his ambiguous language and paradoxical affirmations. On this score, the words of Henri Rondet are worth quoting:

> The father of the Reformation is not a systematizer. He [thinks] intuitively, he is a 'prophet', a tumultuous torrent, he loves crude images, he works his thought into paradoxes, and one commits a serious error by taking what he writes always literally.[2]

Thirdly, because there is the danger of separating Luther's personal experience and religious teachings from the historical context in which he lived. We should bear in mind, when reading his works and appraising his thought, that he appeared at an extraordinary time in history—the height of the Renaissance—when our western civilization was bubbling over with change and fermentation. Everywhere, in Italy, France, Germany, England, scholars of the new humanism were looking back to antiquity for inspiration; they were rediscovering the

---

[1] See p. 57, n. 2   [2] Henri Rondet, *Gratia Christi*, Paris, 1948, p. 258.

ancient poets and philosophers, the Fathers of the Church, indeed, the Bible itself.

Their new discoveries, naturally, made them critical of the *status quo*, of traditional attitudes of mind, of established doctrines; and since this was the age of printing, the carping and criticisms of the scholars and students undoubtedly spread quickly to a new self-conscious bourgeoisie, and from them to the peasants.

Again, new political forces were already at work; the new nationalism, to mention only one, was profoundly modifying the traditional relation of Church and State; the German-speaking peoples were resentful of the Italian dominance of the Church and the heavy exactions of the Roman Curia. At the same time, the Church herself was groaning under clerical abuses and worldly popes. Erasmus, in his *Praise of Folly*, did not spare his words in satirizing monks and clergy, and the reign of the Borgias had only come to an end a few years before Luther entered the Augustinian Order; besides, the practice of simony and the preaching of false theories of indulgences were not uncommon.[1]

Added to this moral decadence was the speculative decadence of scholastic theology. With the teaching of Gabriel Biel, Pierre d'Ailly, and other Nominalist masters, theology reached its lowest point. One of their theories actually encouraged pious men, laymen as well as monks, to indulge in a Pelagian form of asceticism. The theory suggested, among other things, that man could assure himself of salvation through his own personal efforts of self-perfection. That is to say, by virtue of a decree of the divine will, *de potentia ordinata*, he obtained the gifts of Christ's redeeming grace the moment he became morally perfect according to the norms of human reason; if he failed in this respect grace was denied him. (See below, Chapter II, section A.)

[1] For an interesting interpretation of the sixteenth century in Reformation Germany, one should read *Die Reformation in Deutschland*, Freiburg, 1947, in two volumes, by Father Joseph Lortz. Significantly, Lortz stresses the fact that the Church was, at this time, apparently uncertain about some fundamental points of dogma; the universities and the humanists were slow in condemning Luther's doctrines (see Gordon Rupp, *The Righteousness of God*, London, 1953, p. 27). See also G. Ritter, 'Why the Reformation Occurred in Germany', in *Church History*, vol. xxvii, 1958, translated from the original, 'Kirche und geistiges Leben in Deutschland um 1517' (chapter 8 of the author's *Die Neugestaltung Europas im 16. Jahrhundert*, Berlin, 1950), by G. H. Nadel.

Needless to say, such a theology was of little consolation to a world sick with its own decadence, in search of new and better things, and desperately anxious for reform. If anything, it tended to stir up in men's souls an explosive anxiety and great spiritual perturbation, especially in the hearts of the sincere and pious who were humble enough to acknowldge their own lowliness before an all-powerful and all-perfect God.

Apparently this was the case with Martin Luther in his cloister days. Highly strung, afflicted with a sensitive and scrupulous conscience, due perhaps to his Thuringian milieu and severe upbringing, he felt more deeply than others his own lowliness before God and suffered intensely from the semi-Pelagian aberrations of his Nominalist masters. As a monk, he brooded night and day on the realities of sin and damnation, asking himself always if he had done enough to please God, if he had acquired sufficient perfection through prayer and asceticism to win the grace of salvation. His brooding developed into a passionate desire for certitude concerning the justification of his own soul—a smouldering fire that penetrated his whole being and erupted eventually into a volcanic religious experience that shook the foundations of medieval Christendom.

Though this experience belonged to him personally, it was not, for that matter, free from or untainted by the climate of opinion and the historical forces of his age. They, too, undoubtedly contributed to the formulation of a Protestant doctrine and to his eventual revolt. To what extent, however, is not an easy question to answer; this constitutes an additional reason why we hesitate to outline certain essential elements of his Law-Gospel doctrine of salvation in our preliminary chapter. But granting these aspects of the question, and despite the obvious hazards and difficulties involved, we still believe it possible to dive beneath the mass of facts and uncertainties contained in and surrounding Luther's voluminous writings and catch hold of a few basic principles or 'constants' which he persists in defending throughout his life, irrespective of traditional authorities, irrespective of logic and the opinions of men and society—indeed even when he thinks it may cost him his life.

These principles, as we stated above, are mainly three; and they appear in his writings more as descriptions and corollaries of his personal experience than as abstract theses or categorical propositions. To expound them properly, we must place them within the framework of his religious experience[1]—what Strohl calls his *crise de conscience*; perhaps the best way to do this is to allow Luther to speak for himself.

B. *Significance of Luther's religious experience*

In numerous instances, especially in the *Tischreden* and the *Briefwechsel*, he gives us his own account of his spiritual conflict with sin and grace,[2] which seems to reach its climax in the famed *Turmerlebnis* or tower experience. He himself tells us that this latter event is a decisive moment in his life; meditating day and night on the words of Saint Paul, 'the just man lives by faith', he suddenly, as if inspired, passes from a period of despair —almost hatred of God—to the joys of paradise. From that moment on, he no longer doubts his basic religious views. He begins now to defend his personal theology of justification with such passion and energy that one cannot help feel that it springs from a deep-rooted conviction and certitude.

He describes his tower experience towards the end of his life[3] in the preface which he wrote personally for the collected edition of his Latin works, published in Wittenberg in 1545, and in which he reveals his own evolution up to the year 1519. The following extract is significant:[4]

Meanwhile, I had already, for the second time that year [1519], returned to the interpretation of the Psalter, strengthened by the fact that I was better trained, having dealt, in my courses, with Saint Paul's epistle to the Romans [1515–16] and the Galatians [1516–17] and the one on the Hebrews [1517–18].

Assuredly, I had[5] been seized by an astonishing desire to understand Paul in his epistle to the Romans, but until then it was not a

---

[1] 'One thing is more and more clear from recent research: the inner, personal experience of Luther, and his scholarly, theological and above all, exegetical discoveries cannot be separated' (H. Boehmer, *Der junge Luther*, Stuttgart, 1939, p. 362, quoted from G. Rupp, op. cit., p. 102).

[2] Passages bearing witness to Luther's spiritual conflict and personal experience can be found in *W.A.* lviii (i), pp. 6–32; see also p. 15 n. 1, below.

[3] Luther died in the year 1546; he wrote this preface in 1545. The first course on the Psalms had been given from 1513–15; see Henri Strohl, *Luther, sa vie et sa pensée*, Strasbourg, 1953, chapter 3.

[4] *W.A.* liv, 185–6.

[5] Strohl calls our attention to the fact that the verb is in the pluperfect tense.

coldness of the heart that was a hindrance, but the one word in chapter I: 'The justice of God is revealed in Him [Christ]'. For I hated this term 'justice of God',[1] which the usage and custom of all the doctors had taught me to understand philosophically as the justice, formal and active (as they say), whereby God is just and punishes sinners and the unjust.[2]

And I, though a monk living beyond reproach, felt myself to be a sinner before God, troubled in conscience, unable to believe that I had made satisfaction; I did not love, indeed, I detested the just God who punishes sinners; if not by a tacit blasphemy, certainly by a huge murmuring, I was indignant against God, saying: as if truly it were not enough to be miserable sinners, lost for all eternity by original sin, and oppressed by all kinds of calamities because of the Decalogue, but that God, by means of His Gospel should heap sorrow upon sorrow, and also by His Gospel direct His anger and justice towards us. Thus I was furious in my fierce and troubled conscience, and I knocked insistently on the door of Paul's passage yearning ardently to know what Saint Paul meant. . . .

Finally, through the mercy of God, meditating day and night, I paid attention to the connexion of the words: 'the justice of God is revealed in this, as it is written: the just man lives by faith', here I began to comprehend that justice of God by which the just live by the gift of God; to wit, by faith, and that the sense was that the justice of God was revealed by the Gospel, that is passive justice whereby the merciful God justifies us through faith, as it is written: 'the just man lives by faith'. Then I felt wholly reborn and entered into the door of paradise. From that moment on, the entire body of scripture took on a new face for me. . . .

As much as I had previously detested the term, 'justice of God', that much the more, through love, I extolled its sweetness for me. Thus the passage in Saint Paul became for me a doorway to paradise. Afterwards I read Augustine's *De spiritu et littera*, where, against all hope, I hit upon the fact that he interpreted the justice of God similarly: the justice by which God clothes[3] us when He justifies us. And although, concerning this point, he speaks only imperfectly, and

[1] The justice that Luther hates here resembles the Nominalist distributive justice bestowed on the perfect only, as explained below; see Chapter II, section A.

[2] Heinrich Denifle has shown, with much erudition, that most of the theologians and exegetes of the Middle Ages interpreted Saint Paul in the sense that God's mercy justifies, and not in an Ockhamist sense (see *Luther et le luthéranisme*, trans. by J. Paquier, Paris, 1913–16, vol. iii, pp. 109–65).

[3] The word 'clothes' [*induit*] indicates that Luther envisages justification, not as an intrinsic transformation; this pertains to what we have chosen to call the third element of his Law-Gospel doctrine—the imputation of justice—which we discuss below in Chapter II, section C.

does not explain clearly everything about imputation, yet it pleased me that he taught the justice of God by which we are justified.

These words of the Wittenberg monk summarize for us, rather dramatically, what he believed, in later life, to be the central crisis of his soul's search for salvation. This crisis underlies his Law-Gospel doctrine of justification, and likewise its corollary—the eventual repudiation of the traditional organization of the Church, its hierarchical and conciliary authority, ecclesiastical canons, clerical status, medieval monasticism, and the accepted sacramental theology of Catholic doctors. (See below, Chapter VI on the *Smalcald Articles*.)

Admittedly, this autobiographical sketch alone does not suffice to give us an all-round picture of the evolution of his religious experience. This would require a full biographical treatment, involving a serious study of the psychological, cultural, and formative factors that entered into and determined his peculiar religious experience. For information on this score, the reader should consult the seriously written biographies of Henri Strohl, Lucien Febvre, and H. Boehmer, and the more extensive studies of Robert H. Fife, Gordon Rupp, and Father Joseph Lortz (see our Bibliography).

In particular, we refer to Luther's autobiographical account of 1545 in order to show how his discovery of passive justice, through faith and the reading of Saint Paul, comes to him more as the fruit of a personal experience—a sudden illumination—than as the result of theological speculation[1] or a systematic exegesis of Saint Paul's Epistle.

After many days of prayer and meditation, he suddenly sees the light; the exegesis follows the illumination; thus he writes: 'Then I felt wholly reborn and entered the doors of paradise. From that moment on, the entire body of scripture took on a new face for me. . . .' And again at the end: 'Being better armed by these thoughts, I began to interpret the Psalter for the second time, and the work would have terminated in a vast commentary.'

He poses the fundamental problem of salvation not as a

---

[1] In the *Operationes in Psalmos* (1519–21) Luther says 'Vivendo, immo moriendo et damnando fit theologus, non intelligendo, legendo, aut speculando' (*W.A.* v. 163. 28). Elsewhere he speaks similarly: 'Experience . . . is necessary in the Law . . . how much more in theology' (*W.A.* lvi. 447. 11–21).

theologian theorizing on the mysteries of faith, but rather as an afflicted soul pressed on by a deep-rooted frustration. His language underscores an experience: 'I was furious in my fierce and troubled conscience, and I knocked insistently on the door of Paul's passage, yearning ardently to know what Paul meant.'

He is not seeking to penetrate the mysteries of Redemption— to answer the question *quid est*; it is not a matter of *fides quaerens intellectum*, or even less so of conciliating and systematizing the truths of revelation and reason into a *summa* of articles on nature, grace, and sin; he is asking for Paul's meaning as a drowning man cries for help; he is asking for a life-line to drag him out of his depths of despair.

And since the source of his despair, as he tells us himself, in the same autobiographical passage, is the realization of his own sinfulness and the awareness of his total incapacity to please and love God, it is understandable that he should look, not to a theological thesis or abstract doctrine as a solution to his desperate plight, but rather to a substitute experience of certitude and joy.

In a sense, he has to save himself from a kind of impending atheism.[1] This, he feels, is only possible through personal assurance of salvation. The question becomes for him, not what one must do in order to be justified, to be righteous before God; but how to know for certain whether one is indeed justified;[2] whether one has found a 'gracious God'.[3] The fact that he is, so to speak, on the lookout for a reassuring experience explains, to some extent, why Saint Paul's words become so meaningful to him; faith in Christ's promises offers him a more certain means of personal assurance than Ockhamist theology.

[1] We recall Luther's own frank avowal of his hatred of the just God who punishes sinners: '. . . I did not love, indeed, I detested the just God who punishes sinners; if not by a tacit blasphemy, certainly by a huge murmuring, I was indignant, against God . . .' (see the autobiographical fragment (1545), quoted above).

[2] In the *Commentary on Galatians* (1531), 5. 3, Luther tells us about his own experience of spiritual uncertainty. 'Ego Monachus studebam summa diligentia vivere iuxta praescriptum Regulae. . . . Et tamen conscientia mea nunquam poterat certa reddi, sed semper dubitabat . . . igitur longius conabar humanis traditionibus mederi incertae, imbecilli et afflictae conscientiae, hoc in dies magis reddebam eam incertiorem, imbecilliorem et perturbatiorem' (*W.A.* xl (ii), 15. 15–23).

[3] Doing was not enough, he wanted assurance, comfort of soul, and confidence; in a sermon at the end of the 1530's, he says 'Im kloster gedacht ich nicht an weib, gellt oder gutth, sondern das Herz zitterte und zappeltte, wie gott mir gnedig wurde' (*W.A.* xlvii. 590. 6–7).

After all, faith in Christ, for a Christian, is not an abstract or theoretical thesis; it is, on the contrary, an experiential and vital relationship of man to God; a man knows he believes, and though his finite intellect can never hope to penetrate the mysteries of Redemption, he none the less experiences his own assent to these mysteries and to their moral implications, and he senses keenly a new orientation to his Maker. These aspects of faith (not the whole of faith), undoubtedly, appealed to Luther's afflicted soul. Theology alone, it seems, could not have assuaged him.

We should, of course, avoid pushing these reflections too far; there are many imponderables and unknown causes behind Luther's experience. What is certain here is that the principles, or basic elements, of his teachings on justification appear more consistent when viewed within the framework of his religious experience. We shall appreciate this more fully as the chapter proceeds; but at this juncture, we must make some attempt at dating Luther's critical *Erlebnis* and assure ourselves of its genuineness.

C. *The date and authenticity of Luther's* crise de conscience

The exact time of the *Turmerlebnis* is still uncertain. Most historians hesitate to accept Luther's own dating of the event (1519), arguing, for one reason or other, that he did not have a very good memory for dates.[1] While admitting that he describes his tower experience as the crucial turning-point of his career and the dramatic beginning of the Reformation, they none the less prefer to assign it to an earlier period.

Boehmer points to April or May of 1513,[2] Vogelsang to the fall of 1514;[3] Scheel locates it between the autumn of 1513 and that of 1514,[4] Wendorf between 1512 and 1513,[5] and Strake before 1515.[6] Others think that it is impossible to fix the exact time of his experience. More recently, E. Bizer has attempted to

[1] See Chanoine Cristiani, *Luther tel qu'il fut*, Paris, 1955, in footnote, p. 63.
[2] Op. cit., p. 110.
[3] *Die Anfänge von Luthers Christologie*, Berlin–Leipzig, 1929, p. 57.
[4] *Martin Luther*, Tübingen, 1930, vol. i, p. 571.
[5] 'Der Durchbruch der neuen Erkenntnis Luthers . . .', in *Historische Vierteljahr-schrift*, Dresden, 1932–3, vol. xxvii.
[6] *Luthers großes Selbstzeugnis*, Leipzig, 1926.

defend Luther's own date, situating the experience between the years 1518–19.[1]

For our part, we find cogent reasons why the date should be fixed earlier. Already, in his lectures on the Psalms (July 1513), Luther is propounding new Protestant ideas with some waverings[2] and in his lectures on Romans (1515–16) he seems to be in full possession of his theology of passive and imputed justice, which, as we have just seen, is supposed to proceed from his liberating discovery of *justitia dei*—his tower experience. Thus, inasmuch as the tower experience is accepted as the beginning of Luther's new theology, it must have occurred three or more years before the date mentioned in the autobiographical sketch.

However, if historians have sound reasons for fixing the date of this experience as late as 1519, then we must look at Luther's early lectures in a new light. It is possible, for instance, that he was, in his early lectures, not sure of his own interpretations. That is to say, he was teaching his students what he hoped the Bible meant or desired it to mean but without being certain; not of course in the sense that he intended to falsify the texts but rather to find an answer to his own soul searchings for a merciful God. Only later, perhaps in 1519 during the tower experience, did he suddenly become convinced of the truth of his position, the words of Saint Paul bringing him assurance and certitude. In later years he could recall this event as a momentous realization—an unforgettable experience of switching from despair and uncertainty to true faith and conviction.[3] The tower experience, therefore, would be decisive in his life and symbolize dramatically his discovery of the Gospel.

But these opinions and conjectures are inconclusive; they do not settle the exact time of Luther's tower experience. What is certain and most important to our subject is the evidence of a genuine soul-shaking religious crisis in the Reformer's youth. We are inclined to agree with the Protestant historian Boehmer

---

[1] *Fides ex auditu, Eine Untersuchung über die Entdeckung der Gerechtigkeit Gottes durch Martin Luther.* . . . Moers, 1958.

[2] See Strohl, op. cit., pp. 69–70; also Vogelsang, op. cit., p. 32.

[3] Erik H. Erikson says: 'It seems entirely probable . . . that the revelation in the tower occurred sometime during Luther's work on these lectures [on the psalms, 1513]. Alternatively, instead of one revelation, there may have been a series of crises, the first traceable in this manuscript on the Psalms, the last fixed in Luther's memory at that finite event [the tower experience], which scholars have found so difficult to locate in time' [*Young Man Luther*, London, 1958, p. 198].

that Luther, in his last days (the time of the autobiographical sketch), became mythical about himself, recounting the events of his earlier years, however much in good faith, in a manner not strictly historical; yet, notwithstanding, we cannot go as far as Denifle and claim that Luther's account of his crisis is mere fiction.

It is this Dominican's opinion that the principal documents describing Luther's critical experience are posterior to 1530. Thus he argues that the Reformer's personal account of his crisis is a pure invention cooked up afterwards to justify his defection and discredit the Church.[1]

Otto Scheel, refuting Denifle's view, has very carefully singled out significant texts anterior to 1530 which testify to Luther's religious crisis.[2] And Lucien Febvre sees no reason why, after reading Denifle and following the latter's argument, we should abandon the traditional picture of Luther in his early years as an obedient monk, haunted by the sense of his own sinfulness and terrified by the justice of God.[3]

As well, there is much to indicate that Luther, as early as 1505, or even earlier, was going through the initial phases of a religious crisis of which the tower experience could very well have been the definitive symbol and crystallization.

The fact, for instance, that he had been knocked to the ground and almost killed by a lightning bolt, in the year 1505, in the village of Stotterheim, could certainly have shaken his confidence in himself and left him with a weird feeling of being, somehow, marked if not cursed by God.[4] Such a feeling was not unlikely in an age when the consciousness of sin and the fear of eternal punishment were perhaps stronger in men's hearts than their faith in Christ and their love of God.

We know Luther cried out on this occasion: 'Saint Anne help me, I shall become a monk.'[5] To the medieval youth, this

[1] Denifle, op. cit., vol. i, p. xvii.
[2] In his *Dok.*, Otto Scheel assembles a large number of texts by Luther and others which recall the Reformer's soul agonies and sufferings. He divides them into 'Rückblicke' (1513–15) and 'Zeugnisse' (1501–19). The latter are contemporary statements by Luther in Lectures, Letters, and Sermons (see Robert H. Fife, *The Revolt of Martin Luther*, New York, 1957, n. 74, p. 121; also chapter 8 of the same work; also Rupp, op. cit., chapter 5, on the 'bruised conscience', pp. 39–45, and chapter 3, pp. 69–73). [3] Op. cit., p. 31; see also Lortz, op. cit., i, p. 419.
[4] Kierkegaard says: 'Luther, as it is well known, was shaken by the lightning which killed his friend beside him; in the same way, his expressions always sound as though the lightning were continuously striking down behind him' (*The Journals*, 1834–54, Glasgow, 1958, p. 94). [5] See Roland Bainton, op. cit., pp. 21–37.

meant, I shall cease to be worldly and become perfect as Christ is perfect. He strove scrupulously—even stubbornly against the wishes of his parents—to remain faithful to his promise. Is not this fact itself significant? Why should he insist on keeping such a promise, made in a wild moment of fright? It was neither binding nor a sure sign of religious vocation.[1] Does this fact not suggest that he was already, prior to his entrance into the cloister and his subsequent experiences of Pelagian practices and Nominalist theology, obsessed, perhaps tormented, by the problem of his own salvation.[2]

Again, we find witnesses to other critical events in his early monastic life which point to the same basic religious crisis of dreading God's justice and despairing in his own righteousness. Luther's Augustinian confrères recount, to John Cochlaeus, the young monk's fit in the choir during his novitiate year, 1505–6. While one of the friars was reading the Gospel passage in which Christ expels the devil from a deaf mute, the young Luther fell suddenly in the choir crying: 'T'is not I, t'is not I.'[3]

Similar to this event is the terror and nervousness which he experienced during the celebration of his first Mass (1507). His table companions recorded that he was so terrified at speaking directly to God without a mediator that he would have fled from the altar had not his prior admonished him to continue.[4] Also we read that about the year 1515, he was struck with terror at the sight of the Sacrament borne by the vicar-general, Dr. Staupitz, in the Corpus Christi procession.[5] And just at the beginnings of his struggle against the Pope, he is supposed to have locked himself in his room, after fasting for days. When his confrères broke open the door, they found him unconscious on the floor.[6]

---

[1] Admittedly, resort to the cloister was the accepted medieval way of perfection; but there were many holy and pious persons who remained lay Christians in the world; such for instance as St. Thomas More.

[2] '... the complex causes of his [Luther's] conversion to the religious life included not only fears of God but the search for the security which he hoped to find on the path of self-renunciation' (See Fife, op. cit., p. 122).

[3] This is reported by John Cochlaeus in his *Commentaria de actis et scriptis M. Lutheri* . . ., Mainz, 1549, p. 2.

[4] *T.R.* iii, no. 3556A and 3556B (1537).

[5] *T.R.* i, no. 137 (1531).

[6] See Ratzberger, *Handschriftliche Geschichte*, pp. 58; quoted from Fife, op. cit., p. 121.

Moreover, there are repeated references, throughout his later writings, to the sufferings and deep soul agonies of his youth. He speaks often of powerful attacks of depression and moody bouts of melancholy and scruples. Fife contends that 'the early soul experiences, even as they are reflected in the broken mirror of middle life, are too frequent and insistent to be without some factual basis'.[1]

Finally, Luther's account of the *Turmerlebnis*, in the auto-biographical sketch, tallies substantially with the theme and basic elements of his reformation teachings on justification, developed before his definitive break with Rome. Indeed, in the *De libertate christiana* (Oct. 1520), we are left with the impression that he orders his summary of Christian doctrine in accordance with the despair-faith pattern of his own personal experience. Consider, for instance, the following extract, which because of its relevancy, we take the liberty of quoting at length:

8. You ask how it happens [*qua ratione fiat*] that faith alone justifies and gives us, without works, such a treasure of riches, whilst so many deeds, ceremonies and laws are prescribed for us in Scripture. I reply: Before all, be mindful of the fact, as it is said, that faith alone, without works, justifies, delivers and saves; we shall clarify this point further on. In the meantime, we must point out that the whole of God's Scripture is divided into two parts, Commandments [*Praecepta*] and Promises. The Commandments, indeed, teach good works, yet what is taught is not, at once, accomplished, for they show what we must do, but they do not provide the power of doing [*virtutem faciendi*]; in this, however, they are ordained to reveal man to himself, by which means he knows his incapacity [*impotentiam*] to do good and despairs in his own powers. For this reason they are called and are the Old Testament. For example, 'thou shalt not covet' [*non concupisces*][2] is a Commandment by which we are all shown to be sinners [*quo omnes esse peccatores convincimur*], since no one is able not to covet regardless of one's efforts [*quicquid contra molitus fuerit*]. In order not to covet and to fulfil the commandment, it is necessary to despair in oneself and to seek elsewhere and through

[1] Op. cit., p. 121.

[2] In the German text it reads 'Du solt nit boesz begird haben', which Gravier translates into French 'Tu ne convoiteras pas' (see *Les Grands écrits réformateurs*, Paris, 1955, p. 263). The *Bible de Jérusalem* gives the same translation of Exodus and adds the following note: 'C'est le désir tout intérieur, qui est interdit, comme source des péchés contre le prochain.' Woolf translates: 'Thou shalt not have sinful appetites' (*Reformation Writings*, London, 1952, i. 361). The sense is important; we shall come back to it.

another that help which one does not find in oneself, as it is spoken in Osea: 'Perditio tua Israel, tantum in me auxilium tuum.' Now what concerns this one commandment is the same for all the others. Equally are they all impossible for us.

9. When, indeed, by the Commandment, man has been shown [*doctus fuerit*] his own impotence [*impotentiam*] and henceforth made anxious about how to satisfy the Law [*quo studio legi satisfaciat*]— since he must satisfy the Law in such a way that not even one iota or apex be excluded (otherwise he be condemned without hope)— then he is altogether humiliated and reduced to nothing in his own eyes and finds in himself nothing by which to be justified or saved. Here the other part of Scripture intervenes, the Promises of God, which announce the glory of God and say: 'If you wish to fulfil the Law, not to covet, as the Law requires [*exigitur*], then this is for you: believe in Christ in whom you are promised grace, justice, peace, liberty and all things, if you believe you will possess, if you do not believe you will be lacking.' For that which is impossible to you, with all the works of the Law, which are numerous and yet of no avail, you will attain easily by faith [*facili compendio implebis per fidem*]. For God the Father has placed all things in faith, so that whoever does not have faith will have nothing: 'Conclusit enim omnia sub incredulitate, ut omnium miseratur, Rom. 11, 32.' Thus the Promises of God give what the Commandments require, and fulfil what the Law commands, so that everything belongs to God alone, both the Commandments and their fulfilment. He alone commands; also He alone fulfils. Therefore the Promises of God pertain to the New Testament, indeed they are the New Testament.

10. Since these Promises of God are holy words, true, just, free, peace-giving [*pacata*], and entirely good, it happens that the soul which adheres firmly to them by faith is thus united to them, indeed, completely [*penitus*] absorbed by them, so that it does not only [*non modo*] participate but rather is saturated and inebriated by all of their power.

From this it is easy to see from whence faith is able to do so much and why good works, even all of them [*nulla nec omnia bona opera*], cannot equal it, for no work can adhere to the Word of God nor be in the soul, but faith alone and the Word reign in the soul. Such as the Word is, so it renders the soul [*Quale est verbum talis ab eo fit anima*], similar to the hot iron which glows like fire because of its union with fire; thus it is clear to the Christian man that his faith suffices for all things and that he has no need of works [*nec operibus ei opus fore*) to be justified; if he has no need of works, neither has he need of the Law, if he needs not the Law, certainly he is free of the Law; it is true: 'iusto non est lex posita'. Therefore this is that Christian liberty, our

Faith, which does not authorize us to be idle or live in evil, but rather makes [the situation such] that the Law or works are not necessary to anyone as means to justice and salvation.

. . . .

12. The third incomparable grace of faith is the following: It unites the soul to Christ, as the bride is joined to the bridegroom. . . .

Here now is the sweetest spectacle [*dulcissimum spectaculum*] not only of exchange but of salutary war and victory, salvation and redemption [*non solum communionis sed salutaris belli et victoriae et salutis et redemptionis*]. Indeed, since Christ is God and man, a person who has not sinned, does not die, and is not damned, who cannot die even or be damned, whose justice, life and salvation are invincible, eternal and omnipotent, since, say I, such a person makes common and indeed proper to Him, by virtue of the wedding ring of faith [*annulum fidei*], the sins, death and hell which belong to the Bride, and also behaves as if all these things belonged to Him, as if He Himself had sinned, suffering, dying, descending into hell, so that He conquered all of these things, sin, death, hell, and so that they could not absorb Him, these things were, necessarily, absorbed in Him by a stupendous duel [*stupendo duello*]. For His justice is superior to the sins of all, His life more powerful than all death, His salvation more victorious than any hell. Thus the believing soul through the earnest of its faith [*arram fidei*] in Christ its spouse, becomes free of all sin, secure against death, safe from hell, graced by the eternal justice, life, and salvation of its spouse Christ. He presents to Himself a glorious spouse,[1] without spot or wrinkle, cleansing her by the washing in the Word of life; that is through the faith of the Word, of life, of justice and salvation.[2]

These passages conform to the despair-faith pattern of Luther's autobiographical account of his crucial religious experience. Justification begins when the sinner, moved by God, has a deep heartfelt awareness, accompanied by despair, of his moral impotence and depravity before God's Law; in this state, he feels unavoidably condemned by the Law and deserving of damnation; suddenly, he escapes from this despair through 'passive' faith (see Chapter II, section B) in Christ's Word, which not only assures him of salvation but inwardly heals him, if not of sinfulness, at least of the damning consequences of his sins.

[1] This metaphor, obviously, is inspired by Eph. v. 26–27.
[2] We have translated these passages from Luther's *De libertate christiana*, *W.A.* vii. 52–55.

God's Word and grace transform him, mysteriously, so that he becomes capable of observing the Law and producing good works, but without these works being, in any respect, means or prerequisites of salvation, or in themselves intrinsically worthy or meritorious. Out of this transformation emerges the sinner's conviction that his justification—his righteousness—belongs to him in a strictly imputative or extrinsic manner; that is to say, it is the goodness of Christ and the power of Christ alone which justifies and fulfils the Law in him, thereby excluding all claim to intrinsic worth, personal sanctification, and merit.

In short, God's Word, as Law and Gospel, effects in the Christian's soul a threefold dynamic awareness of being, at one and the same time, morally impotent, passively justified, and imputatively righteous before God. For the sake of convenience, we have decided to call the three aspects, or co-parts, of this awareness basic elements or principles of Luther's Law-Gospel doctrine. As stated earlier, they stand out more as descriptive accounts of his own experience than as absolute principles or theses. The three are visible in the above-quoted passages.

The first element is evidenced in the ninth paragraph (numeration by Luther): 'when indeed by the Commandments, he has been shown his own impotence and . . . made anxious about how to satisfy the Law . . .'; and likewise the second element, the saving power of faith, in the description of how faith assures man of salvation and fulfils the Law with 'no need of works to be justified' (no. 10). The third element, the external character of imputative justice, is less conspicuous except for the allusions of the latter paragraph in which he explains how Christ 'absorbs' sin, death and hell and graces the believer 'with His eternal justice . . .'.[1] A more precise knowledge of this aspect of the doctrine is found elsewhere; we shall return to it in section C of Chapter II. For the moment, it suffices to note that the passages quoted from the *De libertate christiana* carry much weight since Luther himself looked upon the work as extremely important for a true understanding of Christianity. To the Pope, he wrote concerning it:

[1] Luther's German version of the same work brings out more forcefully the idea that our sins are 'swallowed up and drowned in', or 'endowed with' and 'decked in' Christ's righteousness [*Gerechtigkeit*]: 'szo mussen die sund ynn yhm [Christ] vorschlunden und erseufft werden, etc.' (*Von der Freiheit eines Christenmenschen*, *W.A.* vii. 25–26, 34–38. 1–10).

This is a small thing [*parva res est*] if you consider merely the paper, [*si corpus spectes*] but the whole Christian life is summed up here [*summa vitae christianae compendio congesta*] if you grasp its meaning.[1]

Taking this statement as a cue from Luther, we intend, by consulting other key writings of his, to grasp the meaning of the three essential elements[2] of his Law-Gospel doctrine, which we have singled out in this small booklet.

[1] *Epistola Lutheriana ad Leonem Decimum* . . ., *W.A.* vii. 48–49. 35–36. Concerning Luther's treatise *De libertate christiana*, Maurice Gravier says the following: 'Luther faisait lui-même remarquer à la fin de sa missive au pape qu'il avait conscience d'avoir écrit sous un petit volume un grand ouvrage. . . . Les théologiens luthériens l'ont bien compris, puisqu'ils considèrent ce petit traité comme le troisième des grands écrits réformateurs. En fait, Luther y exposait pour la première fois sous une forme simple, presque schématique, les thèmes essentiéls de sa théologie et les fondements de la piété nouvelle afin que le simple laïc pût comprendre ce qu'était, aux yeux de Luther, le véritable christianisme' (*Les Grands écrits réformateurs*, Paris, 1955, p. 49).

[2] Henri Strohl, in his biography of Martin Luther, discusses what he calls 'three essential aspects of his religious life', based on Luther's formula 'semper peccator, semper penitens, semper justus'. In some respects these three aspects bear a resemblance to what we have chosen to call 'three basic elements' of Luther's doctrine of justification.

II

THREE INSEPARABLE ELEMENTS OF
LUTHER'S LAW-GOSPEL DOCTRINE

THE key writings to be especially consulted on this topic are the following: *Lectures on the Epistle to the Romans* (1515–16), *De servo arbitrio* (1525), *Commentary on Galatians*,[1] the *Tischreden*, and Luther's correspondence.

The first of these works, written before the posting of the ninety-five theses (1517), and Luther's official break with Rome, 10 December 1520,[2] contains already an essentially Protestant doctrine; it is most revealing on the question of original sin and man's moral impotence. The second work, *De servo arbitrio*, confirms this doctrine and develops it more explicitly, so that we see how men receive faith passively, and why they are utterly powerless to perform meritorious acts. And the *Commentary on Galatians* is helpful in shedding light on the imputative character of Christian righteousness.

The latter work, like the *De servo arbitrio* and the Catechism, was a favourite of Luther's.[3] He wrote it at a time when his convictions were set and definitive—convictions which, over a period of ten years of controversy, he formulated and affirmed, uncompromisingly, against an onslaught of difficulties raised by adversaries on all sides; the *Schwärmerei*, the Antinomians, the Synergists, and the Roman Catholic Schoolmen. These convictions guide him in his interpretation and exposition of Saint Paul's Epistle. We therefore can take what he says in this commentary as truly representative of his heartfelt and fundamental beliefs. Indeed, he tells us, himself, towards the end of

[1] Based on lectures delivered at the University of Wittenberg in the year 1531 and first published in 1535.
[2] This is the date on which Luther burned the Pope's Bull, *Exsurge Domine*, which had been issued on 15 June of that year, and gave the Reformer sixty days to recant of his errors and submit to Rome.
[3] He called it 'my own Epistle, to which I have plighted my troth. It is my Katie Bora' (see P. Watson, Editor's Preface to *Commentary on Galatians*, Eng. trans., London, 1956, p. 5).

his life, that if people took his advice, 'they'd print only the books containing doctrine like Galatians'.[1]

All of these works, we feel, serve to complete each other and to give a fullness to Luther's simpler treatise, *De libertate christiana*, which, otherwise, would be obscured and perhaps misinterpreted if studied solely by itself. In shedding light on our three elements in question, they help us to understand the Law-Gospel relation of Luther's small booklet, and to perceive how the central element of his descriptive account of justification is man's moral impotence before the Law. This element we shall now discuss.

A. *Man's enduring sinfulness*

When we read the works just mentioned, and others besides, we find that Luther's moral pessimism tends to centre everything on man's enduring wickedness. He describes man's moral depravity in such absolute terms as to leave no room for an upward movement of the soul to God. The totality of salvation is downwards—from God to man. Indeed, in this sense it would not be untrue to claim, even though Luther desired ardently to direct the hearts and minds of men to God alone, that his Law-Gospel doctrine of justification is anthropocentric and not theocentric. But we must be careful not to infer from this tendency more than the texts warrant.

What Luther is mainly intent on disproving, with his pessimism, is the uselessness of human works as a means of justification. Good works are excluded from the economy of salvation precisely because human nature (that is the moral self) is powerless to perform them. That is to say, in a way which merits the forgiveness of sin and the beatitude of the soul. These things become clearer when we study the texts relating to Luther's views on original sin and man's moral depravity.

Original sin, Luther tells us in his *Lectures on the Epistle to the Romans*, is the privation in our body and spiritual faculties of all rectitude and efficaciousness, 'an inclination to evil, a distaste for good, a boredom with truth and wisdom, an attachment to error and darkness, a hatred and avoidance of good works and an onrush towards evil'.[2] And a little farther on, in the same

[1] *W.A.* xl (i), 2; quoted by P. Watson in his preface to *C.G.*, p. 5.
[2] Luther asks the question: 'Quid ergo nunc est peccatum originale?' He

text, he adds: 'It is a nausea for all that is good and an inclination to all that is harmful.' This is the reply to what he calls 'scholastic subtleties'—in particular to the thesis that 'original sin is merely a privation in the will of original justice'. His conviction is that the whole man, all the members of his body and all the faculties of his soul, are somehow perverted by original sin.[1]

This celebrated text is often cited, especially by Luther's critics.[2] But unfortunately it is not always prudently interpreted. Admittedly, the language is vehement and the basic idea conveyed pessimistic; it certainly exceeds Saint Augustine's pessimism and the Thomistic contention that original sin consists formally in a *privatio justitiae originalis*.[3] Yet one should not be too

answers: 'Primo secundum subtilitates scholasticorum theologorum est privatio seu carentia iustitie originalis. Iustitia autem secundum eos est in voluntate tantum subjective, ergo et privatio eius opposita. Quia scil. est in predicamento qualitatis secundum logicam et metaphysicam.'

'Secundo autem secundum Apostolum et simplicitatem sensus in Christo Jehsu est non tantum privatio qualitatis in voluntate, immo nec tantum privatio lucis in intellectu, virtutis in memoria, sed prorsus privatio universe rectitudinis et potentie omnium virium tam corporis quam anime ac totius hominis interioris et exterioris. Insuper et pronitas ipsa ad malum, nausea ad bonum, fastidium lucis et sapientie, dilectio autem erroris ac tenebrarum, fuga et abominatio bonorum operum, cursus autem ad malum. Sicut ps. 13 scriptum est: 'Omnes declinaverunt, simul inutiles facti sunt.' Et Genes. 8: 'Sensus enim et cogitatio cordis humani ad malum proni sunt' (*Vorlesung über den Römerbrief* (1515–16), *W.A.* lvi. 312, 1–15).

[1] See p. 30, n. 1; also *S.A.*, pp. 433–5; also our chapter V, section B.

[2] Henri Rondet says; 'Augustin, qui parlait aussi d'expérience, soulignait la misère de l'homme, même racheté, même justifié, et voyait dans la justification moins un état qu'un devenir. Luther va plus loin encore et il assure que l'homme, quoi qu'il fasse, ne sera jamais justifié tant que dure la vie d'ici-bas. Le péché originel, en effet, a corrompu tout son être. Là où il règne, il ne peut y avoir rien de bon, les vertus des païens ne sont que des vices splendides; le chrétien lui-même n'est justifié que par une fiction juridique. Le désordre de la concupiscence suffirait à le constituer pécheur s'il n'était couvert des mérites du Christ. Même couvert par eux, l'homme ne pourrait, en ces actions propres, que pécher mortellement. Un décret divin rend cependant vénielles ces fautes du justifié' (*Gratia Christi*, p. 262). Rondet backs up his statements with a careful selection of texts given in his notes.

[3] 'Respondeo dicendum quod . . . duplex est habitus. Unus quidem quo inclinatur potentia ad agendum, sicut scientiae et virtutes dicuntur habitus. Et hoc modo peccatum originale non est habitus. Alio modo dicitur habitus dispositio alicuius naturae ex multis compositae, secundum quam se habet vel male ad aliquid, et praecipue cum talis dispositio fuerit quasi in naturam versa, ut patet de aegritudine et sanitate. Et hoc modo peccatum originale est habitus. Est enim quaedam inordinata dispositio proveniens ex dissolutione illius harmoniae in qua consistit ratio originalis justitiae, sicut etiam aegritudo corporalis est quaedam inordinata dispositio corporis, secundum quam solvitur aequalitas in qua consistit ratio sanitatis.

(*footnote continued on opposite page*)

quick to conclude that nothing whatever remains of nature in Luther's theology, or that the evil in man is mainly material; that is, localized in the flesh and base affections. Frequently, critics interpret Luther in the latter sense because of his constant use of the term *concupiscentia carnis* which he identifies with sin, and also because he divides the Christian into the interior or spiritual man and the exterior or carnal man.[1]

The Reformer, however, employs these globally to designate man's passion for self or *amour-propre*, which resides primarily in the will and not just in the lusts of the flesh. It is the whole man who is carnal in the sense that he is wholly in love with himself; or it is the whole man who is spiritual in the opposite sense that he is wholly in love with God.[2] Luther focuses the effects of sin more so on the inner heart of man than on the outer members of his body.

His treatise, *De servo arbitrio*, proves the truth of this fact. Here,

Unde peccatum originale 'languor naturae' dicitur) (St. Thomas Aquinas, *S.Th.*, Ia IIae, q. 82, a. 1, corpus).

It is important to point out that Saint Thomas envisages original sin from the perspective of man's supernatural end, and not, as one finds in Nominalist theology, in terms of nature only. The loss of original justice constitutes for human nature an *inordinatio* precisely because man remains ordained, by virtue of God's promises, to the beatific vision. That is to say, it is not nature *qua* nature that is affected by the *privatio originalis justitiae*, but rather the sons of Adam inasmuch as they are destined to see God face to face.

[1] Luther, in his *Randbemerkungen zu den Sentenzen des Petrus Lombardus* (1510–11) (see *W.A.* ix. 75 and 76), uses the terms *concupiscentia* and *carnis* in a limited sense; namely to designate an opposition between the flesh and the spirit, understood literally according to man's composite nature of body and soul. Later, however, after his break with Rome, he will employ these terms in a broader and more universal sense to classify all that is sinful and displeasing to God; especially the sin of pride and self-love (see following note, and p. 32, n. 2).

[2] We must be careful not to interpret Luther's descriptions of the carnal and spiritual man as an opposition between soul and body. Erasmus, apparently, made this mistake and Luther replied '... id observabis in scripturis, ubicunque de carne agitur per antithesin ad spiritum, ibi fere per carnem intelligas omnia contraria spiritus, Ut ibi: Caro non prodest quicquam. [John vi. 63]. Ubi vero absolute tractatur, ibi conditionem naturamque corporalem significare scias, ut: erunt duo in carne una [Matt. xix. 5]. Caro mea vere est cibus [John vi. 55]. Verbum caro factum est [John i. 14]. In his locis poteris mutato Ebraismo corpus pro carne dicere. Ebraea enim lingua uno vocabulo Carnis significat, quod nos duobus carne et corpore significamus. Et vellem sic fuisse translatum distinctis vocabulis totum ubique scripturae canonem. Sic arbitror, locus meus ex Gen. 6. adhuc fortiter stabit adversus liberum arbitrium, quando caro esse probatur, quam Paulus Ro. 8 dicit, nec posse Deo subiici, ut videbimus eo loco, et ipsamet Diatribe [Erasmus' Diatribe on the *Freedom of the Will*] dicit, nihil boni velle posse' (*De Servo arbitrio*, *W.A.* xviii. 735–6, 31–37. 1–5).

he explains more systematically his views on human sinfulness.

He tells us, for example, that man's ignorance and scorn of God's laws spring from the heart of man and his noblest faculties:

And this ignorance, and total scorn, undoubtedly, are not in the flesh and base affections but in the most eminent and noblest faculties in man where justice, faith, fear and knowledge of God should reign; yes, in the reason and the will, therefore even the faculties of free choice, and in the seed of virtue or in the very best which exists in man.[1]

For Luther, the human will is somehow curved in on itself, *incurvatus in se*, and bent ineluctably on earthly goods. This is the concupiscence or carnality that Luther identifies with sin. Even before his break with Rome, he singled out self-love as the worst of vices: '. . . quia homo non potest nisi que sua sunt querere et se super omnia diligere que est summa omnium vitiorum.'[2] The impious, or every natural man born of Adam, is turned in on self; he cannot prevent himself from seeking after his own interest any more than he can cease to be; for he is corrupt (see n. 1, p. 47).

But when Luther says corrupt or 'perverse', he does not mean a physical event—a *corruptio simpliciter*, understood in an Aristotelian sense. He means a moral defect; that is to say, an incapacity of the will to perform good works, as just described. After Adam's fall, man continues to be a rational animal endowed with intellect and will. In terrestrial affairs, especially in matters pertaining to self-interest, he still has a certain faculty of free choice; but morally and spiritually, his nature, unaided by grace, remains a slave to self and powerless to win the favour of God.[3] Likewise, in the order of knowledge, he finds in himself—

---

[1] *De servo arbitrio, W.A.* xviii. 761. 30–37.

[2] 'Quia homo non potest, nisi que sua sunt, querere et se super omnia diligere. Que est summa omnium vitiorum. Unde et in bonis et virtutibus tales querunt seipsos, sc. ut sibi placeant et plaudant' (*Vorlesung über den Römerbrief, W.A.*, lvi. 237. 12–15).

[3] 'Non enim de esse naturae loquimur, sed de esse gratiae . . . Scimus liberum arbitrium natura aliquid facere, ut comedere, bibere, gignere, regere, ne nos delirio illo, velut argutulo, rideat, quod nec peccare quidem liceret sine Christo, si vocem illam nihil urgeamus, cum tamen Lutherus donarit lib. arb. [Here Luther is referring to Erasmus's Diatribe] valere nihil nisi ad peccandum, adeo libuit sapienti Diatribe ineptire etiam in re seria. Dicimus enim, hominem extra gratiam Dei manere nihilominus sub generali omnipotentia Dei facientis [this is Nominalist terminology], moventis, rapientis omnia necessario et infallibili cursu, sed hoc

'written in his heart'—certain self-evident truths; namely, God exists and is omnipotent, human nature depends solely on God's Will,[1] and is under the obligation to obey His Commandments;[2] notwithstanding, this knowledge does not, of itself, make him capable of doing what it tells him should be done.[3] It is in this moral sense that we should understand Luther when he says that man, without grace, can do nothing but sin.[4]

This point is of considerable importance; it means that Luther's position, despite his violent attacks on the merit of human acts, admits of a certain unchanged ontological residuum of human nature.

Luther does not bother to discuss the Law from the point of view of man's ontological structure. As we have already seen, he speaks of the Law as 'showing us what we must do' but not providing the *virtutem faciendi*. His pessimism inclines him to

quod sic raptus homo facit, esse nihil, id est nihil valere coram Deo, nec aliud reputari quam peccatum' (*De servo arbitrio*, W.A. xviii. 753. 6–15).

See also p. 638. 5–11 '. . . bona fide . . . doceamus, ut homini arbitrium liberum non respectu superioris, sed tantum inferioris se rei concedatur, hoc est, ut sciat sese in suis facultatibus et possessionibus habere ius utendi, faciendi, omittendi pro libero arbitrio . . . Caeterum erga Deum, vel in rebus, quae pertinent ad salutem vel damnationem, non habet liberum arbitrium, sed captivus, subiectus et servus est vel voluntatis Dei vel voluntatis Satanae.'

[1] 'Omnes enim homines inveniunt hanc sententiam in cordibus suis scriptam et agnoscunt eam ac probant (licet inviti), cum audiunt eam tractari. Primo Deum esse omnipotentem non solum potentia, sed etiam actione (ut dixi), alioqui ridiculus foret Deus: Deinde ipsum omnia nosse et praescire, neque errare neque falli posse. Istis duobus omnium corde et sensu concessis, coguntur mox inevitabili consequentia admittere, Nos non fieri nostra voluntate, sed necessitate; Ita nos non facere quodlibet pro iure liberi arbitrii, sed prout Deus praescivit et agit consilio et virtute infallibili et immutabili' (ibid., p. 719. 23–30). From the context, it is obvious that Luther wishes to show that man has no freedom of will before God; his purpose is not epistemological; to find out what truths the human mind, by itself, unaided by grace, can know with certainty. Yet the fact that he considers the above truths as self-evident to men proves that his pessimism about human nature does not imply a total perversion of man's power to know and to understand.

[2] '. . . lex (teste Paulo, Ro. 2: 15) in cordibus nostris scripta, tum agnoscitur, ubi recte tractatur, tum obscuratur, ubi impiis magistris vexatur et aliis opinionibus occupatur' (ibid. 33–35). Again; in *Der deutsche Katechismus*: 'Die zehen Gepot sind auch sonst in aller Menschen Herzen geschrieben . . .' (*Bek.*, p. 661, 20–25). When Luther says *aller Menschen*, he is referring to Pagans as well as Christians; consequently, he teaches that the Ten Commandments are, to some extent, known naturally (see below, p. 89, n. 1).

[3] 'Denn so wir künnten aus eigenen Kräften die zehen Gepot halten, wie sie zu halten sind, dürften wir nichts weiter, wider Glauben noch Vaterunser' (*D.C.*, p. 646. 19-21; see also our Chapter IV).

[4] See p. 32 ,n. 2, and p. 34, n. 2.

look upon the Law pragmatically—in so far as it serves to lead man to God by causing him to despair in self. The Decalogue is a striking proof of what man, because of sin, is not and cannot do in the moral or spiritual domain. The following aphorism of Mr. Whale states quite succinctly the essential meaning of Luther's pessimism: 'What man as man must do, man as sinner cannot do.'[1]

Nominalist influence

This moral impotence, perhaps, is better appreciated when related to one of the historical factors which helped to bring on his *crise de conscience*; namely, Nominalist theology. Perhaps more than any other human factor, Nominalism may have been decisive in intensifying his sense of sinfulness and unworthiness before God (*coram deo*). And this we state against conflicting explanations: Denifle does not hesitate to attribute Luther's *Ängst* and pessimism to an inability to control sexual lust;[2] and Grisar to scruples and pathological tendencies.[3] Maritain even goes so far as to accuse the Wittenberg monk of a kind of sour-grapes pride, claiming his frustration and moral defeatism to have resulted from failure to attain the heights of mystical sanctity advocated by such German mystics as Meister Eckhart and Tauler.[4] But these explanations, in the light of modern research, all seem inadequate[5] because they do not point to more radical and likely causes which could very well have conducted an extremely conscientious and sensitive monk on to pessimism and despair.

Certain Pelagian tendencies in Nominalist writings, we think,

[1] J. S. Whale, *The Protestant Tradition*, Cambridge, 1955, p. 26.
[2] See Denifle, op. cit., ii. 391–407. 'In 1908, W. Braun produced an important technical examination of Luther's use of the word "concupiscentia", especially in the Lectures on Romans. Braun showed that Denifle had rightly drawn attention to the great importance of this word for Luther, but that Denifle had completely mis-interpreted its real meaning by confining its meaning to sensual lust' (Rupp, *Righteousness of God*, pp. 24–25).
[3] Hartmann Grisar, *Luther*, trans. by E. M. Lamond, London, 1913–17, vi. 205–6.
[4] See J. Maritain, *Three Reformers*, London, 1928, pp. 3–50.
[5] This is the opinion of Joseph Lortz in his work, *Die Reformation in Deutschland*. This scholar is a Catholic, and much fairer and more objective in his treatment of Luther than his predecessors, Denifle and Grisar. Gordon Rupp quotes him as saying: 'To ascribe Luther's revolt to base motives would be ... grievously to underestimate the depth of the tragedy of the Reformation' (see Rupp, op. cit., p. 27).

suggest a more plausible partial explanation. But before stating our reasons, we would like to recall that Luther was not intimately acquainted with the great Scholastic systems of the thirteenth century. His knowledge of Thomism, apparently, was superficial.[1] What he knew best, outside of the Bible, Saint Augustine,[2] Tauler, and the *Theologia Germanica*,[3] were the Nominalist commentaries on the Sentences of Peter Lombard; in particular, Biel's *Collectorium circa quattuor libros sententiarum...*[4]

[1] 'Luther's knowledge of the *Summa theologica* is not easy to measure.... The lectures and *Table Talk* swarm with references to the great systematist, although none that I have examined show anything more than a superficial acquaintance with Thomas. Father Denifle's *Luthertum* (1906), i. 523 ff., gives a detailed analysis of Luther's references and reaches the conclusion that his understanding of Thomas' ideas is to be rated zero. Despite the bitter tone which disfigures Denifle's discussion, his arguments seem to be convincing. As in the case of Scotus, Luther's attitude toward Thomas bears throughout the stamp of nominalist prejudice' (Fife, op. cit., 47, p. 113).

[2] Jean Cadier, 'St. Augustin et la Réforme', in *Recherches Augustiniennes*, Paris, 1958, vol. iv, has traced the influence of Saint Augustine on the Reformer. He says: 'Luther ... est conduit (c. 1509) par son étude des *Sentences*, à lire les œuvres du grand Docteur africain, il les lit avec passion. "Au début, dit-il dans un propos de table, je dévorais Augustin plutôt que je ne le lisais" ... dans sa vie de Luther, Mélanchthon dit: "il lisait souvent et se rappelait parfaitement tous les écrits d'Augustin"' (p. 358).

It was to be noted, however, that Luther was familiar with Ockhamism before he studied the works of Saint Augustine. Concerning the Nominalist influence on Luther, Father Weijenborg supplies us with the following information: 'A partir de 1502, Luther a incontestablement subi des influences ockhamistes à toutes les étapes de sa formation scientifique. De 1502 à 1505, il suit les cours de philosophie ockhamiste que professent à l'université d'Erfurt ses maîtres Josse Trutfetter et Barthélémy d'Usingen. De la fin de son noviciat (Sept. 1506) à l'été de 1508, il étudie la théologie suivant les directives de Jean Nathin, disciple immédiat de l'ockhamiste Gabriel Biel. En même temps il se prépare à l'ordination sacerdotale par la lecture assidue de *l'Exposition du Canon sacré de la Messe*, ouvrage composé par ce même Biel. Pendant l'année académique, 1508–1509, tout en enseignant comme professeur temporaire l'éthique naturelle à l'université de Wittenberg, il assiste aux cours de théologie ockhamiste de Trutfetter. De retour à Erfurt, il paraphrase dès l'automne 1509, les Sentences, à l'aide des commentaires de Guillaume d'Ockham, Pierre d'Ailly et Gabriel Biel' (R. Weijenborg, 'La charité dans la première théologie de Luther', in *R.H.E.*, 1950, pp. 619–20).

[3] In his 1518 preface to the *Deutsche Theologie*, Luther claims that after the Bible and Saint Augustine, he never learned more from anything than he did from this book on German mysticism: 'Und das ich nach meinem alten narren rüme, ist mir nehst der Biblien und S. Augustino nit vorkummen ein buch, dar auß ich mehr erlernet hab und will was got, Christus, Mensch und alle ding sein' (*W.A.* i. 378. 21–23).

[4] Luther, in his *Randbemerkungen zu den Sentenzen des Petrus Lombardus* (c. 1509–10) (see Paul Vignaux, *Luther commentateur des Sentences*, Paris, 1935, n. 1, p. 5) refers to Biel's *Collectorium*.... It is not certain whether he knew Biel's doctrine, in 1510, from the 1501 edition of Biel's work or simply from the courses of Usingen and

Melanchthon testifies that Luther studied, with pleasure, the commentaries of Biel, d'Ailly, and Ockham, and knew them so thoroughly that in later years he was able to quote them by heart.[1]

Now we observe that Gabriel Biel's *Collectorium* . . . contains certain theses or propositions which Luther grew to dislike extremely and to reject outright;[2] theses which could easily have aroused his own tormented soul to a pitch of agony and near hatred of God.

These theses pertain to the moral goodness of human nature, to the powers of the intellect and the will, *ex suis naturalibus* and *sine gratia*, to perform good works, to avoid sin, to fulfil God's Commandments, if not *quantum ad intentionem praecipientis*, at least *quantum ad substantiam facti*, and also to love God *super omnia*.

The most remarkable and significant of these theses is the one which asserts that man, by virtue of God's decree *de potentia ordinata* and *ex sua liberalitate*, can merit the first grace of salvation by simply doing all that is in him:

Trutfetter (see Vignaux, ibid., p. 46). Concerning the way in which Luther came to know the Collectorium, see H. Degering, *Luther's Randbemerkungen zu Gabriel Biels Collectorium*. . ., Weimar, 1933. Luther's references to Biel are found in *W.A.* ix. 40. 36; and 74. 9.

[1] See Heinrich Boehmer, *Road to Reformation*, Philadelphia, 1957, p. 45. In Melanchthon's own words: 'Gabrielem et Cammeracensem pene ad verbum memoriter recitare poterat. Diu multumque legit scripta Occam. Hujus acumen anteferebat Thomae et Scoto . . .' (Preface to the second volume of the *Opera* of Luther, Wittenberg, 1546, *Corpus Reformatorum*, vi. 159; *Dok.*, p. 532, 199. 37–39; quoted from Vignaux, ibid., p. 145).

[2] In the *Q.J.* we find the following sentences which are remarkably similar to theses which Luther has one of his students (Franz Günther) condemn in the *Disputatio contra scholasticam theologiam, W.A.* i. 221–8. Luther drew up the theses of the *Disputatio* for the latter, who defended them at the University of Wittenberg on 4 Sept. 1517, in fulfilment of the requirements for the degree of bachelor of Holy Scripture (see H. J. Grimm, Introduction to his translation of the *Disputatio*. . . A. xxxi. 6).

Liberum hominis arbitrium ex suis naturalibus sine gratia elicere potest actum moraliter bonum [p. 50]. Liberum arbitrium ex suis naturalibus sine dono gratiae potest quodlibet peccatum mortale novum cavere [ibid.].

Homo per liberum arbitrium ex suis naturalibus potest divina precepta quoad actus substantiam implere, sed non ad intentionem precipientis que est consecutio salutis nostre [p. 51]. Viatoris voluntas humana, ex suis naturalibus potest diligere Deum super omnia [p. 58].

Note. Theses similar to these are condemned by Luther in the *Smalcald Articles*; see *Bek.*, pp. 434–5; and also our Chapter VI, p. 137, n. 6; and *Resolutiones Lutherianae super propositionibus suis Lipsiae disputatis* (1519), *W.A.* ii. 401.

For God accepts the act of the one who does all that is in him [*actum facientis quod in se est*] as a sufficient reason for awarding him the first grace [*ad tribuendum primam gratiam*], not out of justice due but out of his liberality. But the soul, by removing the obstacle, by ceasing from the act or consent of sin, and by turning itself rightly towards God [*eliciendo bonum motum in Deum*] as to its first principle and end, does all that is in it [*facit quod in se est*]. Therefore God accepts the act of removing the obstacle and the turning towards God as a reason for infusing grace [*ad infundendam gratiam*]. Finally, therefore, by removing the obstacle and by turning towards God, one merits grace *de congruo*. . . .[1]

It is argued that this Nominalist idea of merit, when studied in its proper context, and explained with suitable definitions, nuanced meanings, and subtle sub-distinctions, characteristic of the Schoolmen, is not at all incompatible with the traditional teachings of the Church. Vignaux has shown, with careful precision and keen penetration, that, according to the dialectic of God acting *de potentia ordinata* and *de potentia absoluta*, the hypothesis of a *natura pura* brings out the radical gratuitousness of the whole order of grace.[2] But be that as it may, it remains that the emphasis and tendency in this thesis of Biel's is Pelagian; and because of its insistence on doing all that is in one, it presupposes and includes all the other Bielian propositions defending the incorrupt moral capacity of human nature, the highest act of which is to love God above all things.[3]

On reading Biel's account of justification, one is ever conscious of great stress being placed on man's moral capacity to do

[1] Biel, *Q.J.*, p. 31. We read also '. . . anima obicis remotione ac bono motu in Deum ex arbitrii libertate elicito primam gratiam mereri potest de congruo' (ibid.). For a discussion of the Nominalist use of the terms *de congruo* and *de condigno*, see our Appendix I. Biel, of course, does not claim that man can merit grace *de condigno*.

[2] 'C'est *de potentia Dei absoluta* que les "pura naturalia" se détachent de l'ensemble où ils sont engagés de *potentia ordinata*. L'hypothèse d'une pure nature manifeste la gratuité radicale de tout l'ordre de la grâce: si haute que soit la valeur morale de l'amour naturel de l'objet divin: "summe diligibile summe diligendum", elle n'est pas valeur méritoire de la vie éternelle—"actus ille amoris amicitiae, licet esset moraliter bonus, etc. . . . non tamen esset meritorius". Ceci est vraiment d'un autre ordre, absolument surnaturel. . .' (Vignaux, 'Luther et Ockham', in *Wilhelm Ockham*, Münster i. W., 1950, pp. 25–26).

[3] In the *Disputatio* . . . (1517), Luther rejects Biel's theory as false: 'Falsum et illud est, quod facere quod est in se sit removere obstacula gratiae' (thesis 33). Again: 'Actus amiciciae non est perfectissimus modus faciendi quod est in se, Nec est dispositio perfectissima ad gratiam Dei aut modus convertendi et appropinquandi ad Deum' (thesis 26).

good unaided by grace. Now a theoretical or academic over-emphasis on this side of human nature could, in practice, encourage a downright Pelagian approach to God. The thesis on meriting grace *de congruo*, even though it be based on the divine acceptance *de potentia ordinata*, could be taken, by Luther, to mean that man's salvation depends on a human kind of distributive justice. The initial act by which God judges, justifies, and redeems the sinner is determined by the sinner's own personal efforts and merits—by his attempt to do all that is in him—*quod in se est*. The thesis implies that God, *de potentia ordinata*, would have to reward those who do their best *ex suis naturalibus* and curse those who fail to do so. The idea that God grants the first grace even to the unreformed and unrepentant sinner seems, somehow, excluded. Thus Biel's thesis on merit becomes like to the active or formal justice of the doctors which Luther describes and denounces in his autobiographical fragment of 1545.

We can see, therefore, how Biel's moral optimism could affect Luther personally, for as long as he accepted these Nominalist assertions as true.[1] Being himself over-scrupulous about his own unworthiness, as well as desperately eager to experience certitude about God's judgements, Luther would certainly be encouraged by Biel's theology of merit to indulge in a kind of Pelagian effort.

That is to say, it would urge him on to acquiring natural virtue and perfect love of God, not as an effect of grace, but rather as the means of forcing God's hand, so to speak; as if God had to wait for sinners to obtain an ideal natural perfection before bestowing on them the healing and creative merits of Christ's Crucifixion and Resurrection. According to Biel's theory of merit, Luther could argue: If I am absolutely certain I love God *super omnia*, then *ipso facto*, I can claim God's love and reward; namely His justice. Thereby, I shall find certitude of personal salvation in my efforts at human sanctity. But the reverse would also be true, if I am selfish and feel unloved, I would have good reason to think that I was rejected by God.[2]

[1] 'Luther himself repeatedly designates as the chief cause of his distress the notion that man can do everything that he wills to do, and also that he is able to earn the reward of eternal blessedness by his own works' (see Boehmer, op. cit., p. 89).

[2] That Luther reasoned along these dialectical lines is not pure conjecture; in his early commentary on Romans, [in *Die Scholien*] he argues that one who succeeds in

As a matter of historical fact, Luther, before his break with Rome, strove diligently, at times heroically, to attain the heights of sanctity. All historians of our age agree that the material evidence portrays Luther as a zealous and exemplary Augustinian, obedient to his superiors and faithful to the monastic rule.[1] He prayed, studied, and fasted; he preached and taught the Word of God, and performed other works of charity, he punished his body and soul with all manner of penances; in short, he worked, worked, worked to do *quod in se est*; yet never, at any moment, apparently, did he feel in his own heart the perfect love that Biel spoke of. In his own words: 'And I, though a monk, living beyond reproach, felt myself to be a sinner before God, troubled in conscience. . . .'[2]

For Luther, something obviously was wrong with Biel's theories on nature and merit; his own personal experience gave the lie to them. Judging himself in the light of Biel's ideal of perfect love of God, *ex suis naturalibus*, he finds that he is sinful; he discovers selfish motives in his heart, what he calls *concupiscentia*; he does not always observe the Law, he does not always love God disinterestedly; why, he asks himself, can I not be perfect as the theologians and mystics require it? Why do I always fall short of the mark? In a moment of intense frustration, he cries out: my nature is corrupt; without God's favour, I am sinful. It would seem that such an experience was part of him when he interpreted the Bible and concluded that original sin had perverted totally and radically all his moral faculties.[3]

conforming perfectly to God's will cannot be damned: 'Quia impossibile est, ut extra Deum maneat, qui in voluntatem Dei sese penitus proiecit. Quia vult, quod vult Deus; Ergo placet Deo. Si placet, ergo est dilectus; Si dilectus, ergo saluus' (*W.A.* lvi. 391. 13–16). See also Fife, op. cit., p. 215: 'The problem of predestination still causes him anxiety [that is during the time of his commentary on Romans (1515–16)], and the uncompromising position of the Apostle as Martin interprets him on this subject plainly confuses the lecturer. At one point he extricates himself from the contradictions inherent in the conception of predestination by a dialectical explanation. It is impossible that one who conforms fully to the will of God should remain in hell. 'Because he wishes what God wishes, therefore he pleases God. If he pleases God, then he is loved. If he is loved, then he will be saved.'

[1] Lucien Febvre writes: 'Un mauvais moine, non! Un trop bon moine, au contraire. Ou du moins, qui ne péchait que par excès de zèle . . .' (*Martin Luther, Un Destin*, Paris, 1952, p. 31).

[2] Autobiographical fragment of 1545, quoted above, Chapter I, section B.

[3] Similarly the Protestant historian, Henri Strohl, considers Luther's reaction to what he believes to be Pelagian teachings in Biel's theories about nature and merit: 'Il est très compréhensible qu'un moine aussi scrupuleux que Luther, avec une

Having come to this conclusion about man's sinfulness, we are not surprised to find him in the *Randbemerkungen zu Gabriel Biels Collectorium* ... and the *Disputatio contra scholasticam theologiam*, repudiating all the Nominalist theories which defend the capacity of human nature to do good works and to merit grace.[1] In this respect, his attitude is sincere and genuine; he prefers the certitude of his own personal experience and understanding of the Bible to the airy speculations of a decadent theology.[2] But in throwing away Biel's Pelagianism, does he manage to free himself entirely from the former's influence?

Is not his own experience of sinfulness influenced and intensified, even distorted, by what Biel claims to be the ideal perfection of human nature—the love of God *super omnia*? Does he not still continue to ruminate, perhaps at times subconsciously, on what he considers to be the exigencies of this Nominalist ideal, and the distributive justice which it implies? Though he rejects the moral optimism of Biel, does he not judge the corruptness of his own nature by its failure to meet Pelagian standards—what man can and should do *ex suis naturalibus*.[3]

conscience aussi inexorable que la sienne, ait été poussé au désespoir par une telle théorie. Il se martyrisait pour faire "quod in se est", pour mériter la grâce, pour créer par ses propres resources la disposition parfaite que Biel déclarait possible. Une conscience moins sévère eût pu s'accommoder de cette théorie—des milliers d'exemples le prouvent—la sienne non. Sans être "anormal", sans souffrir de "la maladie du scrupule", il devait sentir ce qu'elle avait de décevant pour un homme souffrant de son imperfection, affligé de son péché' (Henri Strohl, *L'Évolution religieuse de Luther*, Strasbourg, 1922, p. 101).

[1] Paul Vignaux has shown that Luther, in the *Disputatio contra scholasticam theologiam*, chose Biel as his principal adversary: 'Luther ... quand il disputera, en 1517, contre la théologie scholastique, le choisira comme principal adversaire" (*Luther commentateur des Sentences*, p. 45); and in a footnote, he writes that the *Disputatio*... 'vise expressément Biel treize fois, dont trois fois en compagnie de Pierre d'Ailly et de Guillaume d'Occam. Les propositions 5–22 suivent Biel, III Sent., d. xxxvii, q. v, a. 3, dub 2 Q–R, que reprennent encore les thèses 26–28 et 54–61: toutes ces propositions concernent le problème de la justification' (ibid., n. 3).

[2] Later, in his *Smalcald Articles*, Luther argues that it is precisely because the 'Sophisten' or Schoolmen have not 'perceived' [*erkenneten*] or recognized real sin that they teach incorrectly concerning repentance (*Bek.*, p. 438. 8–10; see also Chapter V, section C, below).

[3] Fife claims that the Nominalist acceptance of the natural powers of man for good clung to Luther's thinking and 'comes strongly to the fore years later when he breaks with the whole system' (Fife, op. cit., p. 159). See p. 39, n. 3 below. For Luther, the moral impotence of the will consists precisely in the fact that it is not free to tend towards anything [*quodlibet*] presented to it as good: 'Conceditur, quod voluntas non est libera ad tendendum in quodlibet secundum rationem boni sibi ostensum'

We answer that very often Luther's criterion for judging the human will's natural capacity to avoid sin seems to be an ideal or theoretical notion of disinterested love of God;[1] all who fail to observe the Law flawlessly and to remove every trace of self-love from the heart[2] are sinful before God.[3]

(Disputatio . . . (1517), W.A. i. 221, thesis 10). This being the case, the will would be powerless to love God super omnia, inasmuch as such love is presented to it secundum rationem boni.

[1] In the Disputatio . . . of 1517, W.A. i. 221–8, Luther calls Biel's theory about man's ability to love God super omnia a 'fictitious term' and a 'chimera': 'Diligere deum super omnia naturaliter Est terminus fictus, sicut Chimera' (thesis 18). But here he is attacking the will's capacity; he is not denying that the will ought to and should love God super omnia; see n. 3 below.

[2] Such sublime virtue, in our opinion, should only be expected of a living human being endowed with very special graces and divine privileges—the Blessed Virgin Mary, for instance—not a mere creature left to itself. See following note.

[3] We recall what Luther says in the Catechism: If man, by his own powers, could keep the Commandments as they should be kept, there would be no need for faith and the Our Father (see above, p. 31, n. 3). In the Disputatio . . ., however, he is more precise: 'omne opus legis sine gratia dei foris apparet bonum, sed intus est peccatum. Contra Scho.' (thesis 76). The reason for this position, we know from our preceding analysis, is that human nature is always vitiated by self-love or concupiscentia. Consider the following theses from the Disputatio . . .: 'Conversa voluntas ad legem sine gratia dei est affectu commodi sui talis' (thesis 78); again: 'Non est in natura nisi actus concupiscentiae erga Deum' (thesis 21).

Now, notwithstanding the fact that Luther is mainly preoccupied with the Christian's worth before God (coram Deo and erga Deum) and not with his person as he appears before the judgement of his fellow men ('. . . non loquatur de hominibus, quales sunt in oculis suis et coram hominibus, sed quales sunt coram deo, ubi omnes sunt sub peccato . . .' Lectures on Romans, W.A. lvi. 234, 24–25), here in the Disputatio . . . (1517) he is definitely attacking Biel's propositions on the capacity of the human will to do all that is in it, and to perform good works—in particular the allegedly natural power to love God super omnia. In this context, his perspective is not necessarily biblical or supernatural, but somewhat ethical and theoretical; that is to say, it is not a question of how a Christian should love God, by virtue of graces received, but rather what man should do qua man and ex suis naturalibus, but fails to do propter peccatum. What man is really capable of doing in a purely natural state, abstracting from grace and sin, is, we believe, a strictly academic question. The real man is either in a state of grace or a state of sin; historically, the natura pura, without grace or sin, has never existed. Luther, himself, would probably agree with this; but reasoning speculatively on the matter, it would be, perhaps, gratuitous to assume that a man, in such a state of pure nature, and ex suis naturalibus was indeed capable of suppressing, in his heart, all trace of self-love. (We do not think either that this is what Biel meant (see Vignaux, 'Sur Luther et Ockham', p. 29). Equally gratuitous would be the inference that every form of self-love, in man's heart, was truly 'sin', in the ethical sense of that term; namely a wilful transgression against right-reason and nature. In theology, there is room to distinguish between a natural self-love, in keeping with God's plan, and a vitiated self-love, an act contrary to God's Will, and thus properly speaking sinful. When Luther identifies, globally and absolutely, all self-love or concupiscentia with sin, leaving no place for distinctions, he seems to be judging the moral goodness of man according to a

In yet another respect, Nominalism could have intensified Luther's sense of sinfulness and dread of God, in the early cloister years. We are thinking of the priority of the will, in the Ockhamist picture of God,[1] which seems to be pushed to extremes in Luther's writings.[2]

The Ockhamists interpreted predestination principally in terms of an arbitrary divine Will, apparently in no way conditioned by the formal necessities of nature and laws governing creatures. If the Christian, the just man, intrinsically good in his nature and his acts and endowed with divine grace, merits Heaven, it is only due to the fact that God so ordains it *de potentia ordinata*; but He could or might, *de potentia absoluta*, refuse Heaven to the one possessing these qualities; or inversely, even impute justification and the right to Heaven to the sinful man, deprived of grace and devoid of virtue.[3] Nothing necessitates God's taking into account the moral disposition and supernatural qualities of the recipient.[4] Such a picture of God means, to use Febvre's phase, 'unconditioned and unforseen predestination'.[5]

We know, from Vignaux's careful studies, that Luther, from as early as 1510, had rejected the dialectic between 'absolute' and 'ordained' power and was concerned with what in fact God had done.[6] Yet he does not, for that matter, abandon the voluntarism of Ockhamist theology;[7] and it still remains that previous

theoretical standard of ideal natural love of God. Whether this tendency is the result of Nominalist influences only, or to several factors, is not certain.

[1] 'Les disciples d'Occam savaient la contingence radicale de tout l'ordre créé, la liberté du vouloir divin — source de toute loi . . .' (Vignaux, *Luther commentateur des Sentences*, pp. 47–48).

[2] See below, n. 7.

[3] In Appendix I, we discuss the theological implications of the Nominalist dialectic between God's 'absolute' and 'ordained' power; also the 'voluntarism' behind the Ockhamist idea of merit and justification.

[4] 'Ego autem pono quod nulla forma, nec naturalis, nec supernaturalis potest Deum sic necessitare' (Ockham, i, Sent., d. xvii, q. 1, M.; quoted by Vignaux, *Luther commentateur des Sentences*, pp. 90–91).

[5] Febvre, op. cit., p. 33.

[6] 'Nous ne prétendons pas que Luther n'ait point *utilisé* ultérieurement certaines thèses ou expressions nominalistes *de potentia absoluta*; nous constatons seulement qu'en 1510–1511, à la distinction XVII, il ne reprend pas la dialectique dont usaient les occamistes pour "sauver" Pierre Lombard. Cependant le "voluntarisme" divin, qui animait la dialectique *de potentia absoluta*, demeure présent à l'esprit du Sententiaire' (Vignaux, op. cit., n. 1, p. 92; the italics are in text).

[7] The following references are striking examples of extreme 'voluntarism' *W.A., Randbemerkungen zu den Sentenzen des Petrus Lombardus* (1510–11), ix. 60, 5–9; ibid.,

to his rejection of this dialectic, he was troubled and tormented by the spectre of an implacable judge decreeing the eternal fate of men according to mere whims. He tells us, himself, in his autobiographical fragment, that he hated God and God's justice. To what extent, we wonder, was this Nominalist voluntarism responsible for this hatred?

At this stage, we are not prepared to answer this question; but one thing is certain; for a sensitive young monk seeking certitude about his salvation, this Nominalist picture of God, as an arbitrary paradoxical Will, was not calculated to instil much hope; especially in view of the fact that already, *de potentia ordinata*, the implacable divine Will had decreed that men should merit their salvation in a manner which Luther found impossible—namely to love God *super omnia* and *ex suis naturalibus*.

Yet Luther, apparently, instead of questioning the reasonableness of Ockhamist 'voluntarism', seeks rather to escape the incertitude of God's whimsical decrees. The arbitrary divine Will causes in him great perturbation of soul and anxiety; then it is that he turns to the words of Saint Paul; 'the just man lives by faith'; suddenly these words take on new meaning for him— they become meaningful to his experience of sin and his conception of God; they are an escape from self-love, anxiety, and uncertainty; he is overcome by a new discovery, a strange illumination, a vision of God and of self, an intuition; the sinner finds certitude of salvation in faith alone without works—a passive justification which Luther finds he can describe well enough as an imputative effect[1] of the divine Will. Thus God, while

p. 69. 13–16; and p. 88. 1–5; the latter is particularly extreme: 'Christus non potuit peccare propter identitatem personae divinae quae est super omnem legem, sicut dixit: "Dominus est filius hominis etiam sabbati" [Matt. xii. 8]: consequenter et totius legis. Unde si contra totam legem fecisset, non tamen peccasset' (on the Third Book of the Sentences, d. xii, c. 3). This same 'voluntarism' recurs throughout Luther's works and is particularly noticeable in his *De servo arbitrio*.

[1] We deal with Luther's notion of imputed righteousness below; see section C.

The controversial text in Saint Paul, 'Credidit Abraham Deo et reputatum est illi ad justitiam [Rom. iv. 3]' has been subjected to a variety of interpretations. Catholic exegetes do not agree with Luther's insistence on an exclusively and strictly extrinsic imputation of righteousness. The *Bible de Jérusalem* gives the following interpretation of the text: 'Du point de vue strictement grammatical la formule est susceptible de diverses interprétations: en vertu de la foi, Dieu tient Abraham pour juste, sans qu'il le soit réellement; ou bien: en vertu de cette même foi, Dieu confère gratuitement à Abraham une justice qu'il n'avait point quand il croyait;

remaining an arbitrary Will, ceases to be the implacable judge of lawbreakers; he appears to believers as the merciful consoling God of the Gospel.

Our conjectures, here, are not meant to intimate that Luther is formally or officially an Ockhamist.[1] On the contrary, his

ou enfin: au regard de Dieu pour qui les choses sont par définition comme il les voit, la foi se confond concrètement avec la justice. Mais l'ensemble de la doctrine paulinienne permet d'exclure certainement la première interprétation; entendant la foi, surtout quand il est question de justification, au sens de foi vive, elle parait exclure aussi la seconde, et s'accorde parfaitement avec la troisième, celle de saint Thomas' (*Épître au Romains*, trans. by S. Lyonnet, S.J., Paris, 1953, n. (c), p. 80).

Concerning the expressions of the psalmist: 'Heureux ceux dont les iniquités ont été remises, et les péchés recouverts. Heureux l'homme à qui le Seigneur n'imputera aucune offense' [Ps. xxxi (xxxii). 1–2], Lyonnet adds in a subsequent note: 'Les expressions du psalmiste, interprétées dans leur contexte, pas plus que celle de Gen. 15, 6, ne signifient que les péchés demeurent en dépit du pardon de Dieu, mais qu'ils sont "ôtés" "effacés" '[ibid.].

Edouard Tobac, another Catholic exegete, finds that there is a sense in which Saint Paul's teaching on justification in Romans (ii. 13, iii. 20; iii. 28, v. 16) can be interpreted to mean a forensic or declarative righteousness: 'Les théologiens luthériens, en partant de ce caractère forensique de la justification, concluent généralement au caractère extérieur et imputatif de la justice. Les théologiens catholiques au contraire, partant du caractère interne et réel de la justice, en concluent à l'efficacité opérante et non seulement déclarative de la justification. Il nous semble que sans nier au mot *justice* sa formalité de relation normale avec Dieu, on peut parfaitement soutenir que, considérée subjectivement, en la possession de l'individu, cette relation normale avec Dieu est constituée par la présence en lui de l'Esprit de Dieu. Il nous semble aussi dans ces conditions pouvoir maintenir au mot *justifier*, sa signification forensique de "déclarer juste": Dieu reconnait comme juste celui qui par son union au Christ s'est approprié l'Esprit d'adoption' (*Le Problème de la justification dans Saint Paul*, Louvain, 1908, n. (i), p. 212).

It is important to point out these nuances in the interpretation of Saint Paul on justification. They caution us against hasty judgements; such, for instance, as identifying Luther's doctrine of imputation with the teaching of the Nominalists, simply because of verbal resemblances.

Granted, in the Nominalist dialectic between 'ordained' and 'absolute' power, we find that a strictly extrinsic and imputative righteousness is a possibility with God; but for this reason, it does not follow that Luther adopts the latter position as his own; as if, reasoning grammatically, he merely changes the verb tense from 'might' or 'could' to 'is'. We must bear in mind that Luther, within the context of his religious experience and his intense study of the Bible, could have arrived independently at his own understanding of Saint Paul on justification. In his moral frustration and deep agony of soul, the apparent forensic sense of Saint Paul's words should certainly have appealed to him on its own merits.

Of course, it is possible, we think, that the 'voluntarism' of Nominalist theology —which Luther never abandoned—could have affected his thinking during his study of the Bible, at least to this extent; it could have bent his judgement towards stressing and preferring the extrinsic or declarative meaning of Paul's words on imputation, rather than towards accepting the intrinsic and ontological meaning.

[1] Admittedly, Luther, 'more than once in the years of his final break with the

conception of original sin, and its consequences, opposes diametrically the Pelagian tendencies of Ockhamist theology. And
his refuge in faith, accompanied by an impetuous distrust of
philosophy, constitutes a total denunciation of the rationalist
and dialectical excesses of sixteenth-century theology.[1] We have

Church . . . proclaimed himself one of the party of Occam' (see Fife, op. cit., p. 60).
The following examples are well known: 'Sum enim Occanicae factionis . . .'
(*Adversus execrabilem Antichristi bullam* (1520), *W.A.* vi. 600). '. . . Cur et meae sectae
resisterem, scilicet Occanicae seu modernorum, quam penitus imbibitam teneo . . .'
(*Responsio ad condemnationem doctrinalem per Lovanienses et Colonienses factam* (1520),
W.A. vi. 195). In the great controversy over the reality of universals, he seems to
have been on the Ockhamist side: 'Terministen hieß man eine secte in der hohen
Schule unter welchen ich auch gewesen' (*T.R.* iv. 679. 9). And yet other references:
T.R. ii. 516. 6; *W.A.* xxx (ii), 300. 9; *T.R.* ix. 600. 10).

But we should not assume, from such declarations, that Luther's fundamental
and definitive religious teachings are necessarily traceable to or identifiable with
Nominalist theories. As Vignaux wisely warns us: 'Le thème, Luther et Ockham,
n'est pas sans fécondité si, à de séduisantes reconstructions, on préfère l'attention
aux textes' ('Sur Luther et Ockham', *Ock.*, p. 30). A close comparison of Luther's
views with those of his Nominalist Masters usually reveals that we are dealing with
two entirely different approaches to theology, despite verbal resemblances. Gordon
Rupp is getting at this point when he writes: 'The Marginal notes [to Peter the
Lombard's *Sentences*] reveal that Luther's Ockhamist training had come into
collision with a new stress of theological influence [St. Augustine], and one far
more congenial to his own spiritual needs and profoundest intuitions. In the background a third influence is to be observed, Luther's growing acquaintance with
the Bible and his direct appeal to Biblical testimony' (op. cit., p. 92).

In our case, we were mainly interested in showing how certain Ockhamist
theories undoubtedly intensified Luther's awareness of sin and increased his dread
of God; we were not attempting to identify Lutheran doctrine with Nominalist
doctrine.

Moreover, if we find that the 'voluntarism' of Luther's theology smacks of
Ockhamism, we also notice that it is more extreme (see above p. 40, nn. 6 and 7)
than the voluntarism which one discovers in Biel or d'Ailly. This fact would suggest that it stems from another source; perhaps his own experience of sin and faith
joined to an intense study and personal interpretation of Scripture.

[1] In the *Disputatio contra scholasticam theologiam* (1517), (*W.A.* i. 221–8), we find
the following theses against the use of Aristotle and dialectics in theology:

Tota fere Aristotelis Ethica pessima est gratiae inimica. Contra Scholast
[thesis 41].

Error est, Aristotelis sententiam de foelicitate non repugnare doctrinae
catholicae. Contra morales | thesis 42].

Error est dicere: sine Aristotele non fit theologus. Contra dictum commune
[thesis 43].

Nulla forma syllogistica tenet in terminis divinis. Contra Card [d'Ailly]
[thesis 47].

Frustra fingitur logica fidei, Suppositio mediata extra terminum et numerum.
Contra recen. Dialect. [thesis 46].

For anyone who reads the marginal notes to Peter Lombard's sentences, it is
evident that Luther does not relish the invasion of theology by philosophy; and in
this respect he is as critical of the Ockhamists as he is of the Scotists or the Thomists.

(*footnote continued overleaf*)

simply drawn the reader's attention to the more than probable influence which Nominalism exerted on him—how it undoubtedly contributed to his experience of moral frustration and the dread of God. This influence was certainly part of him when he read Saint Paul, Saint Augustine, Tauler, Aristotle, and others; and likewise when he cast a disdainful eye on the crying abuses and abominations of his Renaissance world.

If, indeed, unlike Biel, he bases his religious affirmations, not on dry syllogisms and subtle dialectics, but on faith in the words of Saint Paul, and on the fact that his personal experience of man and God seems to him to be in total agreement with the truths of revelation, we must not, therefore, assume that Nominalism has no influence on him; the traces of Biel's theology are sufficiently present in his training and thinking to colour his vision and affect his experience.[1]

More visible and certain, however, are the implications of Luther's doctrine of original sin. God's justification of the sinner must exclude personal effort and merit. If man is morally depraved, he cannot perform good works until he is justified; he has to be made good, somehow, by divine intervention; in this case by the gift of faith; otherwise all his actions will remain displeasing to God.

Indeed, in the process of being made good, transformed by the power of faith, the sinner can only play the role of a passive subject. Any positive active moral effort on his part such as

Gordon Rupp's remarks on this score are enlightening: 'what no reader of the marginal notes can fail to remark, and a matter on which all commentators seem agreed, is the boldness and acidity of Luther's attack on the invasion of theology by philosophy, and the sharpness with which he turns on philosophers, on Gabriel Biel, on Scotus and on Ockham. Thus he refers to the "rancid rules of logicians", to "those grubs the philosophers", to the "dregs of philosophy" and to "that rancid philosopher Aristotle".'

'These remarkable criticisms are much more than passing observations. They are a studied protest against the aggressions of late medieval philosophy into theology, and if their sharpened edge lies towards Scotus, it is also laid against Ockham and Biel. This is the attempt, aptly described by Vignaux as the detachment of theology from the "envelope" of philosophy. It is a humanist return to the "philosophy of Christ"' (Rupp, op. cit., pp. 92–93).

[1] Here we have been considering only two aspects of the Nominalist influence on Luther's mind; namely, the moral capacity of the human will to do good, and the arbitrariness of the divine Will, both of which seem to have contributed to his feeling of moral frustration and hopelessness before God. There are, of course, other aspects of this influence on Luther, but we do not intend to deal with them in this present study.

co-operating or choosing, would necessarily contradict Luther's contention that human nature is morally depraved. For if the sinful man could choose freely between belief and unbelief when offered to him, it would mean that he is not powerless to pose a morally good act and to arbitrate between good and evil.

We are not saying that Luther reasons out his arguments for passive justification in these simple terms. But the fact is that his doctrine of original sin implies such an argument. Moreover, he himself does insist on the necessity of the sinner's absolutely passive role during the moment when the Word of God transforms him into a 'spiritual man'. This brings us back to the second element of his Law-Gospel doctrine; to understand it properly, we shall treat of it from two angles: the transforming power of faith on the one hand, and the passivity of the sinner on the other.

B. *Transforming power of faith*

Concerning the first point, Luther describes faith as an assurance or guarantee of salvation, and not simply as an *assensus* of the intellect to revealed truths; for him, it is also a kind of force which pulls man to God, fulfils in him the Law, and pushes him on to perform good works. This dynamic aspect of Luther's faith is evidenced in such passages as the following:

Faith, however, is a divine work in us. It changes us and makes us to be born anew of God (John i); it kills the old Adam and makes altogether different men, in heart and spirit and mind and powers, and it brings with it the Holy Ghost. O, it is a living, busy, active, mighty thing, this faith; and so it is impossible for it not to do good works incessantly.[1]

In this way, Luther explains faith, as Strohl would say, not by defining it technically but by describing its effects.[2] Like Saint Paul, he presents faith as a complex reality involving in man an 'ensemble' of diverse psychological elements. Faith engages the mind and heart and all the members of the believer's body, and unites the sinner intimately to Christ so that the soul comes into contact with God Himself.[3]

---

[1] *Preface to the Epistle to the Romans* (1522), *Ph.* vi. 451; see *D.B.* vii. 11.
[2] Henri Strohl, *La Pensée de la Réforme*, Paris, 1951, p. 30; 'Luther n'a pas donné de la foi une définition technique. Vivant par la foi, dans la foi, il l'a décrite.'
[3] Ibid., chapter 3, pp. 29–45.

Passive justification

Yet the sinner, undergoing this transformation, remains passive, and here we have the second aspect of the problem. The sinner can take no deliberate steps to dispose himself for the reception of faith or the first grace.[1] Prayer, fasting, and the like are decidedly ruled out.[2] 'Like to the paralytic with his feet and hands powerless, man must implore the grace which is productive of good works.'[3] Luther, obviously, is rejecting what the early Protestant divines called 'synergism'; more precisely, the Catholic teaching that a man co-operates freely and actively, and in a sense, effectively, with God's grace, in the justification and subsequent sanctification of his soul. Luther will have none of this; as Denifle rightly puts it: everything that stems from the unjustified is sinful.[4]

Of course, there are passages in Luther's works, especially his sermons, where he exhorts the sinner and the unbeliever to make serious and strenuous efforts to understand the Word of God, to accept it and to live by it. He constantly spurs the Christian on to discipline himself, to engage himself in battle against the forces of evil and to tend towards perfection. Yet this manner of exhortation seems to belong more to his preaching technique than to his theological account of justification.

[1] Luther also speaks of a 'passive justification' of God. The Creator is justified passively, as it were, by the sinner's faith and repentance; inasmuch as these acts acknowledge the righteousness of God and the unrighteousness of His creatures. It is in this sense, apparently, that Luther wishes to be understood when he says that we are justified through the fact that God is justified: 'Per hoc autem "justificari Deum" nos justificamur. Et iustificatio [illa] Dei passiva, qua a nobis iustificatur, est ipsa iustificatio nostri activa a Deo' (*Vorlesung über den Römerbrief*, *W.A.* lvi. 226. 24–25). In this chapter, however, we are interested in the passivity of the believing subject. This aspect, we think, is more essential to an understanding of the dramatic psychological tension of the Christian's personal Law-Gospel experience of sin and grace.

[2] 'Ad primam gratiam, sicut et ad gloriam, semper nos habemus passive, sicut mulier ad conceptum. Quia et nos sumus sponsa Christi. Ideo licet ante gratiam nos oremus et petamus, tamen quando gratia venit et anima impregnanda est spiritu, oportet quod neque oret neque operetur, sed solum patiatur. Quod certe durum est fieri et vehementer affligit, quia animam sine actu intelligendi et volendi esse est eam in tenebras ac velut in perditionem et annihilationem ire, quod vehementer ipsa refugit. Ideo sepius nobilissimis sese privat graciis' (ibid., p. 379. 1–10.).

[3] 'Recte ergo dixi, oportere hominem de suis operibus diffidere et velut paralyticum remissis manibus et pedibus gratiam operum artificem implorare . . .' (*Resolutiones Lutherianae super propositionibus suis Lipsiae disputatis* (1519), *W.A.* ii. 420. 6–8).

[4] Denifle, op. cit., vol. iii. 176–7.

From a strictly soteriological point of view, it appears that, for him, man contributes in no active way to his salvation; not even to the extent of corresponding with the initial action of God; in his own words:

We work nothing, we render nothing to God, but only, we receive and suffer the action of another, namely God. Therefore it pleases one to call this righteousness [*justitiam*] of faith or Christian righteousness passive righteousness.[1]

Thus Luther's preaching and exhortations to renounce evil ways and to embrace faith appear as a paradox and not as a mitigation of his theological position. When all is said and done, the sinner's faith and goodness result from a strictly passive submission to the divine action of grace.[2]

The danger here is to infer that Luther is opposed to good works and the observance of the Commandments. Such an inference would run counter to Luther's fundamental intention. He never discountenances good works produced by faith and the Word (see below, Chapter III), nor denounces as useless what is manifestly beneficial to oneself and one's neighbour. He wants simply to point to the true and unique cause of salvation;

---

[1] 'Ista autem excellentissima iustitia, nempe fidei, quam Deus per Christum nobis absque operibus imputat, nec est politica nec ceremonialis nec legis divinae iustitia nec versatur in nostris operibus, sed est plane diversa, hoc est mere passiva iustitia (sicut illae superiores activae). Ibi enim nihil operamur aut reddimus Deo, sed tantum recipimus et patimur alium operantem in nobis, scilicet Deum: Ideo libet illam fidei seu Christianam iustitiam appellare passivam' (*In Epistolam S. Pauli ad Galatas Commentarius*, Preface (1531), 1535, *W.A.* xl (i). 41. 15–21). See following note.

[2] We find the same doctrine of passive justification in Luther's earlier Lectures on Romans, 1515–16. The following texts are significant: 'Et universaliter omnis nostra affirmatio boni cuiuscunque sub negatione eiusdem, ut fides locum habeat in *Deo, qui est negativa essentia et bonitas et sapientia et iustitia nec potest* [*Deus*] *possideri aut attingi nisi negatis omnibus affirmativis nostris*'. (*W.A.* lvi. 392–3. 33, 1–3. The italics are in bold type in the text.)

Again 'Capaces autem tunc sumus operum et consiliorum ejus, quando nostra consilia cessant et opera quiescunt, et efficimur pure passivi respectu Dei, tam quoad interiores quam exteriores actus' (ibid., p. 275. 22–24).

The meaning of these passages is unmistakable: man can do nothing inwardly or outwardly to merit grace or win God's favour. Indeed, what he does himself and by his powers is sinful: 'Quod vero gratia Dei non facit, bonum non est. Quare sequitur, liberum arbitrium sine gratia Dei prorsus non liberum, sed immutabiliter captivum et servum esse mali, cum non possit vertere se solo ad bonum' (*De servo arbitrio, W.A.* xviii. 636. 4–6). In this respect, Luther's teachings on passive justification are quite in keeping with his treatise on the bondage or enslavement of the will.

namely, Christ's righteousness possessed through faith. Un-fortunately, in many instances, his language is over-vehement and misleading; at times he meant it to be interpreted meta-phorically and not literally. But in the treatise *De libertate christiana*, he states his case plainly:

23. Good works do not make a good man, but a good man per-forms good works [*bonus vir facit bona opera*]. Evil deeds do not render a man evil, but an evil man commits evil deeds [*Malus vir facit mala opera*]. Thus, as always, it is necessary that the substance or person be good previous to good works [*ante opera bona*], and that good works follow and proceed [*provenire*] from the person who is good [*ex bona persona*]; 'Mala arbor non facit bonos fructus, bona arbor non facit malos fructus.'

. . . .

Since, therefore, works justify no one and it is necessary for a man to be just before he does a good deed, it is most clear that it is faith alone which, by the pure mercy of God through Christ in His Word [*quae ex mera dei misericordia per Christum in verbo eius personam*] fittingly, and with nothing wanting, justifies and saves the person [*personam digne et sufficienter justificet et salvet*]; also that the Christian man needs no work and no law to be saved [*et nullo opere, nulla lege Christiano homini opus esse ad salutem*]; for, through faith, he is delivered from all law [*ab omni lege*] and by an act of sheer liberty [*ex mera libertate*], he does all things gratuitously [*omnia gratuito facit, quaecunque facit. . .*], seeking in no way either his own interest or salvation; for, already, by the grace of God and through his faith, he has enough and is saved, but solely to please God.[1]

This passage confirms eloquently what has been said on man's moral depravity and the power of faith to heal and transform him; at the same time, it shows clearly that Luther has no intention of doing away with good works.

In addition, we shall see when we deal with the Gospel section of the Catechism,[2] Luther describes sanctification—the work of the Holy Ghost—within the dramatic experiential context of personal struggle against sin, self, and Satan. His language is biblical and psychological rather than philosophical, and lays great stress on the Christian's duty to strive diligently and continually to become holier. Baptism, he tells us, turns the

---

[1] We have translated this passage from Luther's *De libertate christiana* in *W.A.* vii. 61. 26–31 and 62. 7–14.   [2] See Chapter V, section A.

Christian into a soldier of God, engages him in battle against the forces of evil and drives him on to spiritual betterment.[1]

Admittedly, this conscious effort of personal struggle, as well as the need to perform good deeds and observe the Commandments, raises real difficulties for Luther's theology; it seems to contradict his doctrine of absolute passive justice. Yet in his Protestant experiential perspective,[2] it need not appear to him as a contradiction. He does not wish the strivings and efforts of the Christian to be understood in an active sense as a co-operative work in Christ's act of Redemption.

They are not to contribute effectively to the strengthening or weakening of his faith or to the waxing or waning of his holiness. All his righteousness depends solely on God's Will.[3] Though, phenomenologically speaking, the Christian is ever conscious of his struggle and even feels that he is agent of his own acts and making spiritual progress, soteriologically, Luther seems to teach, the struggle is never meritorious *coram Deo*.[4]

Before God, Christ is everything that is true, good, and perfect in the just man's personal life. What is not Christ, or caused directly by Him, belongs properly to the sinful nature[5] of the justified believer, who, as we shall see,[6] remains depraved and vitiated, even after baptism.

Thus the Christian's good works, his striving for perfection, his struggle against sin, his eschatological *attente* of final sanctification have no share in his justification by faith; unless of course for one or other of two reasons: because God imputes justice to them; because they proceed from the believer's absolutely passive submission[7] to Christ's almighty force acting upon him. In this sense, the Christian is a kind of *homo duplex—simul peccator*,

---

[1] See *B.C.*, p. 209, col. 2; also Chapter V, below.   [2] See p. 57, n. 2.

[3] Luther writes: 'Iam illud, ubi Christus (Johannis 6) dicit: Nemo venit ad me, nisi pater meus traxerit eum, quid relinquit libero arbitrio? . . . Nemo potest . . . venire, vis scilicet illa, qua possit homo aliquid conari ad Christum, id est: ad ea, quae sunt salutis, nulla esse asseritur' (*De servo arbitrio, W.A.* xviii. 781. 29–36; see also p. 51, n. 4.

[4] See below, chapter V, p. 92, n. 1.

[5] 'Deinde cum Christus dicatur via, veritas et vita, idque per contentionem, ut, quicquid non est Christus, id neque via, sed error, neque veritas, sed mendacium, neque vita, sed mors est, necesse est liberum arbitrium, cum sit neque Christus neque in Christo, errore, mendacio et morte contineri' (*De servo arbitrio, W.A.*, p. 779. 11–14).

[6] See following section of this chapter.

[7] Luther seems to prefer the word *cedere*—cede to the divine action of Christ

simul justus. He is at one and the same time a spiritual and a
carnal man; a spiritual man in so far as Christ acts in him and
for him, and a carnal man in so far as sin continues to infect
his entire being, and inasmuch as he acts by himself. The battle
between the flesh[1] and the spirit, which endures throughout life,
seems, therefore to be a conflict between Christ's holy Person
and the believer's sinful person. Only when Christ overcomes
the believer's self and compels him, through despair, to reject
his own person,[2] does He declare him to be truly righteous, truly
holy. This, we think, is how Luther wishes to be understood
when he says:

Itaque reiicio me extra omnem activam et meam et divinae legis
iustitiam et simpliciter illam passivam amplector quae est iustitia
gratiae misericordiae, remissionis peccatorum, in summa: Christi et
Spiritus Sancti quam non facimus, sed patimur, non habemus sed
accipimus donante eam nobis Deo Patre per Jesum Christum.[3]

In brief, Luther throws out any form of active justice, whether
it be wilful assent to faith or personal sanctity.[4] There is nothing
active or positive that we can do to merit Christ or our own
holiness; there is only *iustitia passiva.*[5] If we do not believe[6] in
Christ our actions are not meritorious; and if we do believe
in Him it is an effrontery to dare to put alongside His ineffable

(see Strohl, *Pensée de la Reforme*, p. 31). But this word, or the act of ceding, is not
to be understood as a co-operative meritorious work 'coram Deo'. See p. 51, n. 4.

[1] The flesh, in this context, designates the entire egoism of man and not merely
his sexual appetites.

[2] Luther wishes to reject utterly the role of our own person from the work of
justification and sanctification. In his *Commentary on Galatians* (iii. 20) he writes:
'Saint Paul plainly sheweth by what means he liveth in us, and not that which is
in our person. Therefore, when we speak of Christian righteousness, we must
utterly reject the person. For if I hold to the person, or speak thereof, then there
is made of the person, whether I will or no, a worker subject to the law. But here
must Christ and my conscience become one body, so that nothing remain in my
sight but Christ crucified and raised from the dead' (*C.G.*, p. 167; *W.A.* xl (i).
282. 16–22).

[3] Ibid., *W.A.* xl (i). 43. 12–17.

[4] We are not saying that Luther excludes all notion of sanctity from his theology.
Rather that his defence of good works, produced by faith, and his descriptions of
the Christian life, can never be understood in the medieval manner as a personal
meritorious co-operative participation in Christ's work of Redemption.

[5] See below, Chapter V, p. 92, n. 1.

[6] When we say 'believe' here, we mean, of course, a passive acceptance of Christ
and His Word which excludes all personal or possible merit on the part of the
believer. The act of believing is not to be understood as a free personal commit-
ment—*un engagement volontaire.*

merits some paltry acts, vitiated besides by original sin. In the spiritual order—in the realm of grace—Christ alone engages the Christian in battle, Christ alone carries on the struggle against Satan,[1] Christ alone increases the Christian's grace and intensity of faith, Christ alone saves; the moral faculties of man have no role to play.[2]

At this juncture, the reader might object to our exposition of Luther's notion of passive justification. He might feel that we have stretched the point, somewhat, by a too literal interpretation of his statements, or have not made allowances for exaggerations and sweeping affirmations prompted by the historical circumstances. Perhaps his statements on this matter should be seen simply as extreme denunciations of the Pelagian abuses rampant in the monasteries and religious orders of the sixteenth century; they should not be taken at their face value and understood to mean that Luther wanted to exclude absolutely the play of human forces from his description of passive justification.

We would like to think so; but in all fairness to Luther, we cannot admit of any other possible meaning in his teaching. The passivity he speaks of is absolute; indeed it has to be so in order to remain consistent and true to the radical moral pessimism of one of his favourite theological treatises, the *De servo arbitrio* (1525);[3] here he describes the human will's moral depravity in such absolute terms as to leave the sinner before God like to an inert piece of clay.[4]

---

[1] 'In altero (i.e. the world of grace and the spirit as opposed to the world of the flesh where Satan reigns) regnat Christus, quod assidue resistit et pugnat cum Satanae regno, in quod transferimur, non nostra vi, sed gratia Dei, qua liberamur a praesenti soeculo nequam, et eripimur a potestate tenebrarum. Istorum regnorum mutuo tantis viribus et animis perpetuo pugnantium cognitio et confessio sola satis esset ad confutandum dogma liberi arbitrii, quod in regno Satanae cogimur servire, nisi virtute divina eripiamur' (*De servo arbitrio*, W.A., p. 782. 35–40). This divine power—the *virtus divina*—we should add, does not change the fundamental perversity of the human will. After regeneration, the human will cannot be considered sinless, apart from divine imputation. Thus the works of the human person are of no avail before the work and merits of Christ.

[2] See below, Chapter V.

[3] 'A la proposition qu'on lui faisait . . . d'éditer ses œuvres complètes, le Réformateur répondit: "je ne reconnais aucun de mes livres pour adéquat, si ce n'est peut-être le *De servo arbitrio* et le Catéchisme" ' (quoted from the Introduction to the French translation of the *De servo arbitrio*, by Denis de Rougemont, Paris, 1936, p. 17, n. 1).

[4] 'Tum sequitur similitudo, scilicet esse vasa diversa, alia in honorem, alia in

Besides, the third element of his Law-Gospel doctrine, the imputative character of righteousness, which we shall now discuss, gives weight to our interpretation and reveals the degree of his pessimism with regard to the nature of the transformation which faith has wrought in the sinner's soul.

C. *Imputed righteousness*

Though Luther, as we have just seen, depicts faith as a transforming power, he nevertheless seems to compromise his position elsewhere by stating that the man of faith continues to be sinful in nature. In a dualistic paradoxical sense, God's action transforms him imputatively and not qualitatively.

To make the point clearer, let us look, first, at the strange dialogue he had with his wife, set down in the *Tischreden*, January 1537:

Do you not consider yourself a saint, says Martin to Kate, who

contumeliam. His absolvitur doctrina, quod vasa non seipsa parent; sed herus. Hoc vult et Ro. 9, quod figulus potestatem habet et. Sic stat similitudo Pauli efficacissima, quod libertas arbitrii nihil sit coram Deo' (*De servo arbitrio*, W.A. xviii. 728. 27–30; see also pp. 719–20).

Luther also employs the image of the rider and the horse to illustrate how man's will is enslaved either to God or to the devil: 'Sic humana voluntas in medio posita est, ceu jumentum, si insederit Deus, vult et vadit quo vult Deus, ut Psalmus dicit: "Factus sum sicut jumentum et ego semper tecum" (ps. 72: 23). Si insederit Satan, vult et vadit quo vult Satan, nec est in ejus arbitrio ad utrum sessorem currere aut eum quaerere, sed ipsi sessores certant ob ipsum obtinendum et possidendum' (ibid., p. 635. 18–23).

We should add here that Protestant scholars are not in agreement on how to interpret the Reformer's dualistic description of man's struggle with God and Satan. On this particular point Edgar M. Carlson writes: 'The antithesis between God and the devil has its subjective counterpart in Luther's distinction between flesh and spirit. Avid Runestam, Gustaf Lyunggren and Ragnar Bring have made special studies of Luther's use of these terms and they are agreed that they do not refer to a higher and a lower nature of man. Instead, each term represents a total view of man. As ruled by God, man is spirit; as ruled by the devil, he is flesh. The distinction between flesh and spirit is the correlative of the distinction between believer and unbeliever and between the old man and the new man. The essential character of the flesh, unbelief and the old man is egocentricity. Each term includes the total personality as dominated by the ego. It is impossible to ascribe evil to the body or to any other part of man's nature. The ego is active in the inner soul of man no less than his physical nature. In fact, the inner centre of personality may be properly regarded as the citadel of egocentricity. It is man as a person, a self, that is either good or evil. Which he is depends on whether he has allowed God to ascend the throne in his life or insists on occupying it himself. To occupy it oneself is identical with allowing the devil to occupy it, for it is this egocentricity that constitutes the rebellion against God which the devil is concerned to promote' (*Reinterpretation of Luther*, Philadelphia, 1948, p. 51).

startled, replies: A saint? How can I be a saint, I who am such a great sinner. The Doctor then is carried away: There indeed is the papist abomination. How it poisons souls and penetrates to the very depths of our marrow. . . . You believe perfectly well that you are a saint. For the power of baptism is so great it makes your sins such that though they still exist, they do not damn you.[1]

This is one way in which Luther seems to say that the believer's righteousness or justice is not intrinsic or ontological but merely imputed [reputata[2]] or alien[3] The power of Baptism (which gives us faith) is not meant to remove sins but to render them harmless so to speak. God no longer looks upon the believer's sins as meriting damnation; they are cloaked over by the infinite merits of Christ.[4]

Most likely what Luther's exact position amounts to is this: Christ, working in intimate contact with the sinner's soul, not

---

[1] We have translated this dialogue from a French edition of extracts of the *Tischreden*, entitled *Propos de table*, trans. by Louis Sauzin, Paris, 1932, p. 19. This dialogue between Luther and Catherine is recorded in the *Tischreden* for January 1537; and is cited by several editors.

The doctrinal content of this dialogue finds corroboration in Luther's earlier as well as later works. From the Lectures on Romans (1515–16) we have the following example: '. . . baptisatus aut penitens manet in infirmitate concupiscentie, quae tamen est contra legem . . . et utique mortalis nisi Deus misericors non imputaret propter inceptam curationem' (*W.A.* lvi. 513. 17–20; see also p. 46, n. 2). In the *Smalcald Articles* (1537) he teaches the same doctrine about sin remaining in man even though he be transformed by faith (see Chapter VI, p. 137).

[2] Luther employs the biblical terms *imputare* and *reputare* to describe how God declares the man of faith to be just. The following passage, we think, epitomizes his interpretation of Saint Paul's teaching on the imputation of righteousness and the non-imputation of sin to the man of faith: 'Sancti intrinsece sunt peccatores semper, ideo extrinsece iustificantur semper. Hipocrite autem intrinsece sunt iusti semper, ideo extrinsece sunt peccatores semper.'

'Intrinsece dico i.e. quomodo in nobis, in nostris oculis, in nostra estimatione sumus, extrinsece autem, quomodo apud Deum et in reputatione eius sumus. Igitur extrinsece sumus iusti, quando non ex nobis nec ex operibus, sed ex sola Dei reputatione iusti sumus. Reputatio enim eius non in nobis nec in potestate nostra est. Ergo nec iustitia nostra in nobis est nec in potestate nostra' (*W.A.* lvi. 268–9. 31–32, 1–4). Indisputably, Luther understands imputative righteousness as an extrinsic or forensic relation; the believer, though still sinful, becomes just before God by virtue of the fact that God reckons him as just; that is to say, He refuses to regard his sins as damning. See p. 41, n. 1, above.

[3] 'Thou and I are holy, Church, city and people are holy, not by their own but by an alien holiness, not by active, but by passive holiness. . . .' (*C.G.*, p. 39; *W.A.* xl (i). 70, 19–20).

[4] '. . . the justice by which God clothes us when he justifies us . . .' (see the last paragraph of the autobiographical fragment (1545) quoted above, in Chapter I, p. 14).

only fulfils the Law for him but also constitutes the totality of his moral goodness. That is to say, the healing and transforming power of faith is Christ Himself, acting on the soul, pulling and pushing a passive enduringly sinful nature to its ultimate end. Indeed, it would not be untrue to say that the transformation is simply the presence or contact of Christ with the soul.

Luther does not formulate his theology in these simple terms, but it is difficult to understand him otherwise. How else is one to speak of his dualistic assertions that the Christian is, at once, holy in Christ and sinful in nature,[1] forgiven of all his sins and still in possession of them;[2] again how think of a struggle between man and sin if it is Christ alone who does all the fighting.

Plainly, there is no place, here, for entitative and qualitative changes in man, produced by an infused created grace such as the Scholastics define. The Thomistic account of salvation, in terms of entitative and operative habits given initially by Christ and presupposing the free and active participation of man in Christ's Crucifixion and Resurrection, appears to him as pure heresy.

In these respects, Luther's theology is new and revolutionary. Not only does it oppose the idea of Christian merit but also the whole Scholastic account of personal sanctification. His description of passive and imputed righteousness leaves no room whatsoever for modes of being. A man is justified or he is not; and if justified, one cannot distinguish, within his person, between natural and supernatural goodness,[3] mortal and venial sin,[4] actual and sanctifying grace. Such distinctions, for Luther,

---

[1] 'Was ich davon bisher und stetiglich gelehret hab, das weiß ich garnicht zu ändern, nämlich daß wir "durch den Glauben" (wie S. Petrus sagt) ein ander neu, rein herz kriegen und Gott umb Christi willen, unsers Mittlers, uns fur ganz gerecht und heilig hatten will und hält. Obwohl die Sunde im Fleisch noch nicht gar weg oder tot ist, so will er sie doch nicht rechnen, noch wissen' (*S.A.*, p. 460. 7–9; *B.C.*, article 12, p. 148).

[2] When reading Luther on such paradoxical matters as man's sinfulness and God's justice, it is not always easy to understand exactly what he means; one cannot pin him down to clear and precise definitions.

[3] That is to say, ontologically. The believer's nature is sinful and his Christian righteousness is imputed. It is impossible to reduce Luther's notions of redemption and sanctification to the logic of Aristotelian categories. And any attempt to judge his statements in the light of ontological causes would render his theology contradictory and incomprehensible. The context of his thought is fundamentally one of personal experience. See p. 56, n. 1, p. 57, n. 2.

[4] One might say, here, that Luther does not reject the distinction between

are unnecessary and meaningless.[1] Man's perfection is Christ in his sinful soul; there is nothing else to be said.

These views are corroborated, to some extent, by Luther's *post scriptum* to Melanchthon's letter to Brenz, May 1531. Here, he replies to the latter's attempt to compromise his teachings on the matter of the Christian's personal transformation (*renovatio* or *novitas*) subsequent to faith. In our translation, it reads:

I also am accustomed, my dear Brenz, in order to understand better this problem to imagine as if there exists no quality in my heart which bears the name faith or charity,[2] but in their place, I put Jesus Christ, and I say: This is my justice [righteousness]. It is He, Himself, who is the quality and my formal (as they say)[3] justice; so that, in this way, I shall free and rid myself ['me'] of the law and works, and even of the contemplation of that objective Christ, who is perceived as a doctor or giver, But I want Him, by Himself, to be, for me, both the gift itself [*per se*] and the doctrine itself, so that I may possess all things in Him. Thus he says 'I am the way, the truth and the life'; but he does not say: I give unto you the way, the truth, and the life, as if, standing outside of me He [Christ] worked such things within me. It is within me that He should [*debet*] be, should remain, live and speak and not through or in me etc., 2 Cor. 6,[4] so that we should be [*essemus*] Gods' justice in Him, and not in charity or subsequent gifts'.[5]

This *post scriptum* is not meant to be interpreted broadly or synergistically, since Luther, manifestly, is affirming his own position against any Melanchthonian compromise. In such a context, it would be uncalled for and perhaps misleading not to accept his words in their strongest sense. And in this sense, they do not seem to allow at all for the play of human forces and the intrinsic worth of the Christian. Christ alone is just.

mortal and venial sin, but rather treats of the problem differently. But this, we think, is incorrect. In the *Smalcald Articles*, he writes: '. . . . all in us is nothing but sin . . . and there is no use investigating, dividing and distinguishing. . . .' (For the context of this quotation see below Chapter VI, p. 141).

[1] See below Chapter VI, section B.

[2] What the Scholastics call the theological virtues; i.e. supernatural operative habits, disposing us, in a stable way, to believe what God has revealed, to hope in His promises, and to love Him with our whole being.

[3] The Scholastics.

[4] We are not certain what text Luther here is referring to; perhaps it is 2 Cor. vi. 16.

[5] *WAB*, vi. 99–100.

From the foregoing, it would appear that a man, in his upward climb to God, in his spiritual progress and sanctification, does not ascend a stairway of states of perfection; or pass through, what Father Garrigou-Lagrange would call, 'les trois âges de la vie intérieure'. Differences of quality, intensity, and degree, in Luther's vision of salvation, would have to be described as variations in awareness or consciousness.

The individual believer feels more or less intensely that he is living through himself or through Christ. In the former case, he is more or less aware of his own sinfulness; in the latter of Christ's unique righteousness. In either case, the experience or awareness is caused by God's Word, and the total effect of salvation is never definable or describable as a perfection in the order of being but rather a movement or a passage from one kind of awareness to the other.

The experience of being possessed by Christ's righteousness in faith is justification, and any subsequent experience of progressing spiritually in good works and holiness seems to be merely an intensification of the former initial experience. That is to say, the believer is more and more aware of being freed from sin and possessed by Christ, more and more conscious of despairing totally in self and relying completely on God. We find it hard to understand Luther in any other way.

Summing up

Here then, we have a three-sided picture of Luther's experience and description of justification. The Reformer does not define his doctrine in the Scholastic sense of formal definition; he paints a vivid scene of man's moral impotence, and he uses images and examples, such as the 'iron in the fire', the 'spouse of Christ', the 'exchange of the wedding ring', or God's cloak of justice, to portray the transforming effects of faith, the passive role of the believing subject, and the imputative character of justification. And he appeals to scripture and experience, not to universals or syllogisms,[1] to affirm his innermost convictions concerning the justice of God which justifies the sinner.

---

[1] We are not suggesting that Luther was incompetent in logic or incapable of persuasive dialectical argument. Indeed, he taught logic in the Augustinian studentate of Wittenberg, in the year 1508, and also gave lectures on Aristotle's *Nichomachean Ethics*. The handling of these subjects presupposed, on his part, a competent knowledge of the technical language and logical methods of the Schools. More-

Our simplified and rather schematic presentation of the basic elements of his doctrine might tempt one to separate each element from the context of Luther's experience and consider it apart, as a categorical proposition, to be used dialectically in abstract argument.

In abstracto, it is relatively easy for the logician to define the terms of such a proposition (that which the Reformer never did) and juggle them about in clear and distinct syllogisms to prove that Luther was illogical with himself; to argue, for instance, that his pessimism leads to a metaphysical absurdity, or that the third element, the imputative character of righteousness, contradicts the second element, the transforming effects of faith on the sinner, and so on.

Such a procedure has a certain dialectical value in the criticism of a theological system, but in Luther's case, it is not of much use; firstly because his theology is not a system, and secondly because it loses sight of the more fundamental fact that Luther saw both man and God through the light of a vital and personal experience.[1]

The elements, which we have just outlined, hang together and take on more consistency when viewed within the framework of his soul-shaking experience. His pessimistic description of human nature appears as a personal awareness of his own moral incapacity to please and love God disinterestedly, his imputative justice as a heart- and soul-felt assurance that God has accepted him despite his sinfulness, and the passive role of his faculties before the transforming effects of faith as an inner feeling of being entirely dependant on an all-powerful and all-merciful Christ.[2]

over, in what Gordon Rupp has called 'his best and most sustained pieces of theological argument', *Contra Latomum* (1521), the *De servo arbitrio* (1525), and *Of the Lord's Supper* (1528) (op. cit., p. 88), we have clear evidence of Luther's dialectical skill; he could, if he wanted to, argue sharply, penetratingly, and even philosophically. But if he resorted to dialectics or philosophy, when polemicizing, it was more to match his adversaries with their own weapons than to demonstrate the basic convictions of his own faith. In matters of faith, he preferred to lay down and affirm his tenets on the foundation of scripture and experience; and irrespective of human authorities, logical necessities, and philosophical principles (see above, p. 43, n. 1). Thus we find him saying to Erasmus, at the end of his *De servo arbitrio*, after setting out an array of scriptural evidence in favour of his own thesis on the enslavement of the will; 'I have not wanted to compare or to confront but to affirm and I affirm' (*W.A.* xviii. 787. 11–12).

[1] See following note.

[2] On this score, we agree with Henri Strohl's remarks on the formal character

But enough has been said about Luther's religious experience and what we believe to be three basic elements of his Law-Gospel doctrine. By no means do we think that we have exhausted the subject; Martin Luther's life and doctrine is a vast and complicated story. We have simply tried to give unity to and expound those aspects of his life and teachings which, we trust, will help us to trace the Law-Gospel doctrine in Luther's confessional writings.

If we keep in mind what Luther means by man's moral depravity before the Law, man's passive role in the justification of faith, and the external character of this justification, knowing, at the same time, how these three elements stem from and are profoundly related to his personal experience, we shall grasp more readily the dramatic and dynamic sense of his Law-Gospel doctrine of justification. The relation of the Law and the Gospel will appear, not as a logical necessity or dialectical antithesis but as the co-ordinated dual work of God's Word, producing in man's soul a psychological awareness and tension of passing from a state of moral frustration to moral fulfilment, from juridical doubt to Gospel certitude, from the agony of sin to the peace and joy of faith. In this perspective, we shall now undertake to analyse the *Large Catechism* and the *Smalcald Articles*.

of Luther's thought: 'Luther n'a pas bâti un système. Il n'est pas un logicien qui, à l'aide de la méthode déductive, tire d'un principe toutes les conséquences logiques.

'Il n'a pas davantage élaboré une "somme", selon la tradition des écoles médiévales qui s'efforçaient de faire un ensemble cohérent de toutes les données philosophiques et théologiques, transmises par la tradition doctrinale de l'Eglise.

'Il a tout aussi peu essayé de construire, à la façon de Calvin, une théologie biblique dans laquelle devaient rentrer tous les éléments doctrinaux de l'Ecriture sainte.

'Il a été le témoin de son expérience religieuse, qui lui est apparue vraie parce qu'il en constatait toujours à nouveau l'accord avec celle de Paul et celle de saint Augustin, qu'il jugeait être les âmes ayant le mieux saisi l'essence de l'Evangile. Son point de départ a donc été une expérience personnelle, et rien ne devait entrer dans l'exposé de la vérité chrétienne qui ne serait en accord avec cette expérience. C'est ainsi que Luther a tracé le cadre et les limites de son enseignement religieux et théologique. Il se sentait autorisé à repousser le reproche de subjectivisme parce qu'il ressentait un accord total entre son expérience et les données fondamentales de la Révélation. Il attribuait donc cette expérience à l'action directe du Saint-Esprit dans son âme' (*Luther, sa vie et sa pensée*, pp. 74–75).

PART II

LUTHER'S CONFESSIONAL WRITINGS

III

THE PLAN, PURPOSE, AND HISTORICAL SETTING OF LUTHER'S CATECHISMS

A. *The plan*

THE underlying plan and *leit motif* of Luther's *Large Catechism*[1] is the Law-Gospel relation—the Word of God, as Law and Gospel, producing in sinful man the 'despair-faith' experience of salvation. It is precisely in accordance with this relation and despair-faith pattern that it expounds the fundamental tenets of the Christian religion.[2] Thus, in the second part of this confessional writing, immediately following the treatment of the Ten Commandments, we read:

Thus far we have heard the first part of Christian doctrine, in which we have seen all that God wishes us to do or to leave undone.

---

[1] The *Large Catechism* is the English title of *Der deutsche Katechismus* or *Der große Katechismus*. In our thesis we use the English translation, found in the *Book of Concord*, St. Louis, Mo. Concordia Publishing House, 1957. This *Book of Concord* is designated by the abbreviation *B.C.* When we quote from the German version, we use *Der deutsche Katechismus*, designated by the abbreviation *D.K.*, included in the collection: *Die Bekenntnisschriften der evangelisch-lutherischen Kirche*, Göttingen, 1956, designated by *Bek.*

[2] In his long preface to the *Large Catechism*, Luther tells us that the Catechism is a compend and brief summary of all the Holy Scriptures: '. . . welcher [*Katechismus*] der ganzen heiligen Schrift kurzer Auszug und Abschrift ist' (*D.K.*, 'Neue Vorrede', p. 552. 30–34). In the short preface, he explains that the Catechism teaches 'what every Christian must needs know, so that he who does not know this could not be numbered with the Christians nor be admitted to any Sacrament' (*B.C.*, p. 168).

Now, there properly follows the Creed, which sets forth to us everything that we must expect[1] and receive from God and to state it quite briefly, teaches us how to know Him fully. And this is intended to help us do that which according to the Ten Commandments we ought to do. For (as said above) they are set so high that all human ability is far too feeble and weak to . . . keep them. Therefore it is necessary to learn this part as the former in order that we may know how to attain[2] thereto, whence and whereby to obtain such power. For if we could by our own powers keep the Ten Commandments as they are to be kept, we would need nothing further, neither the Creed nor the Lord's Prayer.[3]

These words recall Luther's despair-faith description of salvation, which he outlines in the *De libertate christiana*, and depicts dramatically in his account of the *Turmerlebnis*, about which we spoke in our previous chapter.

By tracing this plan or justification pattern throughout the several parts of the Catechism, and considering how it is further elucidated by the *Smalcald Articles*, we can grasp more clearly the Law-Gospel relation and appreciate how, basically, Luther's doctrine is indeed a Law-Gospel doctrine. But before doing this, we should determine first the origins and historical context of the Catechisms.

B. *The background and purpose*

We know that between the years 1527 and 1529 commissions of inspection were set up by the Elector of Saxony, at Luther's request, for the purpose of visiting and inspecting the parishes of the region. Luther was a member of one of these commissions, in 1528, and he was shocked by his findings.[4]

---

[1] The Göttingen edition of the *Bek.* uses *erwarten*—'expect'—to translate the sixteenth-century meaning of *gewarten* (see *Bek.*, p. 646, n. 3).

[2] '. . . zu lernen daß man wisse, wie man dazu komme . . .' (ibid., pp. 17–18). In the Latin text: '. . . ut compertum habeamus, quinam praeceptis satisfacere queamus . . .' (ibid.).

[3] *B.C.*, p. 192; see also *Bek.*, p. 646.

[4] In his preface to the *Small Catechism*, Luther describes to us his own experience as a 'Visitator': 'Diesen Katechismon oder christliche Lehre in solche kleine, schlechte, einfältige Form zu stellen, hat mich gezwungen und gedrungen die klägliche, elende Not, so ich neulich erfahren habe, da ich auch ein Visitator war. Hilf, lieber Gott, wie manchen Jammer habe ich gesehen, daß der gemeine Mann doch so garnichts weiß von der christlichen Lehre, sonderlich auf den Dörfern, und leider viel Pfarrherr fast ungeschickt und untüchtig sind zu lehren . . .' (*Bek.*, pp. 501–2. 8–16, 1–2). See also the 'Notice historique', by André Jundt, in *L.S.*, vol. ii, p. 7.

The inspections revealed that laymen and ecclesiastics alike were totally lacking in elementary knowledge of the Christian faith. As a consequence, Luther felt an urgent need to give the people a summary exposition of the basic truths of the Christian faith which could become a family book handed down from father to son.[1] He met this need with the publication of his two catechisms, *Der große* or *deutsche Katechismus* and *Der kleine Katechismus*.[2]

Both catechisms came out in the year 1529. A sentence in the preface to the *Small Catechism*, exhorting pastors to instruct themselves by the reading of the *Large Catechism*, allows us to conjecture that the latter was published first.[3] Mr. Allbeck, relying on recent scholarship, claims that the Reformer completed his manuscript of *Der große Katechismus* late in March, and that it came from the press sometime in April, the earliest evidence of this fact being a letter dated 23 April.[4] With this larger work complete, Mr. Allbeck continues, Luther put out briefer forms or charts suitable for use with children, and had them published in booklet form. 'The edition was on sale, on May 16th, according to a letter by Roerer, the proofreader.'[5] This booklet became known as the *Small Catechism*.[6]

Each catechism deals with the five points: the Ten Commandments or Decalogue, the Apostles' Creed, the Lord's Prayer, the Sacraments of Baptism, and the Lord's Supper.

In the second printing of the first 1529 edition of the *Large Catechism*, Luther added a *kurze Vermahnung zu der Beichte*.[7] The 1530 edition of the same work included a secondary lengthy

[1] See the short preface to the *Large Catechism*.

[2] The title-page of the first edition of Luther's German Catechism reads: 'Deutsch Catechismus Mart. Luther'; it became known as the Large Catechism after the appearance of the briefer form in May. An Erfurt reprint of the first edition of the *Small Catechism* gives the title: *Der kleine Catechismus für die gemeine Pfarherr und Prediger Mart. Luther* (see W. D. Allbeck, *Studies in the Lutheran Confessions*, Philadelphia, 1952, p. 216).

[3] No copies of the first edition of the *Small Catechism* are extant; but copies of reprints, made in Erfurt and Marburg, survive.

[4] See W. D. Allbeck, op. cit., p. 216.

[5] Ibid., see also Theo. Kolde, *Historische Einleitung in die symbolischen Bücher der evangelisch-lutherischen Kirche*, Gütersloh, 1907, p. lx.

[6] The first Latin translation of the *Small Catechism* (1529) was appended to a booklet of prayers entitled *Enchiridion piarum precationum* (see Allbeck, op. cit., p. 217). The title *Enchiridion* has since been used to refer to Luther's *Small Catechism*.

[7] See *Bek.*, p. 725; also *L.S.* ii. 227, n. 1. The Latin text is: *Brevis adhortatio ad confessionem.*

preface and an addition to the exposition of the Lord's Prayer. This latter edition, with slight modifications, was used by the German Book of Concord—*das Konkordienbuch*—in 1580.[1]

In the oldest known Wittenberg edition (1529)[2] of the *Small Catechism* there are additional parts: the Morning and Evening Prayers, the 'Benedicite' and 'Gratias', taken from the *Breviarium*, and the Table of Duties. Also, between the article on Baptism and that on the Lord's Supper are inserted a few simple remarks on how to hear confession; other extant ancient editions of this catechism have, in the appendix, formularies for the Marriage Blessing and for Baptism.[3] The German Book of Concord used a 1531 edition of the *Small Catechism*[4] which included Luther's 'explanation of the introduction of the Lord's Prayer'.[5]

These additional parts are found in the critical Göttingen edition of the *Bekenntnisschriften* and André Jundt's French edition of the *Livres symboliques*; we shall consult them when analysing the contents of the *Large Catechism*.[6]

It is a well-known fact that Luther prepared himself gradually for the drawing up of his two catechisms. Three series of sermons, which he gave during the year 1528 on the five catechetical points, form the immediate preparation for the catechisms;[7] but long before these sermons, he had preached and written copiously on the catechetical points: as early as 1516, he had delivered a series of sermons on the Ten Commandments,[8] and in

---

[1] See Allbeck, op. cit., p. 217. The Latin *Book of Concord* used a modified form of a translation made by Vincentius Obsopoeus and published in 1529 (see Allbeck, op. cit., p. 217).   [2] See p. 61, n. 3, above.

[3] We owe this information to André Jundt's 'Notice Historique', in *L.S.* ii. 8.

[4] Two Latin translations of the *Small Catechism* were published in 1529. The second one, by John Sauerman, was more widely used and, with some corrections, accepted in the Latin *Book of Concord* of 1584 (see M. Reu, *Dr. Martin Luther's Small Catechism*, Chicago, 1929, p. 67).

[5] See Allbeck, op. cit., p. 217.

[6] The 1957 reproduction of the English text of the *American Concordia Triglotta* (1917) does not contain the formularies on Marriage and Baptism in the *Small Catechism*, or the short exhortation to confession in the *Large Catechism*.

[7] 'Die unmittelbare Vorbereitung für die Abfassung des Katechismus bilden drei Reihen von Predigten, die der Reformator über die fünf Hauptstücke in der Zeit von 18. bis 30. Mai, 14. bis 25. September und 30. November bis 19. Dezember 1528 in Vertretung des Wittenberger Stadtpfarrers Johann Bugenhagen hielt' (*Bek.*, 'Einleitung', p. xxviii).

[8] Before his Wittenberg congregation (Sept. 1516–Feb. 1517) Luther delivered Sermons on the Ten Commandments, which were published in 1518 (see *W.A.* i. 248).

1517 on the Lord's Prayer;[1] from this date to 1523 he had published charts, sermons, tracts, and treatises on the Ten Commandments, the Lord's Prayer, the Creed, and the Sacraments.[2] The
best known of these are: the explanation of the Creed, published
with previous material under the title *A Short Form of the Ten
Commandments, a Short Form of the Creed, a Short Form of the Lord's
Prayer* (1520):[3] the treatise *On Good Works* (also in 1520),[4] the
special sermons of the year 1519 on the Sacraments of Penance,
Baptism, and the Lord's Supper,[5] and his famous work on the
Sacraments in general, the *De captivitate Babylonica* (1520).[6]
Moreover, before the beginning of 1525, he had already com-
missioned his friends, Justus Jonas and John Agricola, with the
composition of a child's instruction book,[7] which he designated
as 'catechism', and linked up closely with the idea of a *Visitatorenunterricht*.[8] Again, in the *Deutsche Messe* (1526),[9] he had
expressed views on the nature of catechetical instruction, and
co-operated with Melanchthon in the work of the *Visitation*

[1] In 1518 Agricola published a series of sermons on the Lord's Prayer which
Luther had preached in Lent 1517 (see *W.A.* ix. 122). See also Allbeck, op.
cit., pp. 214–15; and Charles M. Jacobs, Introduction to *Eine kurze Form* . . ., in
Ph. ii. 351. This author gives a good outline of the background preparation of
Luther's Catechisms.

[2] See the Table of Contents of vols. i, ii, vi, vii, viii, and ix of the *Weimar Ausgabe*;
also M. Reu's scholarly introduction to the English translation of the treatise *On
Good Works, Ph.* i. 175–83.

[3] *Eine kurze Form der zehen Gebote, eine kurze Form des Glaubens, eine kurze Form des
Vaterunsers, W.A.* vii. 194–230. This work 'is the most important of Luther's
catechetical works prior to the Catechism of 1529, and deserves the name that has
been given to it "the first evangelical catechism" (Cohrs, *Evang. Katechismusversuche,* i. 4)' (introduction to the English translation of the same work, by C. M.
Jacobs, *Ph.* ii. 351).

[4] *Von den guten Werken, W.A.* vi. 192–277. There is also an English translation in
the above-quoted Philadelphia edition, vol. i, p. 184. In the introduction to this
translation, M. Reu says: 'The book, indeed, surpasses all his previous German
writings in volume, as well as all his Latin and German ones in clearness, richness
and the fundamental importance of its contents' (ibid., p. 182).

[5] *Ein Sermon von dem Sakrament der Buße; Ein Sermon von dem heiligen hochwürdigen
Sakrament der Taufe; Ein Sermon von dem hochwürdigen Sakrament des heiligen wahren
Leichnams Christi und von den Brüderschaften;* in *W.A.* ii. 709–38.

[6] *W.A.* vi. 484–574; English translation in B. Lee Woolf's edition of *Reformation
Writings,* i. 201–331.

[7] See *Bek.,* 'Einleitung', p. xxviii. This commission came to a standstill; and it
was not until the publication of the 1529 Catechism that Luther's idea and wish
was realized.

[8] Ibid.

[9] *W.A.* xix. 44; in *Ph.* vi. 177; see also Allbeck, op. cit., p. 215.

Instruction[1] published in 1528, in which a programme for parish instruction was laid down.[2]

These examples of Luther's catechetical work make up a noteworthy portion of the forerunners of his catechisms; there is no point in drawing up a full list of them; what is imperative here is to keep them in mind when studying the catechisms; a consultation of the more important ones[3] will prove helpful in our interpretation of the *Large Catechism*.

The date of the publication of Luther's catechisms (1529) is significant. It means that he composed them at a high point in his break with Rome. This was twelve years after the posting of the ninety-five theses (31 Oct. 1517); since then he had affirmed, unequivocally, his revolutionary views on salvation and on the Roman Church in such famous writings as: *De captivitate Babylonica* (1520), *De servo arbitrio* (1525), *De libertate christiana* (1520), and his *Open Letter to the Christian Nobility* (1520).

Thus long before the appearance of the catechisms, he had formulated and crystallized his religious thinking and beliefs into a definitive Law-Gospel Protestant creed, three basic aspects of which we have outlined in our second chapter. He would naturally attempt to propagate and defend this creed in subsequent sermons, teachings, and polemics. We shall find evidence of this fact as we proceed with our study.

Indeed, leaving aside the author's peculiar and particular description of these elements and his unsparing attacks on monasticism and the Papacy, and also what he excludes from the sacramental life of the Church, there is very little to distinguish Luther's catechisms from earlier catechetical usages. The subjects actually dealt with do not differ materially from the catechetical writings of the fifteenth and earlier centuries. Luther, himself, tells us, in the long preface to the *Large Catechism*, that, of the five points treated, the three most essential ones, the Ten Commandments, the Creed, and the Lord's Prayer, have always been taught by the Church to the faithful.[4]

---

[1] Luther handed over the work of composing a *Visitatorenunterricht* to Melanchthon in 1527, whilst he himself undertook the working out of the catechism (see *Bek.*, 'Einleitung', p. xxviii).

[2] See E. Sehling, *Die evang. Kirchenordnungen des XVI. Jahrhunderts*, Leipzig, 1902, vol. i, p. 149; also *W.A.* xxvi. 195–240; and Allbeck, op. cit., p. 215.

[3] For instance, The *Short Exposition* . . . and the treatise *On Good Works*.

[4] *B.C.*, p. 168.

The informative article, *Catéchisme*, of Mangenot, in the *Dictionnaire de théologie catholique*, helps us discern similarities between Luther's Catechism and the catechetical practices of the Roman Church; the following facts are relevant:

The subjects taught to catechumens, in the primitive Church, were the Symbol of the Apostles, the Paternoster, and the sins and vices to be avoided.[1] These latter, of course, could only be understood in terms of the Ten Commandments, the knowledge of which was undoubtedly presupposed or furnished by the instructor. Again, the Council of Aix la Chapelle, in 836, declares that one must teach children the Lord's Prayer, the Apostles' Creed, and their duties;[2] the word 'duties' implies the Ten Commandments. Saint Thomas in the thirteenth century expounded, among other catechetical questions, the five points. Examples are these opuscules: *Expositio symboli apostolorum*,[3] *Expositio devotissima orationis dominicae vidilicet Pater Noster*,[4] *De duobus praeceptis charitatis et decem legis praeceptis*,[5] and *De articulis fidei et ecclesiae sacramentis*.[6] Moreover, in Luther's own time, there was in use a popular German catechism, the *Christenspiegel*, that came out in 1470; it was the first of its kind in the German language and it dealt with similar catechetical subjects under the heading: 'What one must believe and do in order to live well and die well.'[7] This work was printed in many subsequent editions right up till 1706.

From this list, by no means exhaustive, we see clearly that the five points of Luther's catechisms are not, materially speaking, suggestive of anything typically Lutheran as distinct from Roman Catholicism. The difference is seen in Luther's exclusive Law-Gospel approach to these five points. If we keep in mind Luther's Law-Gospel doctrine and the words of his introduction to the second part of the *Large Catechism*, which we quoted at the beginning of this chapter, we can agree with and appreciate Roland Bainton's interpretation of the plan of the catechism:

[1] *D.T.C.*, article, 'Catéchisme', tome 2, col. 1896.
[2] *D.T.C.*, ibid., col. 1898.
[3] St. Thomas Aquinas, *Opuscula Omnia*, Mandonnet, Paris, 1927, Opusculum 33, pp. 349–89.
[4] Ibid., Opusculum 34, pp. 389–413.
[5] Ibid., Opusculum 35, pp. 413–56.
[6] Ibid., vol. iii, Opusculum 15, pp. 1–19.
[7] *D.T.C.*, ibid., col. 1906.

'Both are built about five points, the Ten Commandments as a mirror of sin, the Apostles' Creed as a proclamation of forgiveness,[1] the Lord's Prayer as an acceptance of mercy and the two sacraments of Baptism and the Lord's Supper as channels of grace.'[2] The plan, in other words, points to the Law-Gospel relation; the Decalogue revealing to man his sinfulness, and the Gospel (professed in the Apostles' Creed, the Lord's Prayer and the Sacraments) transforming him and fulfilling the Law in his heart and members.

We intend to limit our analysis mainly to the *Large Catechism*. This work, in our opinion, contains all the matter of the *Small Catechism* pertaining to the Law-Gospel relation; but handled more fully.[3] On the five main points, the *Small Catechism* is a mere skeleton of the former. Its additional parts, such as the formularies on Marriage and Baptism, do not modify, in any respect, its Law-Gospel plan and content. Perhaps the only advantage the *Small Catechism* has over the large one is the absence of any passionate polemical spirit. But this is incidental to the meaning of Luther's doctrine.

Though our analysis of the *Large Catechism* is based on the German and Latin texts of the Göttingen edition of the *Bekenntnisschriften*, we shall quote, for the sake of clarity and simplicity, from the Philadelphia English edition of the *Book of Concord*.[4] This translation is deemed to be substantially accurate; when we think that it deviates, in any important respect, from the Latin or German texts, we shall say so in the footnotes and offer our own version. Moreover, those German or Latin passages which are difficult to translate or have equivocal meanings will be transcribed in the notes or appendixes.

A final word: when reading the *Large Catechism*, we must

[1] Johannes Meyer claims that the doctrines of the Gospel section of the Catechism are 'all grouped about forgiveness' (*Historischer Kommentar zu Luthers kleinem Katechismus*, Gütersloh, 1929, p. 492).

[2] Roland Bainton, *Here I Stand*, pp. 262–3.

[3] In his preface to the *Small Catechism* Luther, himself, orders the instructor to use the *Large Catechism* to give children a fuller and richer knowledge of the *Small Catechism*: 'Zum dritten, wenn Du sie nu solchen kurzen Katechismum gelehret hast, alsdenn nimm den großen Katechismum für Dich und gib ihn auch reichen und weitern Verstand' (*Bek.*, p. 504, 35–39).

[4] 'The translation used in this edition of the *Book of Concord* was prepared by Professors F. Bente and W. H. T. Dau. It is based on the original German and Latin texts, respectively, and on the existing English translations, chiefly on those incorporated in Dr. Jacob's *Book of Concord*' (*B.C.*, Publisher's Preface).

remember that Luther does not and cannot develop, in an instruction book, a systematic and exhaustive treatment of his theology of salvation. Yet, notwithstanding, he does expect his disciples, especially pastors chosen to teach the faithful, to be in agreement with him on what he considers most fundamental. That is: the Christian, by virtue of his humanity, is always sinful, morally impotent before the Law, an old Adam; at the same time, by virtue of his faith in Christ, he is saintly, transformed imputatively, a new Adam. This dualism is never absent from Luther's thinking; and to understand him, so as not to confuse his Law-Gospel doctrine with medieval Scholasticism or Melanchthonian synergism, we must not exclude it from our interpretation of the catechism texts.

We are now ready to begin our analysis of the first or Decalogue section of the *Large Catechism*.

IV

THE DECALOGUE SECTION OF THE CATECHISM

A. *The plan of this chapter*

THE Decalogue section of the *Large Catechism* deals with the work of God's Word as Law.[1] The Ten Commandments reveal what God wills man to do or not to do in order to please Him and to be righteous.[2] But this Law-revelation does not, as we have seen, bring with it the means which sinful man requires to keep and fulfil these commandments.[3] The Law, thus, becomes for him a mirror of his moral impotence —what he cannot accomplish by himself and without God's help. It also appears to him as a hammer in that he feels crushed by the condemnation of the Law, which causes in him deep frustration and despair. This empties him completely of self so that he is passively disposed to be filled wholly and entirely by Christ's righteousness.

To show this work[4] of God's Word as Law, we have decided to analyse the Decalogue section of the Catechism as follows: we introduce the subject with a skeleton outline of Luther's ordering of the Ten Commandments, showing how he envisages the works of the Law as service to God and to neighbour, the whole of which he centres on the First Commandment or faith in God. Next we consider the force and function of the Law, as we explained in the introduction.

Our aim is not a detailed analysis of each commandment, taken consecutively and related to the Gospel, but an inter-

[1] When we speak of the 'Law' in this chapter, we are referring to the Ten Commandments; we are not concerned with the Jewish rituals and regulations of the Old Covenant.

[2] See below, p. 77, n. 7.

[3] See Chapter I, section C, p. 22.

[4] In our study, we often speak of the 'work of the Word'. The expression is most apt because, for Luther, the revelations of Sacred Scripture are not dead inoperative letters but creative living words effecting redemption and sanctification in our hearts and souls and producing good works pleasing to God (see below, p. 78, n. 2).

pretation of those statements and convictions in which Luther
professes his faith in the divine character of the Decalogue,
describes its role and develops its evangelical import.

B. *Outline of the Ten Commandments*

In the Decalogue section of the Catechism, Luther provides
us with an eloquent defence of the Ten Commandments; he
gives the lie to those who, like Agricola,[1] misinterpret his *sola
scriptura, sola fide* doctrine to declare that the Law is no longer
necessary to the Christian life.

For each commandment, he follows a simple plan: he states
what it is from Scripture; explains its meaning, and what he
believes to be its full positive as well as negative implications; he
announces the divine threats and promises attached to it; gives
examples or draws analogies from Scripture and daily experience to corroborate and clarify his point; and sums up. We
shall survey briefly his ordering of the Ten Commandments.

The first three commandments, he tells us, concern God
directly, the other seven our neighbour.[2] But all of them, he
maintains, 'must flow and proceed' from the First or 'chief'
Commandment[3]; what he calls the *Häuptgepot*,[4] or the *Quellborn*
[fountainhead].[5]

[1] Luther became involved in a bitter controversy with Johannes Agricola
(1499–1566) in the year 1537. The latter was, at the beginning of the Reformer's
career, one of his ardent supporters; but he gradually developed strong antinomian doctrines, arguing that it was no longer necessary to preach the Law, even
its functional role as the mirror of our sinfulness and the means of preparing us for
grace. He thought that repentance should be instilled by preaching the Gospel
alone (Harold J. Grimm, *The Reformation Era*, New York, 1954, p. 231). In the
Smalcald Articles, which we shall study presently, Luther opposes and rejects
Agricola's antinomian theories.
[2] 'Bisher haben wir die ersten drei Gepot gelernet, die da gegen Gott gerichtet
sind ... Folgen nu die andern siebene, gegen unserm Nähisten gestellet ...' (*Bek.*
p. 586. 35–48).
[3] '... des ersten und furnehmsten Gepots, daraus alle andere quellen und gehen
sollen ...' (*Bek.*, p. 642. 46–48). The Latin text reads: '. . . prioris ac praecipui
praecepti ex quo cetera omnia manant et ebulliunt . . .' (*Bek.*, p. 324). The *B.C.*
gives this translation: '. . . of the First and chief Commandment from which all the
others must follow and proceed' (p. 191, col. 1). Again in Latin, Luther refers to
the First Commandment as the head of all the other commandments: '. . . aliorum
omnium caput est' (*Bek.*, p. 567. 34–37).   [4] See *Bek.*, p. 567. 35–36.
[5] At the end of the 'Beschluß' to the Decalogue section Luther writes: 'Also
siehest Du, wie das erste Gepot das Häupt und Quellborn ist, so durch die andern
alle gehet, und wiederümb alle sich zurückziehen und hangen in diesem, daß
End und Anfang alles ineinander geknüpft und gebunden ist' (*Bek.*, p. 644. 17–22).

This First Commandment, he defines as an order to believe
in the one true God '. . . it is the intent [*Meinung*] of this commandment to require true faith and trust of the heart [*rechten
Glauben und Zuversicht des Herzens*] which settles upon the only
true God, and clings to him alone'.[1] Thus the other commandments, stemming from this First Commandment, are simply the
fruit and effect of justifying faith;[2] they are not means to salvation apart from faith and the Word: '. . . where the heart is
rightly disposed[3] towards God and this [First] commandment
observed, all the others follow.'[4] Thus Luther begins and ends
his exposition of the Decalogue with an insistent stress on the
importance of this *Häuptgepot* or 'chief' commandment.[5] Behind
this insistence is the basic conviction which governs his thinking
throughout the whole of the Catechism—*Glauben und Gotteswort
allein*,[6] teach us what we must do to please God; we shall return
to it several times in this and the next chapter.

He summarizes succinctly what he thinks the first three commandments signify: the First Commandment teaches that we
ought to believe in God with all our hearts, and fear and love[7]
Him during our whole lives; the Second, that we ought not to

---

[1] (*Bek.*, p. 560. 30–34; see also *B.C.*, 169).

[2] We must always bear in mind that, for Luther, this justifying faith (the power
to keep the First Commandment) is given solely by the Gospel Word about which
we shall speak in the next chapter.

[3] We recall the findings of our first chapter: the heart of the Christian is only
fully and properly 'disposed towards God' when it is transformed passively and
imputatively. The disposition of the heart cannot be understood ontologically as
an operative or entitative habit inhering really and physically in the Christian's
soul.

[4] '... wo das Herz wohl mit Gott dran ist und dies Gepot gehalten wird, so
gehen die andern alle hernach [folgt die Erfüllung der andern von selbst]' (see
Bek., p. 572. 12–14, and note 4; also *B.C.*, p. 172). The words in square brackets
are the editors' explanation of the text.

[5] 'Also soll nu das erste Gepot leuchten und sein Glanz geben in die andern
alle. Darümb muß Du auch dies Stück lassen gehen durch alle Gepot als die
Schele [hoop] oder Bögel [wreath] im Kranz, daß End und Anfang zuhause füge
und alle zusammenhalte, auf daß man's immer wiederhole und nicht vergesse'
(*Bek.*, p. 643. 24–30).

[6] Again we repeat that this work of faith and God's Word alone must be understood according to the Law-Gospel relation, and in terms of a Law-Gospel experience which God's Word produces in the sinner. We shall see this more clearly as
we proceed with this chapter.

[7] We remind the reader here of what we said in our second chapter concerning
Luther's ideal of pure love of God. We do not fulfil perfectly God's commandment
to love Him as long as we can sense in our hearts the least trace of self-love, however natural such self-love may be.

profane His name in order to commit evil, but only to praise God and help our neighbour; and the Third Commandment, that we should consecrate the Sabbath to meditating and preaching God's Word'.[1]

As for the other commandments, directed at loving our neighbour, Luther considers the Fourth, 'Honour thy father and thy mother', as the first and greatest [hohiste],[2] and allots more space to explaining this commandment[3] than to any other of the remaining seven. For him, it requires more than just a child's duties to his parents; it also implies the reciprocal duties of servants and masters, subjects and rulers.[4] This commandment, therefore, is the bulwark of the family and education, and the divine foundation of all authority, both temporal and spiritual.[5] Obedience to this commandment is a sure sign and proof of

---

[1] In his introduction to the Fourth Commandment, Luther summarizes what he thinks the three previous commandments signify: 'Zum ersten, daß man ihm [Gott] von ganzem Herzen vertraue, furchte und liebe in alle unserm Leben. Zum andern, daß man seines heiligen Namens nicht mißbrauche zur Lügen noch einigem bösen Stücke, sondern zu Gottes Lob, Nutz und Seligkeit des Nähisten und seiner selbs. Zum dritten, daß man an der Feier und Ruge Gottes Wort mit Fleiß handle und treibe, auf daß alle unser Tuen und Leben darnach gehe' (Bek., p. 586. 37–46.).

[2] '... die andern siebene [commandments] ... unter welchen das erste und hohiste* ist: "Du sollt Dein Vater und Mutter ehren" ' (Bek., p. 586. 47–49; see also B.C., p. 176, col. 1).
* 'Summum' is used in the Latin text.

[3] So excellent and important is this Fourth Commandment to Luther that frequently, as we shall see in the next chapter, he employs it as a model in connexion with the New Testament or Gospel commandments. He draws an analogy between it and Christ's evangelical orders to profess one's faith, preach the Gospel, recite the Lord's Prayer, and administer the Sacraments. These latter are, like the Fourth Commandment, divine praecepta to be kept and obeyed and to which are joined specific threats and promises (see below, Chapter V, section B). Using the Fourth Commandment in this way, as a model, he shows us how the Decalogue notion of commandment can be extended to embrace the work of the Gospel. Of course there is this difference: the New Testament commandments, unlike the Old Testament ones, are accompanied by the true and effective means of fulfilment; namely the merits of the crucified and resurrected Christ and the sanctifying powers of the Holy Ghost. But more about this later.

[4] 'In dieses Gepot gehöret auch weiter zu sagen von allerlei Gehorsam gegen Oberpersonen, die zu gepieten und zu regieren haben. Denn aus der Eltern Oberkeit fleußet und breitet sich aus alle andere' (Bek., p. 596. 17–21).

[5] 'Also haben wir dreierlei Väter in diesem Gepot furgestellet: des Gebluts, im Hause und im Lande. Darüber sind auch noch geistliche Väter, nicht wie im Bapsttumb, die sich wohl also haben lassen nennen, aber kein väterlich Ampt gefuhret. Denn das heißen allein geistliche Väter, die uns durch Gottes Wort regieren und furstehen, . . .' (Bek., p. 601. 24–31).

man's willingness to serve God;[1] it is superior to all 'monkish holiness' [ibid.].

Luther's understanding of the Fifth Commandment allows for lawful killing, as in the case of self-defence or the protection of society. He condemns all forms of unlawful killing[2] among which he classes revenge[3] and deliberate refusal to help a neighbour in need.[4] This commandment, he adds, helps us to grasp the others which follow inasmuch as they too specify further ways in which we are forbidden to harm our neighbour.[5]

These are arranged, he says, in a fine order [*fein ordenlich*]:[6] the Fifth Commandment pertains directly to the person of our neighbour, the Sixth to the person closest to him, namely his wife,[7] the Seventh to what is closest to him after his wife—his temporal goods,[8] and finally the Eighth Commandment to his honour and reputation, which goods come next in line.[9]

The Ninth and Tenth Commandments, the Reformer groups together and gives to his exposition of them a characteristic slant, in keeping with his pessimistic view of human nature. He

---

[1] 'Darümb laßt uns einmal lernen ümb Gottes willen, daß das junge Volk, alle ander Ding aus den Augen gesetzt, erstlich auf dies Gepot sehen, wenn sie Gott mit rechten guten Werken dienen wollen, daß sie tuen, was Vater und Mutter, oder den sie an ihr Statt untertan sind, lieb ist' (*Bek.*, p. 589. 40–46). Also when discussing the servant-girl's obedience to her master: 'Ist's nicht ein trefflicher Ruhm, das zu wissen und sagen: "Wenn Du Dein tägliche Hauserbeit tuest, das besser ist denn aller Monche Heiligkeit und strenges Leben"' (*Bek.*, p. 598. 1–3; see also p. 81, n. 1, below.

[2] 'Derhalben, was hie verpoten ist, ist einem gegen dem andern verpoten und nicht der Oberkeit' (*Bek.*, p. 606. 9–11).

[3] He explains that we must not kill 'neither with hand, heart, mouth signs, gestures, help, nor counsel' (*B.C.*, p. 181, col. 1). Nor offend one's neighbour 'on account of any evil deed, even though he may have fully deserved it' (ibid.).

[4] 'Zum andern ist auch dieses Gepots schüldig nicht allein, der da Böses tuet, sondern auch, wer den Nähisten Guts tuen, zuvorkommen, wehren, schützen und retten kann, daß ihm kein Leid noch Schaden am Leibe widerfahre, und tuet es nicht' (*Bek.*, p. 608. 22–27).

[5] 'Diese Gepot [which follow] sind nu an ihn selbs leicht zu verstehen aus dem nähisten; denn sie gehen alle dahin, daß man sich hüte fur allerlei Schaden des Nähisten ...' (*Bek.*, pp. 610–11. 41–43, 1–2).

[6] In the Latin text: '. . . sunt vero eleganti ordine posita' (*Bek.*, p. 611. 1–2).

[7] '... zum ersten [the Fifth Commandment] auf sein eigene Person, darnach fortgefahren auf die nähiste Person oder das nähiste Gut nach seinem Leibe, nämlich sein ehelich Gemahl ...' (*Bek.*, p. 611. 2–6).

[8] 'Nach Deiner Person und ehlichen Gemahl ist zeitlich Gut das Nähiste ...' (*Bek.*, p. 616. 12–13).

[9] 'Über unsern eigenen Leib, ehelich Gemahl und zeitlich Gut haben wir noch einen Schatz nämlich Ehre und gut Gerücht ...' (*Bek.*, p. 624. 28–30).

claims that these latter commandments 'were given strictly speaking to the Jews; nevertheless, in part, they also concern us'.[1]

What he means here is this: the Jews thought that they were righteous before God when they had kept the first eight commandments outwardly;[2] but outward obedience did not prevent them from conniving inwardly after legal tricks and ways of dispossessing their neighbour of his wife and belongings, and such wise as to be acting ostensibly according to one's rights and within the Jewish Law.[3] To offset such evil lusts of the heart, God also promulgated the Ninth and Tenth Commandments, 'in order that it be esteemed as sin and forbidden to desire or in any way to aim at getting our neighbour's wife or possessions'.[4] The Jews, therefore, did not interpret them 'as referring to unchastity or theft, because these vices were sufficiently forbidden by the above commandments'.[5] More radically, they understood them to be aimed at man's inner wickedness and hidden desires. The last two commandments, therefore, forbade them 'to alienate anything' from their neighbour, even though one 'could do so with honour in the eyes of the world'.[6]

But these commandments are meant for us too; because, basic-

[1] 'Diese zwei Gepot sind fast den Jüden sonderlich gegeben, wiewohl sie uns dennoch auch zum Teil betreffen' (Bek., p. 633. 38–40).

[2] '[Jüden] ... hielten's auch dafur, sie hätten jene [the above eight commandments] alle gehalten, wenn sie äußerlich die Werk getan oder nicht getan hätten' (Bek., p. 633. 43–45).

[3] Luther helps to clarify this point by describing the social condition of man and maid servants and married women in the ancient Jewish community: '. . . in dem jüdischen Regiment Knechte und Mägde nicht wie itzt frei waren, ümbs Lohn zu dienen, wielang sie wollten, sondern des Herrn Eigen mit Leib und was sie hatten wie das Viehe und ander Gut. Dazu auch ein iglicher über sein Weib die Macht hatte, durch ein Scheidbrief öffentlich von sich zu lassen und ein andere zu nehmen. Da mußten sie nu unternander die Fahr stehen, wenn imand eins andern Weib gerne gehabt hätte, daß er irgend ein Ursach nähme, beide sein Weib von sich zu tun und dem andern seins auch zu entfrömbden, daß er's mit gutem Fug zu sich brächte. Das war nu bei ihn kein Sunde noch Schande ...' (Bek., p. 634. 3–21).

[4] 'Darümb hat Gott diese zwei [Ninth and Tenth Commandments] hinzugesetzt, daß man's auch halte fur Sunde und verpoten, des Nähisten Weib oder Gutbegehren und einerleiweise darnach zu stehen ...'(Bek., pp. 633-4. 45–47, 1–2).

[5] 'Denn sie [the Jews] legen sie [these two commandments] nicht aus von Unkeuschheit noch Diebstahl, weil davon droben genug verpoten ist ... (Bek., p. 633. 40–43).

[6] 'Hie aber ist auch gewehret, dem Nähisten nichts abzuspannen, ob man gleich mit Ehren fur der Welt dazu kommen kann, daß Dich niemand zeihen noch tadeln tarr, als habst Du's mit Unrecht eröbert' (Bek., p. 634. 38–43).

ally, what Luther points to here is the sinful egoism or perverse selfishness of all men. He emphasizes the word *begehren*, taken from his German translation of the Ninth and Tenth Commandments: *Du sollt nicht begehren . . .*, and best translated into English by 'covet'.[1] This word, along with *concupiscentia*, we have seen in the first chapter, he uses to designate the enduring sinfulness of human nature—the love of self and self-reliance, which is an abomination in the eyes of God, the source of all sin and evil, and most condemned by the commandments.[2]

We are not surprised, therefore, to find him saying, in connexion with these two commandments, the following:

> . . . we are so inclined by nature that no one desires to see another have so much as himself, and each one acquires as much as he can, the other may fare as best he can. And yet we pretend to be godly [*fromm*], know how to adorn ourselves most finely and conceal our rascality [*Schalk*.] . . .
> This last commandment therefore is given not for rogues in the eyes of the world, but just for the most pious, who wish to be praised and be called honest and upright people. . . .[3]

And still further on, just before the 'Beschluß', he sums up:

> Thus these commandments are especially directed against envy [*Abgunst*][4] and miserable avarice [*leidigen Geiz*], God wishing to remove all causes [*Ursach*] and sources [*Wurzel*] whence arises everything by which we do injury to our neighbour, and therefore He expresses it in plain words: *Thou shalt not covet*, etc. For He would especially have the heart pure, although we shall never attain to that as long as we live here; so that this commandment will remain, like all the rest, one that will constantly accuse us [*ohn Unterlaß beschuldigt*] and show how godly we are in the sight of God.[5]

The final words of this quotation exemplify a recurring theme of the *Large Catechism*, about which we shall speak again; namely the Law's function as a mirror of our sinfulness. It is an essential part of Luther's despair-faith pattern of salvation, and pertains directly to our Law-Gospel problem.

[1] The Latin text reads: 'Non *concupisces* domum proximi tui nec *desiderabis* uxorem ejus . . .' (*Bek.*, p. 633. 31–34). The italics are ours.

[2] See above, Chapter II, section A.

[3] *Bek.*, pp. 634–5. 43–46, 1–6; for the English translation, see *B.C.*, p. 189, col. 1.

[4] Envious in the sense of being ill-disposed towards someone's well-being and fortune.

[5] *Bek.*, pp. 638–9. 36–44, 1–5.

But more immediately, our skeleton outline of Luther's exposition of the Ten Commandments reveals, as would be expected, the same basic opposition between the redemptive work of God's Word and the damning efforts of man's will.[1] Right from the start, he centres the keeping of the Commandments on an inner act of faith in God's Word; this, in a sense, is another way of telling us that, without faith and God's help, our good works are meaningless; and in his summing up, he declares men to be morally impotent, having nothing to boast of before God but their own self-love and covetousness.

As always, we sense the personal pattern of despair and faith involving man's enduring sinfulness and his passively and imputatively acquired righteousness. These latter are criteria by which we can judge whether a Christian's obedience to the Ten Commandments is properly the result of the exclusive work of the Word. That is to say, whether he relies on his own sinful efforts to attain righteousness, in which case, as we shall see, the Law will crush and terrify him; or obeys the Commandments through faith and dependence on divine help alone, and thus experiences spiritual comforts and assurance of salvation.

We should add, at this juncture, that Luther expands the brief imperatives of the Mosaic Law, as formulated in the Book of Exodus.[2] He shows how they take in what he believes to be the full range of man's moral duties and God-pleasing works. He is obviously not content to limit the Ten Commandments to simple 'don'ts' and to stick slavishly and narrowly to the single sentence 'thou shalt not'. On practically every page of the Decalogue section of the Catechism, he exhorts us energetically to attend to our positive obligations—to anticipate God's Will, to look to the welfare of our neighbour, to contribute our share to the corporal works of mercy. This is particularly manifest in his interpretation of the last two commandments, where he condemns, outright, all sham self-complacency in a purely negative and outward obedience to God's laws.

Here, one might raise an objection: Luther's treatment of the Decalogue implies distinctions and amplifications based, to some extent, on common sense, a sound experience of men and a shrewd knowledge of nature; could this mean that his theology is not a matter exclusively of the Word?

[1] See section C of this chapter, and p. 79, n. 1, p. 80, n. 5.   [2] Exod. xx. 1–21.

We answer no, if we keep close to our original soteriological meaning of 'exclusive'; for first of all, human experience and knowledge, for Luther, will never suffice to uncover the evangelical core of the Law—the paradoxical way in which it is ordained to our salvation;[1] secondly, because he could, indeed does, refer to other scriptural texts,[2] besides the mere Mosaic list from Exodus, to support most of the positive duties mentioned; and finally, his exposition of the latter still does not allow for any description of human nature as a source or cause of merit and an active means of salvation.[3] In these respects, his theology remains exclusively a theology of the Word—the Word alone revealing and providing the sole and unique means by which we are saved. His tireless attack on monasticism (see below) is a clear-cut example of how he wishes to exclude everything from his theology that is not in accordance with what he believes to be 'the pure Word of God'. Now we are ready to discuss Luther's remarks on the force of the Law or the Ten Commandments.

C. *The force of the Law*

He accounts for the force of the Law in three ways: by its divine origins, its sanctions, and the evidence of daily experience.

(1) *The divine origins*

Concerning the divine origins of the Law, Luther has no doubts about the matter; the Ten Commandments belong to

---

[1] 'Denn wir künnden ... nimmermehr dazu kommen, daß wir des Vaters Hulde und Gnade erkenneten ohn durch den, Herrn Christum, der ein Spiegel ist des väterlichen Herzens, außer welchem wir nichts sehen denn einen zornigen und schrecklichen Richter. Von Christo aber künnten wir auch nichts wissen, wo es nicht durch den heiligen Geist offenbaret wäre' (*Bek.*, p. 660. 38–45.)

[2] Concerning obedience to civil authorities, for instance, Luther writes: '... wiewohl es in zehen Gepoten nicht ausgedruckt stehet, ist es doch sonst an vielen Orten der Schrift reichlich gepoten' (*Bek.*, p. 603. 22–25). This practice Luther follows with respect to the implied duties of the other commandments.

[3] At one point, Luther describes creatures as means: 'Denn die Kreaturn sind nur die Hand, Rohre [channels] und Mittel, dadurch Gott alles gibt, wie er der Mutter Brüste und Milch gibt ...' (*Bek.*, 1 Gepot, p. 566. 20–23). But these are to be understood as God-given means: 'Derhalben soll sich kein Mensch unterstehen, etwas zu nehmen oder zu geben, es sei denn von Gott befohlen, daß man's erkenne fur seine Gaben und ihm darümb danke, wie dies Gepot fodert. Darümb auch solche Mittel durch die Kreaturn Guts zu empfahen nicht auszuschlagen sind noch durch Vermessenheit andere Weise und Wege zu suchen, denn Gott befohlen hat; denn das hieße nicht, von Gott empfangen, sondern von ihm selbs gesucht' (ibid., 26–37).

the divinely inspired books of Holy Scripture.[1] In the long preface to the Catechism, he says that 'whoever knows the Ten Commandments perfectly must know all the Scriptures ...;'[2] and adds that the 'entire Psalter' is nothing but 'thoughts and exercises upon the First Commandment'.[3] And in the same sense, he calls the whole of the Catechism a 'compend and brief summary of all the Scriptures'.[4] Furthermore, he says, we should 'feel sufficiently constrained by the commandment of God alone' to read the Catechism daily;[5] for God 'has solemnly enjoined us in Deut. vi. 6, to meditate upon His precepts, sitting, walking, standing, lying down and rising, and have them before our eyes and in our hands as a constant mark and sign'.[6] In the 'Beschluss', he states that the Ten Commandments are the only good works pleasing to God precisely because they are ordained by His Divine Will:

> Thus we have the Ten Commandments, a compend [*Ausbund*] of divine doctrine [*göttlicher Lehre*], as to what we are to do in order that our whole life may be pleasing to God, and the true fountain and channel from and in which everything must arise and flow that is to be a good work, so that outside the Ten Commandments no work or thing can be good or pleasing to God, however great or precious it be in the eyes of the World.[7]

The Ten Commandments, therefore, by virtue of their divine origin, determine exclusively what works are pleasing to God. As always, it is a question of faithful obedience to the divine Word—what God has willed and taught; for the Word of God

---

[1] Luther, of course, is aware of the fact that Jesus later explained the commandments in the form in which we are to keep them (Matt. xii. 1–13; John v. 1–17; also Paul in Col. ii. 16, 17 and Eph. vi. 2, 3).

[2] 'Denn das muß ja sein: wer die zehen Gepot wohl und gar kann, daß der muß die ganze Schrift können ...' (*Bek.*, p. 552. 16–18). The Latin text reads: 'Nam illud sane certum atque indubitatum est, quod, qui decem praecepta probe norit ac perdidicerit, is totam etiam scripturam sciat . . .' (ibid.). See also *B.C.*, p. 167.

[3] 'Und was ist der ganze Psalter denn eitel Gedanken und Ubunge des ersten Gepots ...' (*Bek.*, p. 552. 24–26).

[4] '. . . welcher [*Katechismus*] der ganzen heiligen Schrift kurzer Auszug und Abschrift ist' (ibid. 31–33).

[5] Ibid.

[6] '... so sollt' doch uns allein gnugsam zwingen Gottes Gepot, welcher Deutero. 6, [7–8], ernstlich gebeut, "daß man solle sein Gebot sitzend, gehend, stehend, liegend, aufstehend immer bedenken und gleich als ein stetigs Mal und Zeichen fur Augen und in Händen haben"' (*Bek.*, pp. 550–1. 39, 1–6; see also *B.C.*, p. 167).

[7] *Bek.*, p. 639. 11–19; see also *B.C.*, p. 190, col. 1.

'is the sanctuary above all sanctuaries'[1] and 'the treasure which sanctifies everything, and by which even all the saints themselves were sanctified'.[2]

Those works devised by man, which Luther claims not to be comprehended in the Ten Commandments, are false and idolatrous, having no redemptive effect; such things as the intercession of the saints,[3] the Holy Sacrifice of the Mass,[4] ecclesiastical orders,[5] and every Pelagian form of seeking, in one's own works, consolation and salvation.[6] The force of the Law is such that it excludes from the work of salvation all traditional ideas of personal merit and effort. This exclusive aspect of his theology appears in his treatment of every commandment; its full revolutionary implications are stated unequivocally in his exposition of the Fourth and Sixth Commandments, which, we believe, suffices to illustrate the point: 'What God commands must be nobler than everything that we may devise ourselves....'[7] Keeping the Fourth Commandment is 'far better than all the holiness of the Carthusians';[8]

---

[1] Luther employs this metaphor when discussing the Third Commandment: 'Denn das Wort Gottes ist das Heiligtumb* über alle Heiligtumb ...' (*Bek.*, p. 583. 26–27).
* 'Sacrum' in the Latin text.

[2] '... Gottes Wort ist der Schatz, der alle Ding heilig machet, dadurch sie selbs, die Heiligen alle, sind geheiligt worden' (ibid. 33–36).

[3] In his explanation of the First Commandment, Luther says that we are to rely solely on God for our spiritual consolation and security; not on riches, talents or the merits of the saints. Concerning the latter, he calls the various devotions of the saints, especially the practice of appealing to them for help, in times of trouble, instead of directly to God, 'countless abominations' [... *des Greuels unzählich* ...] (see *Bek.*, p. 562. 10–30).

[4] See below, p. 136, n. 3.   [5] See following notes [6], [7], and [8].

[6] 'Darüber ist auch ein falscher Gottesdienst und die hohiste Abgötterei, so wir bisher getrieben haben und noch in der Welt regieret, darauf auch alle geistliche Stände gegründet sind, welche allein das Gewissen betrifft, das da Hülfe, Trost [consolation] und Seligkeit suchet in eigenen Werken, vermisset sich Gott den Himmel abezuzwingen, und rechnet, wieviel es gestiftet, gefastet, Messe gehalten hat etc., verlässet sich und pochet darauf, als wolle es nichts von ihm geschenkt nehmen, sondern selbs erwerben oder überflüssig verdienen, gerade als mußte er uns zu Dienst stehen und unser Schuldner, wir aber seine Lehenherrn sein' (*Bek.*, pp. 564–5. 40–43, 1–11).

[7] 'Denn was Gott gepeut, muß viel und weit edler sein denn alles, was wir selbs mügen erdenken' (*Bek.*, p. 589. 4–6).

[8] 'Siehe, das ist besser denn aller Karthäuser Heiligkeit, ob sie sich gleich zu Tod fasten und ohn Unterlaß auf den Knien beten. Denn hie hast Du ein gewissen Text und gottlich Zeugnis, daß er dies geheißen hat, aber von jenem [the religious state] kein Wort befohlen' (*Bek.*, p. 591. 18–24).

likewise the Sixth Commandment is superior to the religious state which has been chosen 'without God's Word and command'.[1] These commandments sanction the married state and elevate it above all other states.[2]

Faithful obedience to the Sixth Commandment is impossible outside the married state:[3] 'In order that it may be more easy in some degree to avoid unchastity, God has commanded the state of matrimony';[4] and yet this is not enough, 'God's grace besides is required in order that the heart may also be pure'.[5] He does not hesitate to condemn as false and sinful the life of priests, monks, and nuns who 'resist God's order and command, inasmuch as they despise and forbid matrimony, and presume and vow to maintain perpetual chastity ...'.[6] Consistently, with

[1] 'Da hast Du abermal ein köstlich, ja viel und große gute Werk, welche Du fröhlich rühmen kannst wider alle geistliche Stände, ohn Gottes Wort und Gepot erwählet' (Bek., pp. 615–16. 42, 1–4).

[2] 'Dieweil aber dies Gepot [Sixth] so eben auf den Ehestand [see Luther's Work, Vom ehelichen Leben (1522), W.A. ix (ii), 275–304] gerichtet ist und Ursach gibt, davon zu reden, sollt Du wohl fassen und merken: Zum ersten, wie Gott diesen Stand [married state] so herrlich ehret und preiset damit, daß er ihn durch sein Gepot beide bestätigt und bewahret. Bestätigt hat er ihn droben im vierden Gepot ... Hie aber hat er ihn ... verwahret und beschutzet ... er ihn [married state] erstlich vor allen andern eingesetzt hat ...' (Bek., p. 612. 13–26).

[3] Unless it be manifestly clear that God wills otherwise; see below, n. 6. This point is highly significant for Luther's biography, see following page.

[4] 'Derhalben, auf daß deste leichter wäre, Unkeuschheit etlicher Maße zu meiden, hat auch Gott den Ehestand befohlen ...' (Bek., p. 614. 1–4).

[5] '... wiewohl noch Gottes Gnade dazu gehöret, daß das Herz auch keusch sei' (ibid. 5–6). Here again we see how Luther insists on the purification of the inner man; exterior acts and the appearance of goodness are not enough; God's grace and Spirit must be present to purify the heart and justify the inner man. This purification, however, must not be understood ontologically or entitatively, as we explained in the second chapter. God declares the inner man just or righteous and Christ, as it were, becomes the sole agent and active subject of all his good works.

[6] 'Daraus siehst Du, wie unser bäpstischer Hause, Pfaffen, Monche, Nonnen wider Gottes Ordnung und Gepot streben, so den Ehestand verachten uns verpieten und sich ewige Keuschheit zu halten vermessen und geloben ...' (Bek., p. 614. 13–17).

On the Christian obligation to marry, Luther recognizes ['some exceptions (although few)] '... welche Gott sonderlich ausgezogen, daß sie zum ehelichen Stand nicht tüchtig sind, oder durch hohe, übernatürliche Gabe befreiet hat, daß sie außer dem stande Keuschheit halten können' (Bek., p. 613. 40–44). The former exceptions could refer to the impotent, the insane, and the like; but the latter are definitely persons having a special calling, requiring Christian celibacy. Luther, therefore, seems to admit the principle, here, that certain men, aided by special graces, can remain chaste outside the married state; but in making these distinctions, it is obvious from the context, he does not wish to condone monasticism or ecclesiastical orders in general. What he probably means here is that a chosen

his doctrine of enduring sinfulness, he argues that however much monks may abstain from the external act, 'their hearts are so full of unchaste thoughts and evil lusts that there is a continual burning secret suffering which can be avoided in the married life'.[1] For this reason he concludes that 'all vows of chastity out of the married state'[2] are condemned by the Sixth Commandment, and 'free permission is granted ... even the command is given to all poor ensnared consciences to abandon their vows and embrace the married state'.[3] People who remain under vows 'only sin more and more against this commandment'.[4]

Here, we are not dealing with a mere impatient outburst against monasticism or clericalism.[5] The matter at stake is much

few, men such as Saint Paul or John the Baptist, are exempted from the married state to carry on some unique mission; but the Reformer, apparently, does not extend the principle to justify a whole community of friars or religious. He did not think that the monasticism of his time was sufficiently centred on God's Word to convince him that religious vows were really worth while, and truly inspired by the Holy Ghost.

[1] 'Und kurzlich, ob sie gleich des Werks sich enthalten, so sticken sie doch im Herzen voll unkeuscher Gedanken und böser Lust, daß da ein ewigs Brennen und heimlichs Leiden ist, welchs man im ehelichen Leben ümbgehen kann' (*Bek.*, p. 614. 26–31). Denifle made too much of passages like this one to relate the origins of Luther's new theology to sexual lust. But we recall to the reader what we said earlier; namely, that we must not interpret Luther apart from the historical context of his religious experience. As we saw, he had been trained in Nominalist theories of merit and imbued by an ideal of pure love of God *super omnia* which tended to make one regard the most natural acts, desires and thoughts, and undoubtedly physiological reactions of the body—innocent in themselves—as signs of sinful egoism. In actual fact, Luther may not have experienced temptations of the flesh beyond the ordinary, if measured by a saner and more wholesome theology than Nominalism.

[2] 'Darümb ist durch dies Gepot aller unehlichen [*sic*] Keuschheit Gelübd verdammpt und Urlaub gegeben, ja auch gepoten allen armen gefangenen Gewissen, so durch ihre Klöstergelubde betrogen sind, daß sie aus dem unkeuschen Stand ins eheliche Leben treten ...' (*Bek.*, p. 614. 31–37).

[3] Ibid.

[4] '... ob sonst gleich das Klosterleben göttlich wäre, doch nicht in ihrer Kraft stehet, Keuschheit zu halten, und, wo sie darin bleiben, nur mehr und weiter wider dies Gepot sundigen müssen' (ibid. 38–42).

[5] Luther's attack on ecclesiastical orders is not incidental to his catechism treatment of the Decalogue; it is too frequent and persistent to be merely incidental. During his exposition of nearly every commandment, and also of the five parts of the Gospel section, he returns to this theme, and never misses an opportunity to contrast the fruitful living works and blessings of the Ten Commandments with what he considers the dead Pelagian works of monks and nuns. His renunciation of monasticism, indeed of any form of organized or institutionalized religion, not explicitly commanded by the Word, is perfectly consistent with his exclusive Law-Gospel theology of the Word.

more basic and significant; it is really a kind of *Apologia suae vitae*—a frank statement of the convictions which undoubtedly motivated his stand against the papal doctrine of works, his eventual renunciation of the Augustinian vows, and subsequent marriage to Catherine Bora.

Holding sincerely to the above convictions, he could surely argue that his own vows are invalid for these four reasons: they are opposed to the Fourth and Sixth Commandments,[1] and thus God's Word; they are based on the 'cursed presumption' that religious life is a 'higher and better life and estate' than the Ten Commandments teach;[2] they are Pelagian attempts to attain righteousness without God's help;[3] and they are contrary to the basic needs of human nature.[4]

[1] An incident in Luther's life, which seems to have impressed upon his mind the possibility of a real conflict between the genuine good works commanded by God's Law and what he later considered to be the vain fruitless works of religious orders, was the conversation with his father on the day he celebrated his first Mass. Roland Bainton depicts the scene very vividly: '. . . he came from the altar to the table where his father and the guests would make merry with the brothers. After shuddering at the unapproachableness of the heavenly Father [during his Mass] he now craved some word of assurance from the earthly father. How his heart would be warmed to hear from the lips of old Hans that his resentment [over the fact that he had disobeyed his wishes and entered the cloisters] had entirely passed, and that he was now cordially in accord with his son's decision. They sat down to meat together, and Martin, as if he were still a child, turned and said, "Dear father, why were you so contrary to my becoming a monk? And perhaps you are not quite satisfied even now. The life is so quiet and godly!" '
'This was too much for old Hans, who had been doing his best to smother his rebellion. He flared up before all the doctors and the masters and the guests, "You learned scholar, have you never read in the Bible that you should honor your father and your mother? And here you have left me and your dear mother to look after ourselves in our old age" ' (*Here I Stand*, p. 31).
Behind Luther's Scriptural arguments against Pelagian practices and religious orders lies this biographical fact. To some extent, it may explain the strong personal tone of his attacks. Throughout the Catechism, he never tires of pointing out a diametrical opposition between God's commandments and the obligations of the religious life.
[2] We find this remark in his Conclusion to the Ten Commandments: 'Siehe aber, ist es nicht ein verfluchte Vermessenheit der verzweifelten Heiligen, so da sich unterstehen, ein höher und besser Leben und Stände zu finden, denn die zehen Gepot lehren ...' (*Bek.*, p. 640. 31–35).
[3] This is clear from what has already been said.
[4] 'Denn wo die Natur gehet, wie sie von Gott eingepflanzt ist, ist es nicht müglich, außer der Ehe keusch zu bleiben; denn Fleisch und Blut bleibt Fleisch und Blut, und gehet die natürlich Neigung und Reizung ungewehret und unverhindert, wie idermann siehet und fühlet' (*Bek.*, p. 613. 44–50). In this passage, we have a good example of Luther's understanding of God's Law; it commands us to do what experience teaches us we cannot do without God's help.

Admittedly, no Catholic theologian will be convinced by these arguments against monastic vows, but none the less they do illustrate two things relevant to our subject: for Luther, the force of the Law derives solely from God's Word,[1] as he interprets it; and its corollary, the Ten Commandments not only exclude but also condemn 'human holiness' and the pursuit of personal merit[2]—especially the 'supererogatory' works[3] of religious orders. These things he sees as attempts to replace God's Law and work by man-made ordinances. It is in this exclusive sense that we must understand him when he says that the Ten Commandments determine what work is to be done in God's name.

(2) *The divine sanctions*

In his 'exposition of the Appendix to the First Commandment',[4] Luther shows us how the divine sanctions enforce the Law of God. He introduces the Appendix in the following words. 'In order that it may be seen that God will not have this commandment thrown to the winds, but will most strictly enforce it, He has attached to it first a terrible threat, and a beautiful, comforting promise. . . .'[5] He then quotes the Appendix in full:

For I am the Lord thy God, strong and jealous, visiting the iniquity of the fathers upon the children unto the third and fourth generation

---

[1] 'Widerümb, was fur Wesen und Werk außer Gottes Wort gehet, das ist fur Gott unheilig, es scheine und gleiße, wie es wolle ...' (*Bek.*, pp. 583–4. 46–48, 1–2).

[2] At the end of his exposition of the works comprehended in the Fifth Commandment, he writes: 'Du aber wisse, daß dies die rechte, heilige und göttliche Werk sind, welcher er sich mit allen Engeln freuet, dagegen alle menschliche Heiligkeit Stank und Unflat ist, dazu nicht anders denn Zorn und Verdammnis verdienet' (*Bek.*, p. 610. 25–30).

[3] Underlying Luther's arguments is the pessimistic element of his Law-Gospel doctrine of justification—man's enduring sinful egoism. Because of this, no person, monk or laymen, 'can get so far as to keep one of the commandments as it should be kept, but needs the Lord's Prayer, and the Apostles' Creed to obtain the strength to keep them' (*B.C.*, p. 190, col. 2). To attempt to observe the difficult obligations and complicated rules of the religious life is presuming to go beyond a point that one can never reach. Thus Luther compares the monk to a beggar who says: 'I have not a penny to make payment with but I confidently undertake to pay ten florins' (ibid.). It is only when the Christian despairs totally in himself that he realizes the absurdity of personal merit and abandons himself completely to Christ in an act of faith. This despair-faith pattern of salvation remains constant throughout the Catechism.

[4] See *B.C.*, p. 171, col. 1; the words in quotation marks are a translation from the Latin text: 'Primi praecepti appendicis expositio' (see *Bek.*, p. 567).

[5] *Bek.*, p. 567. 14–21.

THE CATECHISM 83

of them that hate Me; and showing mercy unto thousands of them that love Me and keep My commandments.[1]

He goes on to say that though 'these words relate to all the commandments' they are joined to this 'chief [First] commandment because it is of the first importance that men have a right head, for where the head is right the whole life must be right, and vice versa'.[2]

Now, we have just seen, to have a right head and obey the First Commandment, one must fear and believe entirely in God,[3] and distrust and despair completely in self and in creatures;[4] so that, fundamentally speaking, the threats and promises contribute to the work of the Word producing in us the despair-faith experience of salvation.

Moreover, this retributive theme runs throughout the entire Catechism, the Gospel section as well as the Decalogue section. Luther dwells upon it as he expounds each Decalogue commandment and each Gospel commandment;[5] and in the 'Beschluß', he repeats, in full, the text of the Appendix, reaffirming that these words must be considered affixed to each commandment in particular, 'so that it inheres and pervades them all'.[6]

[1] 'Denn ich bin der HERRE, Dein Gott, ein starker Eiferer, der da heimsuchet der Väter Missetat an den Kindern bis ins dritte und vierde Gelied, die mich hassen, und tue Barmherzigkeit an viel tausend, die mich lieb haben und meine Gepot halten' (Bek., p. 567. 26–33). Luther's translation here is in keeping with his Bibelübersetzung (Ex. xx. 5). He requotes this Appendix from Exodus in the 'Beschluß' to the Decalogue section of the Catechism (see Bek., p. 641. 38–44).

[2] 'Wiewohl aber diese Wort auf alle Gepot gehen ... so sind sie doch eben zu diesem Häuptgepot gesetzt, darümb daß daran am meisten liegt, daß ein Mensch ein recht Häupt habe; denn wo das Häupt recht gehet, da muß auch das ganze Leben recht gehen, und widerümb' (Bek., p. 567. 34–40). In the 'Beschluß' he repeats himself on this score (Bek., p. 644. 17–22; also p. 642. 22–31).

[3] 'Also hat die ganze Schrift überall dies Gepot [First] gepredigt und getrieben, alles auf die zwei Stück, Gottes Fürcht und Vertrauen, gerichtet ...' (Bek., p. 643. 8–11). Luther says this while insisting on the value and importance of the divine threats and promises.

[4] 'Wiederümb wer etwas anders [creatures] in Himmel und auf Erden fürchtet und liebet, der wird wider dieses [i.e. the First Commandment] noch keines [any other commandment] halten (ibid. 5–7).

[5] We use the expressions 'Gospel or evangelical commandments' to refer to Christ's New Testament imperatives: these are to be distinguished from the 'Decalogue or Old Testament commandments'. On no account, however, are they to be divorced from each other; together they produce in the Christian's soul the awareness of his own sinfulness and his confidence in Christ's righteousness (see below, Chapter V, section A).

[6] '... also daß es [the Appendix] in und durch sie [the commandments] alle gehe' (Bek., p. 642. 7–8).

(3) *Experience corroborates the truth of the divine sanctions*

To illustrate and confirm the truth and force of these sanctions, Luther points to the lessons of daily experience: '... I have seen, he says, in the case of many who perjured themselves in their marriage vows, that they have never had a happy hour or a healthful day, and thus perished miserably in body, soul and possessions';[1] or again as a warning against stealing, '... we see and experience this being fulfilled daily before our eyes, that no stolen or dishonestly acquired possession thrives...';[2] and again with the Fourth Commandment: 'Where come so many knaves that must be daily hanged ... but from disobedience (to their parents) ... the godly and obedient have this blessing, that they live long in pleasant quietness, and see their children's children to the third and fourth generations';[3] and so on for the other commandments.

On the surface, these remarks look very much like a film version of 'crime does not pay'—a reduction of Christian morality to a kind of eighteenth-century bourgeois virtue, motivated by servile fear and *amour propre*; this would seem all the more so since Luther lays a certain amount of stress on the material and temporal benefits of the good life—not just the spiritual ones.[4] But deep down, nothing is farther from Luther's mind.

He wants, as we have often observed, religion and Christian conduct to spring spontaneously from an inner heartfelt[5] faith

---

[1] In connexion with the Second Commandment Luther makes this remark: '... wie ich an vielen erfahren habe, die ihr eheliche Gelübd verschworen haben, daß sie darnach keine gute Stunde oder gesunden Tag gehabt haben und also beide an Leib, Seele und Gut dazu iämmerlich verdorben sind' (*Bek.*, p. 577. 19–25).

[2] Here he is dealing with the Seventh Commandment: 'Solchs sehen und erfahren wir zwar fur Augen täglich erfullet werden, daß kein gestohlen und fälschlich gewonnen Gut gedeihet' (*Bek.*, p. 621. 33–36).

[3] *Bek.*, p. 595. 5–30.

[4] There are many instances in the Catechism where Luther describes the material benefits and rewards of God's promises. The following one, however, should suffice to illustrate the point: 'Da hast Du nu die Frucht und das Lohn, daß, wer es hält, soll gute Tage, Glück und Wohlfahrt haben, wiederümb auch die Strafe, daß, wer ungehorsam ist, deste ehe ümbkommen und des Lebens nicht froh werden soll' (*Bek.*, p. 594. 32–37). Luther also quotes Saint Paul, Eph. vi. 2, 3, in support of his statement: 'Das ist das erste Gepot, [Fourth Commandment], das eine Verheißung hat, auf daß Dir's wohlgehe und lange lebest auf Erden' (ibid. 20–22).

[5] That is to say, spontaneous and free in the sense that Christ alone is the active subject and cause of the Christian's good works and obedience. This spontaneity

in the divine Word and Love of God.[1] This is abundantly clear from his treatment of the First Commandment, not to mention a spate of other examples. We cannot appreciate this fact if we limit our view to isolated texts on the divine sanctions; we must read them within the *ensemble* of the Catechism; then we shall see why Luther urges us so strongly to meditate on God's threats and promises.

In the first place, because they are, like the commandments themselves, God's Word, and therefore must be revered and taught to the faithful; in the second place, because these sanctions, however much they promise to reward or punish us, are meant to illustrate how greatly and 'earnestly' God esteems and cherishes His commandments,[2] so that we may gather, from the importance which he Himself attaches to them, that keeping them is the best way to please Him. In this sense, the sanctions should make us act out of a desire to please rather than to escape chastisement or merit a prize.[3]

If he cites incidences of divine retribution in the daily lives of men, it is more to frighten and entice the wicked[4] to faith and good works than to encourage the truly Christian man. Being a man of the Bible, Luther obviously knew that the faithful, in this world, do not always enjoy temporal happiness;[5] God's

and spiritual freedom is not to be understood in a Catholic sense which teaches that man retains, however limited, the power of choice in accepting or refusing God's gifts and co-operating with and corresponding to the promptings of the Holy Spirit.

[1] In the 'Beschluß', he says: Damit [i.e. by the promises and the threats] er [God] will gefodert haben, daß sie [our works] alle aus solchem Herzen gehen, das alleine Gott furchtet und fur Augen hat und aus solcher Furcht alles lässet, was wider seinen Willen ist, auf daß ihn nicht erzürne, und dagegen auch ihm allein vertrauet und ihm zu Liebe tuet, was er haben will, weil er sich so freundlich als ein Vater hören lässet und uns alle Gnade und Guts anbeut' (*Bek.*, p. 642. 22–31; see also p. 644. 10–23).

[2] 'Nu ist ... in diesen Worten zusammengefasset [he is referring to the Appendix] beide ein zornig Draüwort und freundliche Verheißung, uns zu schrecken und warnen, dazu zu locken und reizen, auf daß man sein Wort als ein göttlichen Ernst annehme und groß achte, weil er selbs ausdrücket, wie groß ihm daran gelegen sei und wie hart er drüber [*sic*] halten wolle ...' (*Bek.*, p. 642. 8–16; see also p. 598. 14–26).

[3] 'Derhalben sollt Du von Herzen froh sein und Gotte danken, daß er Dich dazu erwählet und wirdig gemachet hat, ihm solch kostlich, angenehme Werk zu tuen' (*Bek.*, p. 590. 24–27).

[4] 'Denn diese sind's auch, die er meinet, als er spricht: "die mich hassen", das ist, die auf ihrem Trotz und Stolz beharren' (*Bek.*, p. 569. 13–16).

[5] Luther attempts to explain this fact by the world's failure to see through

prophets are stoned, Christ's disciples martyred, and His
Holy Church persecuted throughout history. The persevering
Christian, consequently, requires more than material benefits
and temporal promises to incite him to live up to his obligations;
he needs faith and love. The sanctions, while important, are
secondary, and do not supplant the Spirit of God and the
deeper inner work of the Word.[1] The ideal Christian perfection,
produced by the fullness of God's Word, is to obey His commandments free of constraint 'with joy and pleasure because it is
God's commandment . . . and a work most pleasing to Him'.[2]

We must be careful, therefore, not to misunderstand Luther—
to see an inconsistency in the contrasts between the ideal
Christian obedience and his passing observations on daily
retributions. Many apparent inconsistencies will vanish if we
adopt, what may be called, *a split perspective*; that is to say, a view

appearances: 'Es feilet aber leider daran, daß die Welt der keines nicht gläubt
noch fur Gottes Wort hält, weil sie siehet, daß, die Gott und nicht dem Mammon
trauen, Kümmer und Not leiden und der Teufel sich wider sie sperret und wehret,
daß sie kein Geld, Gunst, noch Ehre, dazu kaum das Leben behalten. Wiederümb,
die dem Mammon dienen, haben Gewalt, Gunst, Ehre und Gut und alle Gemach
fur der Welt. Derhalben muß man solche Wort fassen eben wider solchen Schein
gestellet, und wissen, daß sie nicht liegen noch triegen, sondern wahr müssen
werden' (*Bek.*, p. 570. 17–30).

Then follow a series of examples from experience and Scripture—in particular
the story of Saul and David. The important thing here is that the Christian, in
times of suffering and tribulation, must continue to believe firmly in God's promises. But, if necessary, Luther states elsewhere, he has to be ready to risk and
disregard everything upon earth to remain faithful to God: '... daß das Herz kein
andern Trost noch Zuversicht wisse denn zu ihm, lasse sich auch nicht davon
reißen, sondern darüber wage und hindansetze alles, was auf Erden ist' (*Bek.*,
p. 563. 31–35).

[1] 'Widerümb hat es die Kraft, wo man's mit Ernst betrachtet, höret und handlet,
daß es nimmer ohn Frucht abgehet, sondern allezeit neuen Verstand, Lust und
Andacht erwecket, rein Herz und Gedanken machet. Denn es sind nicht faule
noch tote, sondern schäftige, lebendige Wort. Und ob uns gleich kein ander Nutz
und Not triebe, so sollt' doch das idermann dazu reizen, daß dadurch der Teufel
gescheucht und verjagt, dazu dies Gepot erfüllet wird und Gott gefälliger ist denn
alle andere gleißende Heuchelwerke' (*Bek.*, p. 586. 10–22).

[2] Advising parents how to train their children to keep the Fourth Commandment, not from compulsion and with reluctance but with pleasure and joy, Luther
says: '... nicht aus Zwang und Widerwillen, sondern mit Lust und Freuden, eben
ümb voriger Ursach willen, daß es Gottes Gepot ist und ihm fur allen andern
Werken wohl gefället ...' (*Bek.*, p. 597. 17–21).

Again we repeat that the Christian's freedom and spontaneity of action should
be understood in a passive sense, such as we described in Chapter II. Christ is
always the sole warrior, the sole doer, and the sole victor in matters of forgiveness,
merit, and redemptive fulfilment.

of the Law as it applies firstly to the believer or redeemed person, and secondly to the non-believer; this brings us to the next question—the role or function of the Law.

D. *The function of the Law*

For the man of faith, the fulfilment of the Law, and all that belongs to it in the way of rewards and blessings, follows as a kind of effect of the believer's inner act of faith and passive justification, as we saw in our second chapter.[1] In this sense, the just man, the one made righteous by the 'power of God's Word', is bound to observe the Law as a living tree is bound to bring forth good fruit;[2] his observance of the Commandments, his good deeds, flow from his heart as a matter of course, freely and naturally,[3] not as a result of violence or constraint. And also for the rewards or divine benefits accruing; these are bestowed upon him, not as a payment due, but rather as part of the initial gift of faith and the entirety of Christ's work which has fulfilled the Law in him.

Besides, the Christian, though endowed with these blessings, remains for obscure reasons, the subject, or rather arena, of the inner struggle between the old Adam and the new.[4] In this struggle, the divine sanctions play their role; at those moments when the Christian succumbs to the temptations of the old Adam, when he ceases to rely solely on God's Word and Grace and turns back to his own devices and personal efforts to seek consolation and salvation, the divine sanctions rise up again in his conscience to warn and accuse him, the threats to frighten him and the promises to incite him into true obedience and faith. We shall find ample confirmation of this in the next chapter on the Gospel section.

In the case of the obdurate unrepentant non-believer (the wicked), the Law, with its sanctions, is functional in a different sense; it is a kind of check to crime.[5] That is to say, the Law

[1] See above, Chapter II, section B.
[2] This point is made most explicit in Luther's treatise *On Good Works*.
[3] Again we say, in Luther's theology, the 'free and natural' performance of good works excludes any meritorious form of consent, assent, or co-operation with the unique work of Christ.   [4] See below, p. 95, n. 1.
[5] This functional role of the Law, applying differently to the penitent and impenitent, the righteous and unrighteous, cannot be shown by quoting isolated texts from the Catechism. It is best seen and appreciated within the overall perspective that one reaches on reading the Catechism from beginning to end.

weighs heavily upon the soul of the sinner and constrains him to keep the Commandments under pain of punishment; the transgressor is condemned by the Law; he merits the chastisement meted out to him both by the justice of this world and the wrath of God in the next.[1]

However, in the case of the sinner who is predestined to repentance, the Law plays yet another role; it becomes more than just a guide to Christian living—a list of what to do and not to do in order to please God; but a means to faith and salvation. It reveals to him his sinfulness and prepares him for the Work of the Gospel Word. As Mr. Whale puts it,[2] the Law, in a threefold manner, brings the sinner to God; it mirrors his moral impotence, it crushes him into a state of total despair, proving thereby his need for God, and masks, so to speak, the passive justification taking place in his soul at the very moment when the Law, paradoxically, seems to render him more wicked, or at least, more conscious of his wickedness; the moment when God ushers in the work of the Gospel. We shall substantiate and develop these points further, when we deal with the *Smalcald Articles* in the last chapter.

The *Large Catechism*, itself, does not discuss explicitly or systematically this question of the threefold function of the Law; that is to say, we do not find such statements as: the Law is necessary to man for three reasons; or the Law has three purposes in the work of salvation. Rather, it treats of the Law, as we have so far expounded, and shall continue to expound, in terms of the Word of God establishing, enforcing, and fulfilling it. Yet the personal pattern of despair and faith, pervading the whole of the Catechism, which we have illustrated with numerous passages, presupposes and is inseparable from these dynamic and functional properties of the Law. We shall return to them in the subsequent chapters.

The preceding analysis, we think, constitutes the main content of Luther's Decalogue section of the *Large Catechism*, at least for what concerns our particular problem—the Law-Gospel relation. We can surely now state, without hesitation, that faith in the Decalogue is as much a part of Luther's

---

[1] This point will be discussed more fully in the last chapter on the *Smalcald Articles*.

[2] See below, Chapter VI, section C, p. 144, n. 2.

theology as faith in the New Testament. The Ten Commandments belong to the fullness of divine revelation; they have the
sanctions of God's threats and promises, which, to some degree,
are made manifest in the daily experience of human society.

Decidedly, the Law, with its sanctions, applies to all men,
binding them equally to observe every commandment, but to
different effects according as men are sinfully obdurate in their
unbelief or saved through faith in the Word working within
their hearts.

Luther's approach to the Decalogue, therefore, is biblical
and soteriological: biblical because he affirms and argues from
the Scriptural Word—the revelation of what God has said and
done for us; and soteriological because he envisages the Ten
Commandments functionally and evangelically—in so far as
they necessarily produce in us a despair-faith experience of
salvation.

His point of view is not a philosophical one; he does not
develop and determine man's duties from a systematic analysis
and definition of human nature and the human act as such, as
we would find in Aristotle's *Nicomachean Ethics* or Saint
Thomas's *Prima Secundae*. Nor does he attempt to classify human
acts in genus and species; nor again to distinguish between the
natural and supernatural operative habits of Christian conduct.

Of course it is not the purpose of his Catechism to deal with
the Ten Commandments in this speculative fashion; but even
so, we feel, from the general tenor of the entire work, this kind
of approach has little appeal to him personally. He prefers what
may be termed a biblical existentialist account of sin and grace.
Besides, his idea of sinful nature and imputative righteousness
does not admit of any consideration of the human act as intrinsically worthy before God.[1] The act is worthy only because God

[1] We are not implying that Luther sees no *fundamentum* in human nature for the
Law; on the contrary, he states with Saint Paul that the Law is written in the hearts
of all men: 'Die zehen Gepot sind auch sonst in aller Menschen Herzen geschrieben
[Röm. ii. 15], den Glauben aber kann keine menschliche Klugheit begreifen und
muß allein vom heiligen Geist gelehret werden' [*Bek.*, p. 661. 25–29]. Here Luther
draws a clear distinction between what can be acquired through nature and what
comes from above or is supernatural. This Pauline text reminds us of Saint Augustine's remark: '. . . lex tua scripta est in cordibus hominum, quem nec ulla quidem
delet iniquitas' [Confess. II, iv, 9]; or a similar text from Saint Thomas: '. . . lex vetus
manifestabat praecepta legis naturae, et superaddebat quaedam propria praecepta'
[*S.Th.* Ia IIae. q. 98, a. 5, c.]; and also the following from the *Catechism of the*

commands it, enforces it and, in a certain exclusive sense, fulfils it. We shall find further evidence of this in the Gospel section of the Catechism, which we shall now consider from the viewpoint of the fulfilment of the Law.

Council of Trent: '. . . For it is not the fact that Moses has given them to us, but because they are, as it were, stamped on the heart of every man.' The point is this: Luther's experience and knowledge of human nature is inseparable from his faith in the Word, and never excludes his moral pessimism; however much they prove the reality of the Ten Commandments and manifest the necessity and obligation to keep them (such, for instance, as the need to marry in order to fulfil the requirements of the Sixth Commandment), they nevertheless do not permit us to conclude that we are capable of keeping them ourselves by virtue of our own powers. Experience makes us ever conscious of what we cannot do because of sin rather than what we are *per se*; if it shows us, in certain respects, what we are, it is only to expose our radical moral weakness and corroborate the teachings of the Word; namely, that we depend solely on God for our salvation.

V

THE GOSPEL SECTION OF THE
LARGE CATECHISM

OUR analysis of the Gospel section of the Catechism aims, we repeat, at showing how it explains the work of the Gospel with respect to the sinner who despairs in his own efforts to obtain the righteousness of the Law; in other words, it will explain the Law-Gospel relation according to which the sinner is made righteous through faith in Christ from whom comes the power to keep the Commandments. Consequently we shall deal next with the four latter parts of the Catechism— Part Two on the Creed, Part Three on Prayer, and Parts Four and Five on the Sacraments—inasmuch as they bring out this relation and throw light on our subject.

On the matter of keeping the Commandments or fulfilment of the Law, a word of caution is necessary: by this is not meant that the sinner becomes just by managing through faith to keep the Commandments; that is to say, it is not his own personal work that renders him righteous, even though this work follows justification, but uniquely the redeeming merits and saving powers of Christ. The keeping of the Commandments, itself, results from Christ moving our heart and our members: '. . . Christus expellit Adam de die in diem magis et magis, secundum quod crescit illa fides et cognitio Christi . . .'[1] The

---

[1] Martin Luther makes this point clear in his small treatise *On the Two Kinds of Righteousness* (Sermo de duplici justicia), in which he differentiates 'between Christ's righteousness by means of which He justifies, sanctifies and redeems, and the righteousness of a believing Christian which is made possible by the righteousness of Christ' (see Lowell J. Satre, *Introduction to Two Kinds of Righteousness* in A. xxxi. 245).

He draws a parallel between these two kinds of righteousness and two kinds of sin—alien righteousness and personal or 'proper' righteousness—original sin and proper or 'actual' sin: 'Haec igitur iusticia aliena et sine actibus nostris per solam gratiam infusa nobis, trahente intus scilicet patre nos ad Christum, opponitur peccato originali, quod alienum similiter est sine nostris actibus per solam generationem nobis cognatum et contractum. Et ita Christus expellit Adam de die in diem magis et magis, secundum quod crescit illa fides et cognitio Christi. Non enim tota simul infunditur sed incipit, proficit et perficitur tandem in finem per mortem.

'Secunda iusticia est nostra et propria, non quod nos soli operemur eam; sed quod cooperemur illi primae et alienae. Haec nunc est illa conversatio bona in

man of faith cannot lay claim to righteousness on the basis of his personal obedience or good works—on the basis of what Luther calls active justice: '. . . in eam [iusticiam activam] non possum confidere neque per eam consistere coram iudicio Dei'.[1]

operibus bonis, Primo in mortificatione carnis et crucifixione concupiscentiarum erga seipsum . . .

'. . . Haec iusticia opponitur peccato actuali et proprio nostro, ut ad Ro. VI. Sicut exhibuistis membra vestra servire iniquitati ad iniquitatem, ita nunc exhibete membra vestra servire iusticiae ad sanctificationem . . .' (*W.A.* ii. 146–7. 29–38, 1–25).

It is worth noting here that Luther uses the word 'cooperemur', and describes our personal or 'proper' righteousness—our doing of good works—as a surrendering of ourselves over to Christ as in a marriage union: 'Igitur per iusticiam priorem oritur vox sponsi qui dicit ad animam "tuus ego"; per posteriorem vero vox sponsae quae dicit "tua ego": tunc factum est firmum perfectum atque consummatum matrimonium . . .' (ibid., p. 147. 26–29).

This plainly is the language of Saint Paul, but we feel, for reasons already stated in the second chapter, that this union or relation cannot be understood in the Catholic sense of meritorious co-operation or a meritoriously acquired sanctity; that is to say, in the sense that the creature is a secondary cause of personal betterment in the order of grace, his spiritual faculties of intellect and will being allowed to share effectively in God's holy work. We shall come back to this point later on.

This *Sermo de duplici iusticia* was written as early as 1519, two years before the famous Diet of Worms, and ten years before the appearance of Luther's German Catechism. It illustrates well how his conception of the true righteousness of the Gospel was already clearly formulated in his earlier sermons; we shall find the same doctrine underlying the Gospel section of the Catechism.

[1] *W.A.* xl. (i). 42–48. 26–. Luther is much more explicit on this point in his later work, the *Commentary on Galatians* (1535). Here, he describes the afflicted conscience despairing in its own moral weakness and misery before the exigencies of the Law, and shows how it finds consolation and strength in the righteousness of Christ alone: 'Quare nullum remedium habet afflicta conscientia contra desperationem et mortem aeternam, nisi apprehendat promissionem gratiae oblatae in Christo, hoc est hanc fidei, passivam seu Christianam iustitiam, quae cum fiducia dicat: Ego non quaero iustitiam activam [i.e. salvation of works], deberem quidem habere et facere eam, et *posito, quod eam haberem et facerem, tamen in eam non possum confidere neque per eam consistere coram iudicio Dei. Itaque reiicio me extra omnem activam et meam et divinae legis iustitiam et simpliciter illam passivam amplector quae est iustitia gratiae, misericordiae, remissionis peccatorum, in summa: Christi et Spiritus Sancti quam non facimus,* sed patimur, non habemus sed accipimus, donante eam nobis deo Patre per Iesum Christum' (*W.A.* xl. (i). 42–43. 26–30, 12–17). The italics are not in the text.

Manifestly, Luther is here rejecting any form of active justice whether it be understood in the order of sanctification or justification; there is nothing active or positive we can do to merit Christ or personal holiness; there is only *iustitia passiva*. A few paragraphs farther on he adds: 'Sed sicut terra non profert fructus, nisi prius irrigata et foecundata e coelo . . . ita per iustitiam legis multa faciendo nihil faciamus et implendo legem non implemus, nisi prius sine nostro opere et merito iustificati simus per iustitiam christianam nihil pertinentem ad iustitiam legis seu ad iustitiam terrenam et activam. Ista autem est iustitia coelestis et passiva quam non habemus, sed e coelo accipimus, non facimus sed fide apprehendimus, per quam ascendimus supra omnes leges et opera . . .' (ibid. 46. 22–30).

With this in mind, we recall again the passage, quoted above in Chapter III, which joins the Decalogue section to the Gospel section of the *Large Catechism*, explaining how the former teaches us 'what God wishes us to do or leave undone' and the latter 'whence and whereby' we receive the power to keep the Commandments; which theme, moreover, is reiterated by the Reformer at the end of the second part dealing with the Creed: '. . . the Creed[1] is a doctrine quite different from the Ten Commandments; for the latter teaches indeed what we ought to do, but the former tells us what God does for us'.[2] This serves as an appropriate transition from our commentary on the Decalogue section to our study of the remaining parts of the Catechism.

These quotations are taken from the published text (1535) of the Commentary in the Weimar edition, based on lectures delivered in 1531, at the University of Wittenberg, only two years after the publication of his German Catechism, and prepared for the press by George Rörer (see Philip S. Watson, *C.G.*, London, 1953, pp. 1–15).

Luther tells us himself, in his preface to the 1535 edition, that the Commentary truly represents his thought: 'Vix ipse credo, tam verbosum fuisse me, cum enarrarem publice hanc Sancti Pauli ad Galatas Epistolam, quam hic me libellus exhibet. Et tamen sentio meas cogitationes esse omnes quas in hoc scripto per fratres tanta diligentia signatas reperio, ut fateri cogar vel omnia vel etiam plura fortasse in ista publica tractatione a me esse dicta' (*W.A.* xl (i). 33. 1–15).

He also tells us in his introductory annotations to the Commentary that his purpose is to defend the pure doctrine of faith against the doctrine of works and man's traditions: '. . . sed quia ut saepe moneo, periculum hoc maximum et proximum est, ut diabolus ablata pura fidei doctrina rursus invehat doctrinas operum ac traditionum humanarum' (ibid., p. 39. 16–18).

[1] Belief in the Father as Creator (*Schepfer*), Christ as Redeemer (*Erloser*), and the Holy Ghost as Sanctifier (*Heiligmacher*).

[2] 'Aus dem siehest Du nu, daß der Glaube gar viel ein andere Lehre ist denn die zehen Gepot. Denn jene [die 10 Gepot] lehret wohl, was wir tuen sollen, diese aber sagt, was uns Gott tue und gebe. Die zehen Gepot sind auch sonst in aller Menschen Herzen geschrieben [see also *W.A.* xvi. 372. 1–3], den Glauben aber kann keine menschliche Klugheit begreifen und muß allein vom heiligen Geist gelehret werden. Darümb machet jene Lehre [of the Law] noch keinen Christen; denn es bleibt noch immer Gottes Zorn und Ungnade über uns, weil wir's nicht halten können, was Gott von uns fodert. Aber diese [namely the doctrine of faith] bringet eitel Gnade, machet uns fromm ['just'] und Gott angenehme. Denn durch diese Erkenntnis kriegen wir Lust und Liebe zu allen Gepoten Gottes, weil wir hie sehen, wie sich Gott ganz und gar mit allem, das er hat und vermag, uns gibt zu Hülfe und Steuer [Stütze], die zehen Gepot zu halten ...' (*Bek.*, p. 661. 20–25).

One finds the very same doctrine, expressed in almost identical words, in Luther's *Sermon on Good Works* and his treatise *On the Liberty of a Christian Man*. We wish to call attention to the fact that it follows the same dynamic pattern of despair and faith which the Reformer describes in his autobiographical account mentioned above (see Chapter I).

We are of the opinion that Luther's teaching on the work of the Gospel and its relation to the Law emerges from the latter four parts of the Catechism in three significant ways:

Firstly, the Gospel reveals to us what God has done for sinners in the order of Creation, Redemption, and Sanctification, proving thereby that we owe everything to God and nothing to ourselves; our natural gifts, our Christian righteousness, our personal betterment, our good works and keeping of the Commandments, do not result from our own efforts or strivings but uniquely from God's holy work. To preach this is to preach the Gospel, and to believe in this is to fulfil the Law. Thus the Law and the Gospel remain, as stated earlier, exclusively a matter of the Word preached, believed in and practised.

Secondly, believing in God's work, preaching God's work, and praying and praising God in accordance with His work, and administering the Sacraments, possess the character of Decalogue precepts; like them, they are actions commanded by God and sanctioned by Holy Scripture; Christians are bound in duty to carry them out; indeed, for the Christian, these actions are the true and proper fulfilment of the First Commandment. Thus duty and obligation, commandment and obedience, remain, paradoxically,[1] an essential part of the Christian life. We shall see how Luther, on more than one occasion, argues analogically that Christ's exhortations to have faith, to recite the Lord's Prayer, to receive and administer the Sacraments, are as much precepts and obligations as the keeping of the Fourth Commandment; they are never without the divine promises and threats. We shall single out these instances as we deal with each part.

And thirdly, the force and function of the Ten Commandments, such as we have earlier described, still play their fundamental role in the drama and psychology of salvation; we are thinking, of course, of the dual character of the Christian, of his inner struggle with the old Adam and the new. That is to say,

[1] The paradox is this: the Christian is obliged to do what he, by himself, cannot do; whereas he is aware of his duties and obligations, stemming from his faith, he is, at the same time, warned that God alone causes in him true obedience and trust and fulfils the Law in his members; there is no place here for Melanchthonian synergism or Roman Catholic merit. His obedience and trust are the spontaneous fruit or result of unmerited righteousness.

the Christian's evangelical faith, while obtaining for him remission of sin, does not cut at the roots of sin but only cuts them
down so to speak,[1] and weakens their effects; his 'Adamic'
nature and personal sinfulness—disobedience and self-love—
endure until his death. And all this makes for the spiritual
tension of relying on self (the work of the old Adam) or relying
solely on God (the work of the new Adam or Christ), in which
drama the Ten Commandments continue to hold their proper
place. In the event that the Christian weakens in his faith or
relies again on his own efforts to seek righteousness, they loom
up anew in his conscience to terrify and crush him, to remind
him that he is a sinner dependent solely on God's work for
salvation. These points become clearer as we proceed with our
analysis.

A. *The command to believe in the work of the Blessed Trinity.*

The totality of God's work is best shown in the second part of
the Catechism on the Creed. Luther sums it up briefly in three
chief articles, according to the three persons in the Godhead
to whom everything is related, so that the first article on God
the Father explains Creation, the second article on the Son,

---

[1] Rudolf Thiel, discussing original sin in his biography of Luther writes: '. . . he
[Luther] found most objectionable in Augustine that he did not carry his condemnation of human nature far enough. Augustine wanted to make an exception
for reason, and praised it as a light in the darkness to lead us to God, so he bore
the real responsibility for bringing the church into such useless chattering.'
   'Luther brooked no compromise. His doctrine was: "All of human nature has
been stunted by the guilt of man's first sin, and become corrupted and hostile to
God to its unfathomable depths." When Augustine maintained that Baptism
destroyed sin down to its roots so that it could no longer grow like a hair on one's
head or ever need cutting—then Luther would say: "original sin is like a man's
beard. Clean shaven today, it grows again tomorrow. It never stops as long as one
lives" ' (see Rudolf Thiel, *Luther*, trans. by Gustaf Wienke, Philadelphia, 1955,
p. 123).
   Rudolf Thiel's description of Luther's doctrine of original sin is quite accurate
and apropos; we should never lose sight of it when the Reformer speaks of the
righteousness, the freedom, or the holiness of the Christian man. If evangelical
faith renders the Christian righteous before God, it does not purify him of the roots
of sin; if the Gospel frees him from the false righteousness of the Law, it does not
remove the sinful chains of his 'Adamic' nature—at least in this world; and if the
Holy Ghost transforms him into a conscious state of personal or 'proper' holiness,
He does not perfect him entitatively or ontologically. Aware of this pessimism, it
is hard for us to see how human nature, and all that it entails in the personal
life of a saint, has any positive moral role to play in the search and struggle for
salvation.

Redemption, and the third, on the Holy Ghost, Sanctification;[1] and he goes on to say that this creed is 'nothing other than the answer and confession of Christians arranged with respect to the First Commandment'.[2]

Here, in the last statement, we have evidence of our second main point; that to believe in the articles of the Creed is quite simply obedience[3] to God's Commandments. We know, from the Decalogue section, that the First Commandment includes all the others, so that we may add that the Creed is arranged with respect to the whole Decalogue. Thus the Creed, far from dispensing us from the Ten Commandments, moves and compels us to keep them.[4] We are beholden to God for all that He has done for us and given us 'to do all, those things as He demands and has enjoined in the Ten Commandments'.[5]

His discussion of the First Article recalls the ever-recurring drama of depending solely on God and despairing completely in self.

To believe in God the Father Almighty, Creator, is to believe that we receive everything from God and nothing from ourselves,[6] that consequently we owe Him all our praise, our love,

---

[1] B.C., p. 192; see also Bek., p. 647. 3–12. Note: as early as 1520, Luther had divided the Creed into 'drei Häuptstück, nachdem die drei Person der heiligen, göttlichen Dreifältigkeit drein erzählet werden, das erst dem Vater, das ander dem Sohn, das dritt dem heiligen Geist zuzueigen' (W.A. vii. 214. 25–27).

[2] B.C., p. 192; see also Bek., 'Also daß der Glaube nichtes anders ist denn ein Antwort und Bekenntnis der Christen, auf das erst Gepot gestellet ...' (p. 647. 36–38).

[3] The frequent occurrence of such words as dienen, gehorsam, &c., illustrates how the Creed, for Luther, includes obligation and service; the Christian's obedience, however, unlike the Pharisee's, is never sought for its own sake; knowing that his salvation depends uniquely on Christ's merits, he realizes that his obedience to precepts, duties, or obligations is the fruit of rather than the means to unmerited righteousness. (See p. 94, n. 1, p. 129, n. 1.)

[4] B.C., p. 193; see also Bek., p. 649. 21–23: 'Denn wo wir's ['es', stands for all that God the Creator has done for us] von Herzen gläubten, würden wir auch darnach tun und nicht so stolz hergehen ...' In other words, if we really had faith in this article, we would automatically and spontaneously do what God expects of us. Luther, in this passage, is speaking of Creation, but the argument applies all the more so if we bring in the work of Redemption and Sanctification.

[5] B.C., p. 193; see also Bek., p. 649. 7–15: 'Hieraus will sich nu selbs schließen und folgen: weil uns das alles, so wir vermügen [besitzen] dazu was in Himmel und Erden ist, täglich von Gott gegeben, erhalten und bewahret wird, so sind wir ja schüldig, ihn darümb ohn Unterlaß zu lieben, loben und danken und kürzlich ihm ganz und gar damit zu dienen, wie er durch die zehen Gepot fodert und befohlen hat.'

[6] 'Was ist's nu gesagt [was bedeutet] oder was meinest Du mit dem Wort:

and our obedience, and He owes us nothing. All is comprehended in the word 'Creator' [*Schepfer*].[1] God gives us all that we are and possess 'out of pure love and goodness, without our merit as a benevolent Father . . .'.[2] The worth and blessings of nature are exclusively God's, just as in the order of grace, righteousness and sanctity come respectively from the merits of Christ and the special work of the Holy Ghost (see below).

The personal element of despairing in self appears inasmuch as Luther argues that this article, fully believed in, 'ought to humble and terrify us all' who 'sin daily with all that we possess'.[3] These points apply equally well to the other articles of the Creed.

On the Second Article of the Creed, Luther follows the same Law-Gospel line of exposition, stressing always the strictly gratuitous character of God's mercy and gifts to men.[4] It is a simple reaffirmation of his fundamental position, excluding all semblance of merit: Christ alone is *unser Herr und Erlöser*,[5] because He alone, without any help from us, 'redeems us from sin, from the devil, from death and from all evil'.[6] Due to Adam's sin and our own personal sins, we are like a dead corpse, helpless before God's wrath and the condemnation of the Law, powerless to do anything to save ourselves from eternal doom,

"Ich gläube an Gott, Vater allmächtigen, Schepfer ..." Antwort: Das meine und gläube ich, daß ich Gottes Geschepfe bin, das ist, daß er mir geben hat und ohn Unterlaß erhält Leib, Seele, und Leben ...' (*Bek.*, p. 648. 9–15).

[1] 'Also daß man aus diesem Artikel lerne, daß unser keiner das Leben noch alles, was itzt erzählt [aufgezählt] ist und erzählt mag werden, von ihm selbs hat noch erhalten kann, wie klein und gering es ist. Denn es alles gefasset ist in das Wort "Schepfer" ' (ibid., 26–32).

[2] *B.C.*, p. 193, col. 1.

[3] 'Darümb sollt' uns dieser Artikel alle demütigen und erschrecken, wo wir's gläubten. Denn wir sundigen täglich mit Augen, Ohren, Händen, Leib und Seele, Geld und Gut und mit allem, das wir haben, sonderlich diejenigen, so noch wider Gottes Wort fechten. Doch haben die Christen den Vorteil, daß sie sich des schüldig erkennen, ihm dafur zu dienen und gehorsam zu sein' (*Bek.*, p. 649. 32–41).

The passage illustrates how faith, far from giving the sinner any self-confidence in his own spiritual goodness, makes him despair all the more in self so as to attain to the truly Christian perfection of depending solely on God.

[4] See p. 109, n. 1, p. 98, n. 2.

[5] 'Das sei nu die Summa dieses Artikels, daß das Wortlin "HERR" aufs ein'-fältigste soviel heiße als ein Erloser, das ist, der uns vom Teufel zu Gotte, vom Tod zum Leben, von Sund zur Gerechtigkeit bracht hat und dabei erhält' (*Bek.*, p. 652. 25–30).

[6] 'Was ist nu das, ein Herr werden? Das ist's, daß er mich erlöset hat von Sunde, vom Teufel, vom Tode und allem Unglück' (*Bek.*, p. 651. 33–36).

until Christ comes to help us[1] and redeems us with His Crucifixion and Resurrection.

In this way, we see what we have from the Second Person of the Godhead, over and above the temporal goods of Creation; how Christ 'completely poured forth Himself and withheld nothing from us . . .'.[2]

In place of sin, death, the captivity of the Law and God's wrath, has come 'Jesus Christ, Lord of life, righteousness, every blessing and salvation, and has delivered us poor lost men from the jaws of Hell, has won us, has made us free and brought us again into the favour and grace of the Father, and has taken us as His own property [sein "Eigentumb"] under His shelter [Schirm] and protection [Schutz],[3] that He may govern us by His righteousness, wisdom, power, life, and blessedness'.[4]

The other points of the Creed, pertaining to Christ as Erlöser[5] serve simply 'to explain and express the redemption and how and why it was accomplished . . .'.[6]

[1] Because of man's sin, after Creation, we fell under God's wrath and were doomed to 'ewigem Verdammnis, ..., wie wir verwirkt und verdienet hatten. Da war kein Rat, Hülfe noch Trost, bis daß sich dieser einige und ewige Gottessohn unsers Jammers und Elends aus grundloser Güte erbarmete und von Himmel kam, uns zu helfen' (Bek., p. 651. 47–51 and p. 652. 1–2).

[2] 'Hie lernen wir die andere Person der Gottheit kennen, daß wir sehen, was wir über [außer] die vorigen [vorhergehenden] zeitlichen Guter von Gott haben, nämlich wie er sich ganz und gar ausgeschüttet [ausgegeben] hat und nichts behalten, das er nicht uns gegeben habe' (ibid., p. 651. 10–15).

[3] We would like to know more fully what Luther means here by Christ taking us as his 'Eigentumb unter seinen Schirm und Schutz' (Bek., p. 652. 9–11). The metaphor itself is unobjectionable, but what Luther wishes to imply by it may raise serious difficulties; such for instance as the problem of how to define or describe the character of imputative and passive righteousness. These are matters which the Reformer does not choose to discuss at any length in an elementary Catechism book. Undoubtedly, like the other 'single points' of the Creed, he would prefer to leave these difficult matters to be treated in more ample sermons during the liturgical year. (See following note.)

[4] B.C., p. 194, col. 1. Speaking of the other points of the Creed that pertain to the life and work of the Redeemer, Luther writes: 'Aber diese einzele Stück alle sonderlich auszustreichen [besonders auszulegen] gehöret nicht in die kurze Kinderpredigt, sondern in die großen Predigte über das ganze Jahr [im Verlauf des ganzen Jahres], sonderlich auf die Zeit [Weihnachten, Passionzeit, Ostern, Himmelfahrt] so dazu geordnet sind, ein iglichen Artikel in die Länge [ausführlich] zu handeln von der Gepurt, Leiden, Auferstehen, Himmelfahrt Christi etc.' (Bek., p. 653. 4–10).

[5] Namely, that the Second Person of the Trinity became man, was conceived by the Holy Ghost, born of the Blessed Virgin, suffered under Pontius Pilate, was crucified, died and buried, rose again from the dead, ascended into heaven and sitteth at the right hand of the Father . . . to judge the living and the dead . . .'.

[6] B.C., p. 194, col. 1.

The important or central truth throughout this article, as with the others, is that God's work, in the Person of Christ, is gratuitous, in no way dependent on our own efforts or merits: '. . . for He did none of these [birth, death, and resurrection] for Himself, nor had He any need of them'.[1]

It is to be understood that since Luther is describing articles of the Creed—what one must believe to be saved—the foregoing is only redemptive to those who *obey* the Commandment to believe; that is to say, those who profess their faith, inwardly, in Christ as Lord and Saviour. The idea of precept and obligation still obtains.

But this faith and the very power to believe—the fulfilment of the Commandment—is given by the Holy Ghost who inspires us to believe in the Word, to preach the Word and to administer the Word; and this brings us to the Third Article of the Creed, the Holy Ghost as Sanctifier or *Heiligmacher*: 'Darümb mussen wir fußen auf das Wort: Heiligen Geist ...'[2]

How does the Holy Ghost sanctify? Luther's answer to this question, in the Catechism, reveals to us how the Gospel saves the sinner and fulfils the Law, without the need of our good will or good works considered as means or requisites: 'Just as the Son obtains dominion . . . through His birth, death, and resurrection . . . so also the Holy Ghost effects our Sanctification [*Heiligung*][3] . . . by the Communion of saints . . . the forgiveness of sins, the resurrection of the body and life everlasting . . .'.[4]

He explains himself more fully:

For neither you nor I could ever know anything of Christ or believe in Him and obtain Him for our Lord, unless it were offered to us and granted to our hearts by the Holy Ghost through the preaching of the Gospel. The work is done and accomplished [by Christ]. . . . But if the work remained concealed so that no one knew of it, then it would be in vain and lost ... therefore sanctifying [*heiligen*] is

---

[1] Ibid.   [2] *Bek.*, p. 653, 36-37.

[3] Catholic theologians employ the word 'sanctification' in a particular sense. Whereas, strictly speaking, sanctification includes the initial graces of Baptism and justification—the work by which God raises the Christian from the state of sin to the state of grace—it is more customary to use the term to designate the spiritual growth and perfection of the individual Christian following upon his Baptism, and which presupposes the free operation of his spiritual faculties of intellect and will as secondary causes of his Christian perfection. (See p. 107, n. 4 and p. 109, n. 1; also Appendix IV.)

[4] *B.C.*, p. 194, article 3.

nothing else than bringing us to Christ to receive this good, to which we could not attain ourselves.[1]

What is significant here is that *Heiligung* is described simply as the gift of Christ, offered and accepted through the influence and mysterious workings of the Holy Ghost; like justification, it is again exclusively the work and Word of God preached and believed in; one wonders to what extent this work of the Holy Ghost causes a real physical and inner transformation of the believing subject (see p. 101, n. 4).

This then is the total work of the Gospel—the revelation and acknowledgement of what God has done and does for us as Creator, Redeemer, and Sanctifier. It stands in marked contrast to the false righteousness of the Law, which is the revelation of what we, by ourselves, cannot do. At the same time, we learn that faith in God's work is an obligation and a commandment. Obedience is not excluded but rather more fully produced by the Gospel. In other words, the articles of the Creed are both a commandment and a fulfilment; by professing our faith in them, we obey God's Commandment, and yet the very work of obeying arises from the power of God the Sanctifier to the exclusion of any merit on our part; our obedience is not a means but a gift.

With regard to the dual character of the Christian, and its implications for the role of the Law, the second part of the Catechism provides us with only intimations. The significant passages are those on forgiveness of sin.

Luther tells us that the work of the Holy Ghost comprises, among other things, the formation of the Christian Church (*ein christliche Gemeine oder Sammlung*[2]): through which 'we have forgiveness of sin wrought by the Holy Sacraments, Absolution and all manner of consolatory promises of the entire Gospel'.[3] And, in this connexion, he speaks of the *Vergebung der Sunde* in his peculiarly characteristic way.

It does not seem to be a removal or absolute extirpation of

---

[1] In Appendix II, we give the German text of this quotation and compare it with similar passages from the *Catechism of the Council of Trent*.

[2] Also: eine 'heilige Christenheit' (*Bek.*, p. 656. 25–26).

[3] *B.C.*, p. 195, col. 2; see also *Bek.*, 'Darnach weiter gläuben wir, daß wir in der Christenheit haben Vergebung der Sunde, welches geschiehet durch die heiligen Sakrament und Absolution, dazu allerlei Trostsprüche des ganzen Evangelii' (p. 658. 10–14).

sin but rather a shield against the ill effects of sin, a kind of weakening of the force of sin: 'For although the grace of God is secured through Christ and Sanctification is wrought by the Holy Ghost through the Word of God in the unity of the Christian Church, yet on account of our flesh[1] which we bear about us, we are never without sin'.[2] And a few sentences on, he adds: 'Thus, although we have sins, the [grace of] the Holy Ghost does not allow them to injure us, because we are in the Christian Church, where there is nothing but [continuous, uninterrupted][3] forgiveness of sins . . .'.[4]

For our purpose, these passages betoken the duality of the Christian man, he is at one and the same time sinner and saint: *simul justus simul peccator*; sinner by virtue of his 'Adamic' nature and saint by virtue of his faith. But because his sinfulness endures, he inevitably falls back on his own efforts to seek righteousness. And thus Luther, in the same breath, warns us: 'Therefore all who seek and wish to merit holiness [*Heiligung*], not through the Gospel and forgiveness of sin, but through their works, have expelled and severed themselves [from the Church].'[5]

Though he does not say it in so many words, we can see, in this particular context, how the Law can retain its force and function for the lapsed Christian. It remains written in his heart and sanctioned by the Word, and continues to crush and terrify him for as long as he persists in self-reliance and turns his back on the Gospel. We shall say more about this point when we deal with the fourth and fifth parts on the Sacraments.

[1] We recall again what was said in the second chapter about sinful flesh; for Luther, this embraces the whole man as self-seeking and egotistical and not merely the sexual appetite; it is a question of the human will, as well as the bodily members, being curved in on itself—*incurvatus in se*—and bent ineluctably on earthly goods.

[2] *B.C.*, p. 195, col. 2; 'Denn wiewohl Gottes Gnade durch Christum erworben ist und die Heiligkeit durch den heiligen Geist gemacht durch Gottes Wort in der Vereinigung der christlichen Kirchen, so sind wir doch nimmer ohne Sund unsers Fleischs halpen, so wir noch am Hals tragen [mit uns herumschleppen]' (*Bek.*, p. 658. 19–25).

[3] In the Latin text we read: 'ubi nihil aliud quam assidua et indesinens est peccatorum remissio . . .' (ibid., 37–39).

[4] *B.C.*, p. 195, col. 2; 'Also machet der heilig Geist, daß, ob wir gleich Sunde haben, doch sie uns nicht schaden kann, weil wir in der Christenheit sind, da eitel [lauter] Vergebung der Sund ist ...' (*Bek.*, p. 658. 30–33).

[5] *B.C.*, p. 195, col. 2; *Bek.*, p. 658. 38–42.

Another aspect of the Third Article is the total absence of any positive comment on hierarchical jurisdiction and episcopal authority, such as one would find in a Catholic Catechism. The Church is simply a 'peculiar congregation in the world', which is the mother who 'begets and bears every Christian through the Word of God'.[1] Wherever the Word of God is preached and believed in, the Church exists; and wherever the Holy Ghost 'does not cause it to be preached and made alive in the heart, so that it is understood it is lost . . .'.[2] The emphasis is always on the exclusive work of the Word or the Gospel; the human element seems to have no intermediary or effective role in God's economy of salvation.

B. *The command to pray*

The third part, dealing with the obligation and duty to pray, 'to call upon God in every need',[3] reveals the same despair-faith tension of the previous part. Indeed, it is only inasmuch as the Christian recognizes his need of God and despairs in himself that his prayer becomes truly effective[4]—that is to say, a genuine heartfelt and total acknowledgement that God gives

[1] *B.C.*, p. 194, col. 2; '... Denn ... hat er [the Holy Ghost] ein sonderliche Gemeine in der Welt, welche ist die Mutter, so ein iglichen Christen zeugt und trägt durch das Wort Gottes ...' (*Bek.*, p. 655. 2–5).

[2] *B.C.*, pp. 194–5; 'Denn wo er's [the Holy Ghost] nicht predigen lässet und im Herzen erweckt, daß man's fasset, da ist's verloren . . .' (*Bek.*, p. 655. 11–15).

[3] See below, p. 103, n. 2.

[4] 'Wo aber ein recht Gebete sein soll, da muß ein Ernst sein, daß man seine Not fühle und solche Not, die uns drücket und treibet zu rufen und schreien. So gehet denn das Gebete von sich selbs, wie es gehen soll, daß man keines Lehrens darf, wie man sich dazu bereiten und Andacht schepfen soll. Die Not aber, so uns beide fur uns und idermann anliegen soll, wirst Du reichlich gnug im Vaterunser finden ... Darümb auch Gott haben will, daß Du solche Not und Anliegen klagest und anziehest [zur Sprache bringst], nicht daß er's nicht wisse, sondern daß Du Dein Herz entzündest, deste stärker und mehr zu begehren, und nur den Mantel weit ausbreitest und auftuest, viel zu empfahen' (*Bek.*, p. 668. 19–40).

From this it follows that the more we feel our needs the more we realize our dependence on God and give ourselves entirely to Him and to His Word. The Lutheran pattern of despairing in self is expressed in these words: '... uns drücket und treibet zu rufen und schreien'; that is to say our needs, in particular our moral impotence before the Law, press and compel us to call and cry out. Again we see how essential the element of despair is to Luther's understanding of the work of the Gospel. We cannot embrace the articles of the Creed until we first of all despair in our own sinful attempts to keep the commandments; and we cannot pray efficaciously unless we cry out from the depths of our own needs and failures. The German word 'Not' means much more than just 'need'; it signifies an extreme distress or urgent necessity, a state in which man is conscious of his insufficiency.

him everything and he gives God nothing.¹ In this respect, prayer is not distinct or separable from faith in the Creed but a kind of daily profession of it. More precisely, we may say, it is the Christian fulfilling the obligation of the Second Commandment: 'Das heißet aber gebet, wie das ander Gepot [Second Commandment] lehret: "Gott anrufen in allen Nöten".'²

Moreover, this part illustrates plainly how the work of the Gospel, for the Reformer, does not exclude, by any means, God's Commandments; the Decalogue notion of commandment is still here:

This [prayer] He [God] requires of us, and has not left it to our choice. But it is our duty and obligation to pray if we would be Christians, as much as it is our duty to obey our parents and the government. . . . Thou shalt and must do it, so also here it is not left to my will to do it or to leave undone, but prayer must be offered at the risk of God's wrath and displeasure.³

In short we have the commandment and the promise.⁴

¹ See p. 105, n. 1.
² *Bek.*, p. 663. 40–43. The context in which Luther makes this statement is concerned with showing that prayer is as 'strictly and earnestly commanded as all other commandments' (see *B.C.*, p. 197, col. 1). The German text, in length, reads as follows: 'Und soll nämlich das erste sein, daß man wisse, wie wir ümb Gottes Gepots willen schüldig sind zu beten. Denn so haben wir gehört im andern Gepot: "Du sollt Gottes Namen nicht unnützlich führen", daß darin gefodert werde, den heiligen Namen preisen, in aller Not anrufen oder beten. Denn anrufen ist nichts anders denn beten. Also daß es streng und ernstlich geboten ist, so hoch [sehr] als alle andere [Gebote], kein andern Gott haben, nicht töten, nicht stehlen etc., daß niemand denke, es sei gleich soviel, ich bete oder bete nicht ...'
'Das ist aber je wahr: Was man bisher fur Gebete getan hat, geplärret und gedönet in der Kirchen etc., ist freilich kein Gebete gewesen. Denn solch äußerlich Ding, wo es recht gehet, mag ein Ubung fur die jungen Kinder, Schüler und Einfältigen sein und mag gesungen oder gelesen heißen, es heißet aber nicht eigentlich gebetet. Das heißet aber gebet, wie das ander Gepot lehret: "Gott anrufen in allen Nöten" ' (*Bek.*, p. 663. 2–43).
³ *B.C.*, p. 197, col. 1.
⁴ Observe here how Luther draws an analogy between the duty to pray and the Fourth Commandment, and speaks of it in exactly the same terms; namely, as a divine precept joined to the promises (see also p. 112, n. 3, p. 114, n. 1, p. 127, n. 6). The sanction of the promise, moreover, plays the same role as the sanctions joined to the Decalogue commandments; they 'encourage and kindle our hearts to pray with pleasure and delight' because we see from the promise what importance God Himself attaches to His commandment, and how assuredly our prayer will be heard and granted: 'Zum andern soll uns deste mehr treiben und reizen, daß Gott auch eine Verheißung dazu getan und zugesagt hat, daß es soll Ja und gewiß sein, was wir beten, wie er spricht im Psalm [Ps. l. 15]: "Rufe mich an zur Zeit der Not, so will ich Dich erretten" und Christus im

And what makes prayer a good and holy work, pleasing to God, as with other works mentioned in the Decalogue section, is the fact that it is commanded by God;[1] the worthiness of our prayer and the power to pray comes from the Word and not from our own personal worth or deeds:[2] 'God does not regard prayer on account of the person, but on account of His Word and obedience thereto'.[3]

The 'howlings' and 'growlings' of monks and ecclesiastics are

---

Evangelio [Matt. vii. 7]: "Bittet, so wird Euch gegeben etc. Denn ein iglicher, wer da bittet, der empfähet!" Solchs sollt' je unser Herz erwecken und anzünden, mit Lust und Liebe zu beten, weil er mit seinem Wort bezeuget, daß ihm unser Gebete herzlich wohl gefalle, dazu gewißlich erhöret und gewährt sein soll, auf daß wir's nicht verachten noch in Wind schlagen und auf ungewiß beten' (Bek., pp. 666-7. 42-50, 1-2). The threat is also part of the sanction; it is there to strike fear into the heart of the unrepentant sinner who refuses to turn to God and pray forgiveness: '. . . prayer shall and must be offered at the risk of God's wrath and displeasure' (B.C., p. 197, col. 2).

[1] B.C., p. 198, col. 1. To appreciate the full significance of this idea, we should read the whole of the Third Part on Prayer; but the following passage sums up the main point: 'Das Werk ist ein Werk [Prayer] des Gehorsams und, das ich tue, tue ich nicht anderer Meinung, denn daß in dem Gehorsam und Gottes Gepot gehet, darauf ich künnde gründen und fußen, und solchs groß achte nicht ümb meiner Wirdigkeit willen, sondern ümb des Gepots willen ... Meinethalben wäre es nichts, aber darümb soll es gelten, daß Gott geboten hat' (Bek., p. 665. 6-18).

[2] This aspect of unworthiness is very much in keeping with Luther's more explicit teachings set down in his Commentary on Galatians (1535): 'I say these things to the end that we may diligently distinguish Christian holiness from other kinds of holiness. The monks called their order holy (although they durst not call themselves holy); but they are not holy; because Christian holiness is not active, but passive holiness. Wherefore let no man call himself holy on account of his manner of life and works, if he fasteth, prayeth, scourgeth his body, giveth alms to the poor, comforteth the sorrowful and afflicted, etc. Else should the Pharisee in Luke (18. 11) also be holy. The works indeed are good, and God straightly requireth them of us, but they make us not holy. Thou and I are holy, Church, city and people are holy, not by their own, but by an alien holiness, not by active, but by passive holiness, because they possess divine and holy things, to wit, the vocation of the ministry, the Gospel, baptism, etc., whereby they are holy' (C.G., p. 39; W.A., xl (i) 70. 11-22.)

The work of prayer, we believe, should be understood in the same way; it is not our effort at praying or personal prayer that makes the work holy but uniquely the commandment and the promise embraced and fulfilled in the passive righteousness of the Gospel.

[3] B.C., 198, col. 1. In this context, Luther argues that prayer done in obedience to God's Law is 'as precious, holy and pleasing to God as that of Saint Paul or the most holy saints' (ibid.). It is the Word of God—in this case His commandment—which makes prayer efficacious and not the personal goodness or holiness of the individual: '... denn ich will ihn [St. Paul] gerne lassen heiliger sein der Person halben, aber des Gepots halben nicht, weil Gott das Gebete nicht der Person halben ansiehet, sondern seines Worts und Gehorsams halben' (Bek., p. 666. 1-5).

to be rejected[1] because they are based on the false doctrine of good works, on self-reliance; they do not spring spontaneously from the heart in distress, and from an inner genuine obedience to God's Word and Commandment, and from faith in Christ's promises.[2] Likewise, as with other good works, mere external actions, such as 'bawlings' and 'babblings' in churches, do not constitute the fulfilment of the commandment to pray; the Christian, to pray properly, must experience the obligation to obey God's Word and feel the deep need for prayer; it must not be done out of a desire to appear holy or to prove oneself to be righteous (ibid).

Since we know from the first part that the commandment imposes the obligation and reveals the need, and since, also, we know from the second part that the Gospel-faith in the total work of the Blessed Trinity provides the power to fulfil and obey the Word, we can see, once more, in the instance of prayer, how Luther's Catechism is built around the Law-Gospel relation; out of the transition from despairing absolutely in self to believing in and depending solely on God comes the Christian's prayer, his cry for help. It is in this sense, we believe, that one should interpret Luther when he declares that we should be 'incited' to pray because of the commandment and the promise and because God Himself

... anticipates us and Himself arranges the words and form of prayer for us, and places them upon our lips as to how and what we should pray, that we may see how heartily He pities us in our distress, and may never doubt that such prayer is pleasing to Him and shall certainly be answered.[3]

The seven Petitions or 'Bitte' [*precatio*], into which Luther divides the Lord's Prayer, are not a typically Lutheran division. Saint Thomas, and other theologians before him, adopted the

---

[1] 'Darümb haben wir billich der Münche und Pfaffen Gebete verworfen, die Tag und Nacht feindlich heulen und murren, aber ihr keiner denket ümb ein Haar breit zu bitten. Und wenn man alle Kirchen sampt den Geistlichen zusammenbrächte, so müßten sie bekennen, daß sie nie von Herzen ümb ein Tröpflin Weins gebeten hätten. Denn ihr keiner je hat aus Gottes Gehorsam und Glauben der Verheißung furgenommen zu beten, auch keine Not angesehen, sondern nicht weiter gedacht (wenn man's aufs beste ausgericht hat), denn ein gut Werk zu tuen, damit sie Gott bezahleten, als die nicht von ihm nehmen, sondern nur ihm geben wollten' (*Bek.*, pp. 667-8. 42-46, 1-11).
[2] ibid.
[3] *B.C.*, p. 198, col. 1.

same obvious divisions. What is characteristically his own is the way he presents each petition as a particular application of the command to pray, joined to the threats and promises of God's Word and the strong personal emphasis, as usual, on depending solely on God and despairing totally in self.

We do not intend to enter into a detailed analysis of each petition; this would involve us in superfluous reiterations of the Law-Gospel theme such as we have already seen.[1] Suffice it to say that Luther's handling of each petition corroborates our previous observations with regard to the worthiness and right-eousness of God against the sinfulness and unrighteousness of His creature, the promises and fulfilment of the Gospel against the threats and despair of the Law, and also, at least implicitly, the force and function of the Commandments as related to the dual character of the Christian.[2]

We should mention, however, that his treatment of the last four petitions bears significant traces of the peculiar pessimism we have seen elsewhere; we are thinking of man's moral de-pravity, the unhealing character of forgiveness of sin, and the inner tension of the Christian life. Let us consider, for instance, the following text:

---

[1] Luther's treatment of the Seven Petitions may be summarized as follows: the first two petitions 'comprehend all that pertains to the honour of God and to our salvation, that we receive as our own God and all His riches' (B.C., p. 200, col. 2). In short, they are an eloquent appeal to let God be God, as Watson would express it; and acceptance of His mercy and acknowledgement of our own plight without Him. Likewise the third petition, 'Thy will be done . . .', is related to God Himself, yet for the sake of sinners (ibid., p. 201). Through faith and prayer the sinner fulfils God's Will and finds refuge in God's Holy Word and the grace and strength to conform his own will to God's Word: 'For where the Word of God is preached, accepted, or believed, and produces fruit, there the holy cross cannot be want-ing . . .' (ibid.). As with the previous articles, these petitions are described as 'duties' and 'obligations' to which the Christian must attend. What is important to bear in mind, in this connexion, is that obedience to these duties or obligations is not a self-reliant means to grace but rather God-given blessings fulfilled in faith (see above, p. 104, n. 2).

The remaining petitions touch upon our temporal and spiritual needs; the fourth one embracing all that belongs to the welfare of the state and the individual; the others, upon all that is required to obtain forgiveness of sin and to fight the three 'Bekoerunge' or temptations against the commandment and the Word; namely the temptations of the flesh, the world, and the devil.

[2] We recall what we said in the previous chapter concerning the fact that the Law is still in force for the Christian man and continues to loom up in his con-science if and when he resorts to his own efforts to attain righteousness and abandons faith in the Word and the promise (see above, Chapter IV, pp. 87–88).

The flesh in which we daily live is of such a nature that it neither trusts nor believes God, and is ever active in evil lusts and devices, so that we sin daily in word and deed, by commission and omission, by which the conscience is thrown into unrest, so that it is afraid of the wrath and displeasure of God and thus loses the comfort and confidence of the Gospel.[1]

Here, we have the moral pessimism of Luther's doctrine of original sin, and a reiteration of the crushing personal terrifying role of the Law mirroring our sinfulness.

Moreover, this state of nature, as Luther describes it, does not seem to be healed even by baptism and the Word. We are never without sin,[2] we must cry continually unto God to forgive us our sins.[3] Though we have accepted and believe the Word of God, Luther tells us, the flesh is itself indolent and inclined to evil and the world perverse and wicked.[4] In this world, there is no complete removal of sin[5] or real transformation of the believer's being.[6]

[1] *B.C.*, p. 203, col. 1; *Bek.*, p. 683. 24–32.

[2] See p. 95, n. 1. Also the following: 'Dies Stück [the fifth petition] trifft nu unser armes und elends Leben an, welchs, ob wir gleich Gottes Wort haben, gläuben, seinen Willen tuen und leiden und uns von Gottes Gabe und Segen nähren, gehet es doch ohn Sunde nicht abe, daß wir noch täglich straucheln und zuviel tuen ...' (*Bek.*, p. 683. 1–7).

[3] *B.C.*, p. 203, col. 1. In *Bek.*, 'So ist nu die Meinung [Sinn] dieser Bitte [5], daß Gott nicht wollt' unser Sunde ansehen und fürhalten, was wir täglich verdienen, sondern mit Gnaden gegen uns handeln und vergeben, wie er verheißen hat, und also ein fröhlich und unverzagt Gewissen geben, fur ihm zu stehen und zu bitten. Denn wo das Herz nicht mit Gott recht stehet und solche Zuversicht schepfen kann, so wird es nimmermehr sich türren unterstehen zu beten. Solche Zuversicht aber und fröhlichs Herz kann nirgend herkommen, denn es wisse, daß ihm die Sund vergeben seien' (p. 684. 16–28). Compare this passage to p. 108, n. 6, where we see how Luther describes the sanctifying work of the Holy Ghost in similar terms.

[4] 'Denn unser Fleisch ist an ihm selbs faul [schlecht] und zum Bösen geneigt, ob wir gleich Gottes Wort angenommen haben und gläuben. Die Welt aber ist arg und böse' (*Bek.*, p. 676. 46–50). See also p. 108, n. 2.

[5] Here, we think, is the basis of imputative and passive righteousness in Luther's theology. Luther does not use these expressions in the Catechism, but they follow from his description of human nature and the forgiveness of sin. The crux of the problem is that the old Adam endures until the day of judgement. The sinner's transformation is, in a mysterious manner, passive and imputative, not entitative; he simply stands in a new relation to God, not because of anything he has done himself or wished to do, or can do now, enabled by grace, to please God, but solely because God no longer regards his sins as damning. The intent of the fifth petition, 'forgive us our trespasses', is to ask God not to 'regard our sins and hold up to us what we daily deserve, but would deal graciously with us, and forgive, as he

(*footnotes 5 and 6 continued overleaf.*)

Equally significant are his remarks about consenting to temptation and resisting temptation when discussing the petition 'lead us not into temptation'. Whereas he paints a black picture of human nature, exhorting us to rely solely on God for the 'power and[1] strength to resist temptations',[2] he none the less says, that the feeling of temptation, 'as long as it is against our will and we would rather be rid of it', cannot harm us. It is only harmful when we 'consent' to it (ibid.), 'when we give it the reins and do not resist or pray against it'.[3]

In this respect, he seems to admit of a certain spiritual free-

promised, and thus grant us a joyful and confident conscience to stand before him in prayer. For where the heart is not in right relation towards God, nor can take such confidence, it will never more venture to pray but such a confident and joyful heart can spring from nothing else than the [certain] knowledge of the forgiveness of sin' (Bek., p. 684. 16–28). From this passage, one will observe that the emphasis is subjective and psychological, not ontological in the Scholastic sense. The transformation is in the order of opposing states of consciousness—of passing from a personal awareness of self as sinful and damned to a personal awareness of God as merciful and forgiving—the inner mood of the soul changes from despair, sorrow, and anxiety to hope, joy, and peace.

[6] In article 3, while describing the progress of the Christian's sanctification, Luther says: 'Indes aber, weil die Heiligkeit angefangen ist und täglich zunimmpt, warten wir, daß unser Fleisch hingerichtet und mit allem Unflat bescharret werde, aber herrlich erfurkomme und auferstehe zu ganzer und volliger Heiligkeit in einem neuen ewigen Leben. Denn itzt bleiben wir halb und halb reine und heilig, auf daß der heilig Geist immer an uns erbeite durch das Wort und täglich Vergebung austeile bis in jenes Leben, da nicht mehr Vergebung wird sein, sondern ganz und gar rein und heilige Menschen, voller Frommkeit und Gerechtigkeit, entnommen und ledig von Sund, Tod und allem Unglück in einem neuen unsterblichen und verklärten Leib' (Bek., p. 659. 1–16). From this passage, it appears that, for Luther, the Christian is only completely and physically purified by forgiveness of sin and grace on the day of judgement and in the next world. In this world, the Christian carries the old Adam around his neck, as we have seen elsewhere, and is, as it were, half pure; the dualism and struggle of the inner self is never absent.

---

[1] 'Solchs heißet nu "nicht einführen in Versuchunge", wenn er uns Kraft und Stärke gibt zu widerstehen, doch die Anfechtung nicht weggenommen noch aufgehaben' (Bek., p. 687. 26–29). Luther prefers the word *Anfechtung* for which there is no English equivalent. 'It may be a trial sent by God to test man, or an assault by the Devil to destroy man. It is all the doubt, turmoil, pang, terror, panic, despair, desolation, and desperation which invade the spirit of man' (Roland Bainton, op. cit., p. 31).

[2] For Luther, temptations—in Old Saxon *Bekoerunge*—are of three kinds, 'namely of the flesh, of the world and of the devil' (see *B.C.*, p. 203).

[3] 'Darümb ist's viel ein ander Ding, Anfechtung fühlen und darein verwilligen oder Ja dazu sagen. ... Aber solch Fühlen, weil es wider unsern Willen ist und wir sein lieber los wären, kann niemand schaden. Denn wo man's nicht fühlete, künnde es kein Anfechtung heißen. Bewilligen aber ist, wenn man ihm den Zaum lässet, nicht dawider stehet noch bittet' (Bek., pp. 687–8. 36–47, 1–4).

dom of the Christian's inner self or ego, capable of working and co-operating with grace. Yet one finds great difficulty in reconciling this manner of speaking with the despair-faith pattern of his theology,[1] and in particular with the imputative and passive character of righteousness. Having made a clear distinction between 'feeling temptation' and wilfully consenting to it, he concludes strangely: '. . . if you venture to help yourself by your own thoughts and counsel, you will only make the matter worse and give the devil more space . . .'.[2]

[1] We realize, of course, that Luther's point of view on the matter of resisting temptation and the forgiveness of sin is not easy to get at and explain. Lutheran scholars themselves are not in agreement. But, notwithstanding, we cannot help feeling that it is precisely here that his theology differs basically from the traditional Catholic stand. What does the Reformer mean when he says the Christian resists temptation and refuses to consent to sin and sinfulness? Does he mean that he acts freely, enabled by grace, and as subject of his own acts, or is he simply moved passively by the indwelling God? How shall we determine Luther's meaning and answer to these questions? Perhaps the best way is to consider the implications of his doctrine—that is to say, what he himself attacks in Roman Catholicism as being against God's Word and God's work.

He attacks and throws out of the work of Redemption the intercession of saints, monasticism, the doctrine of Purgatory, the sacrificial role of the Mass, the special powers of an ordained clergy and the meritorious work of penance and personal effort; also he treats of the sacraments in an untraditional scheme (see below, next section) refusing to acknowledge Marriage, Extreme Unction, and Holy Orders as true Sacraments, and condemning outright the divine prerogatives of Papal authority and jurisdiction. Why? Is it not because all of these teachings presuppose that human beings, members of the Church of Christ, share in the work of Redemption as instrumental and secondary causes of grace? For Luther, it seems, these things threaten to undermine the exclusive work of the Gospel as he understands it. That is to say, they introduce into God's work the efforts and strivings of sinful man. This, he considers blasphemous; for nothing sinful can be of God. Now resisting temptation is either God's work or man's work or both.

We do not wish to beg the question and make Luther say more than he intended; but should we not conclude, from his picture of human nature and his description of forgiveness of sin, that the Law-Gospel relation excludes meritorious and personal effort entirely from the work of Redemption, even from the necessary act of resisting temptation?

Cut off from the Gospel, devoid of faith in the forgiveness of sin, a man's deeds, in relation to God, are evil, vitiated by self-love; with the Gospel, all that we do pleasing to God and deserving of grace, results from a purely passive suffering of the inner workings of the Three Persons of the Blessed Trinity. God becomes, in a mysterious inexplicable fashion, the subject of our Christian thoughts, words, and deeds. (See Regin Prenter, *Spiritus Creator*, chapter 1.) The inner self, the substance of self, so to speak, remains non-participant, non-co-operating, and non-availing; faith in the Gospel, both in itself and in relation to the Law, is a God-commanded God-fulfilled work.

[2] 'Sonst, wo Du mit Deinen Gedanken und eigenem Rat unterstehest, Dir zu helfen, wirst Du's nur ärger machen und dem Teufel mehr Raum geben ...' (*Bek.*, p. 688. 29–32).

For our subject, we should notice, in these passages, that the Law and the Gospel—the Word as command and the Word as fulfilment—are inseparable from the Christian's experience of himself as *Sünder und Gerecht*, from his awareness of a dynamic dualism and spiritual tension within his soul. It is never absent from Luther's treatment of the separate parts of the Catechism. As with the former parts, so too with this part on prayer, the Christian is engaged in the struggle between sinful self and saving grace. If he relies on his own efforts and works, he will not see the need for prayer and will not obey the commandment to pray; but if he believes sincerely in God's Word and promise, prayer will spring up spontaneously from his heart[1]—it will be a crying out from the depths of his anguish and sinfulness. In this sense, the command to believe in prayer and to recite the *Our Father* is a declaration of war against ourselves, the world, and the devil. The following passage, found at the beginning of the third part, contains the essential Law-Gospel meaning of Luther's teachings on the command to pray:

... For since we are so situated [in the state of sin] that no man can perfectly keep the Ten Commandments, even though we have begun to believe, and since the devil with all his power, together with the world and the flesh, resists our endeavour, nothing is so necessary as that we should continually resort to the ear of God, call upon Him and pray to Him, that He would give preserve and increase in us faith and fulfilment of the Commandments.[2]

On the negative side, we find, of course, no comment on the intercession of saints, the role of the Blessed Virgin, and the need to pray for the souls in Purgatory.[3] Luther, undoubtedly,

---

[1] See p. 102, n. 4; also *B.C.*, pp. 197–8.

[2] *B.C.*, p. 197; *Bek.*, p. 662. 20–29.

[3] Concerning the doctrine of purgatory: Luther is against its being imposed by Rome as an article of faith on the grounds that he can find no evidence for it in Scripture. Thus he writes, in the year 1521, against the Papal Bull, *Exsurge Domine* (1520), condemning its teachings: 'I have never yet denied that there is a purgatory and I still hold that there is, as I have many times written and confessed, though I have no way of proving it incontrovertibly, either by Scripture or reason. I find in the Scriptures, indeed, that Christ, Abraham, Jacob, Moses, Job, David, Hezekiah and some others tasted hell in this life. This I think to be purgatory, and it is not incredible that some of the dead suffer in this manner. Tauler has much to say about it and, in a word, I have decided for myself that there is a purgatory, but I cannot force any others to the same decision. There is only one thing that I have attacked, namely the way in which they apply to purgatory passages of Scriptures so inapplicable that it becomes ridiculous.'

(*footnote continued on opposite page.*)

intended to exclude these beliefs as they are opposed to his
principles *sola fide, sola scriptura, sola gratia*, as we explained
above. And although he asserts the Christian obligation to pray
for others,[1] it is indeed hard to understand the value or merit[2]

And a few lines farther: '. . . no one is bound to believe more than what is based on
Scripture, and those who do not believe in purgatory are not to be called heretics,
if in other respects they hold to the entire Scriptures, as the Greek Church does'
(*An Argument in Defence of All the Articles of Dr. Martin Luther wrongly condemned in the
Roman Bull*, Ph., iii. 111–13; see also *W.A.* vii. 450–1).

In this matter, as with all matters of faith, Luther is arguing exclusively from his
understanding of the written Word of God. We are surprised, however, that, at
this point in his career, he does not reject completely the whole notion of purgatory. Already, at this early date, his Law-Gospel theology is definitely established
and it has no use or need for a doctrine of purgatory. As we have endeavoured to
explain in the first and final chapters of our thesis, his theology teaches that Christ's
righteousness is all-embracing and all-sufficient for the full redemption of sinners.
If the Christian believes in Christ's righteousness, he is totally saved; if he refuses
to believe, he is totally damned; not only is there no place here for human merit
coram Deo, either in this or the next world, but no point in distinguishing between
poena and *culpa*, and mortal and venial sin (below, Chapter VI, section B).* Thus
strictly speaking, Luther should not even hold to the opinion that there is a purgatory. Perhaps, in this instance, he is speaking with tongue in cheek, or perhaps
has not yet grasped the full implications of his own theology.

Later, 1538, in the *Tischreden*, he rejects the doctrine of purgatory altogether,
contending that God, in Scripture, has proposed only two ways: 'Deus in suo
verbo duas nobis proposuit vias: salutem per fidem, damnationem per incredulita-
tem. Nihil mentionis facit de purgatorio' (*T.R.* iii, 'Anton Lauterbachs, Tagebuch,
aus Jahr 1538', no. 3695, p. 539. 14–16; see also *Propos de table*, pp. 309–10). He
goes on to say that we are not to admit this doctrine which obscures the grace and
benefits of Christ: 'Neque admittendum est purgatorium, quod beneficia et
gratiam Christi obscurat' (ibid.).

We feel that this latter argument is more in keeping with Luther's fundamental
Law-Gospel theology of salvation. While belonging to his personal interpretation
of the Bible, it cannot be divorced from his soul-shaking experience of sin and grace,
of despair and faith.

We should add, moreover, that oral tradition and the authorities of the Fathers
are unacceptable to him when their statements do not tally with his fundamental
position. Saint Gregory's views on purgatory, for instance, are not taken seriously
by him (*see T.R.* iii, no. 3695).

[1] Every one, Luther declares, 'should accustom himself to pray for all his wants,
whenever he is sensible of anything effecting his interests or that of other people
among whom we may live, as for preachers, the government, neighbours, domes-
tics . . .' (*B.C.*, p. 198, col. 2).
[2] Catholic theologians distinguish between grace merited *de condigno* and *de
congruo* to account for the value of human intercession. But Luther, understanding
these terms, perhaps in a Nominalist fashion, rejects them outright in his *Commentary on Galatians* (see Appendix I). The way to see how his community praying

* Catholic theologians employ these distinctions to account for the necessity
of a purgatory. One can refer to the article 'Purgatoire', in *D.T.C.*, tome
13, cols. 1167–1357, for a fuller treatment of the Catholic position on
purgatory.

of such prayer in the context of his exclusive theology of the Word.[1]

In the Fourth and Fifth Parts on the Sacraments, which we shall now study, we shall meet with the same Law-Gospel approach to fundamental doctrine.

C. *The command to administer the Sacraments*

Luther divides his remarks on the Sacraments into three questions: what are the Sacraments, what are their benefits, and who is to receive them?[2] His answers to these questions reveal to us how the Sacraments belong exclusively to the work of the Word and should be related to the fulfilment of the Law.

His definition of the nature and efficacy of the Sacrament rests, in his own words, on the 'Word and command',[3] or more

for others fits best into his account of salvation is to look upon it simply as an outward manifestation of Christ's Will. That is to say, as Christ desires the salvation of sinners, so too, the Christian community desires it and proves it through praying for others. Its prayer, in this sense, is a sign that God is present in the community of believers. But, for this matter, prayer cannot be considered meritorious or efficacious in the normally accepted meaning of that term. That is to say, as meriting grace for another.

Here, we are not speaking of the efficacy of prayer, *generaliter*; Luther believes most strongly in it (see *B.C.*, p. 198, col. 1), but that efficacy which, to some extent, is related to the man who prays. As far as Luther is concerned, as stated above, prayer is efficacious not because of the worth or qualities of him who prays, but solely because of the Word of God believed in and obeyed. Indeed, the very act of praying for forgiveness is not a means to righteousness, but rather a consequence thereof. Thus when we pray 'Dear Father forgive us our trespasses', we do not perform a meritorious work by which we, of our own efforts, obtain forgiveness, we simply recognize and accept such forgiveness. Our sin is forgiven before we even pray by the power of the Gospel: 'Therefore there is here again great need to call upon God and pray: Dear Father, forgive us our trespasses. Not as though He did not forgive sin without and even before our prayer (for He has given us the Gospel, in which is pure forgiveness before we prayed or even thought about it). But this is the intent that we may recognize and accept such forgiveness' (*B.C.*, pp. 202–3).

[1] That Luther recognizes the efficacy of godly men praying for others is clear from the following passage: 'Denn was meinest Du, daß bisher so groß Ding ausgerichtet habe, unserer Feinde Ratschlagen, Furnehmen, Mord und Aufruhr gewehret oder gedämpfet, dadurch uns der Teufel sampt dem Evangelio gedacht hat unterzudrücken, wo nicht etlicher frommer Leute Gebete als ein eiserne Mauer auf unser Seiten darzwischen kommen wäre' (*Bek.*, p. 669. 26–34).

[2] See p. 119, n. 3.

[3] From the outset, in the section on Baptism, Luther lays down the principle of his sacramental theology, based on Matt. xxviii. 19, and Mark, xvi. 16: 'In diesen Worten sollt Du zum ersten merken, daß hie stehet Gottes Gebot und Einsetzung, des man nicht zweifele, die Taufe sei ein göttlich Ding, nicht von Menschen erdacht noch erfunden. Denn so wohl als ich sagen kann, die zehen Gebot, Glauben und Vaterunser hat kein Mensch aus seinem Kopf gespunnen,

explicitly, we know from the preceding parts, on the Word commanding and fulfilling man's justification, redemption, and sanctification.

The Word of God joined to the external element or sign (water, bread, and wine) and accompanied by a promise of grace (forgiveness of sin) institutes the Sacrament[1] and com-

sondern sind von Gott selbs offenbaret und gegeben, so kann ich auch rühmen, daß die Taufe kein Menschentand sei, sondern von Gott selbs eingesetzt, darzu ernstlich und streng geboten, daß wir uns müssen täufen lassen oder sollen nicht selig werden ... Aber laß äußerlich Ding sein,* als es immer kann, da stehet aber Gottes Wort und Gebot, so die Taufe einsetzet, gründet und bestätigt' (*Bek.*, pp. 691–2. 37–41, 1–20).

We should note in this passage, the recurrence and insistence on *Gottes Gebot* [or *Gepot*]—God's commandment or command, a further instance of the fact that Luther's evangelicalism does not exclude the Decalogue notion of commandment. Indeed he draws an analogy, such as we have cited previously, between the Ten Commandments and God's 'solemn and strict' commandment to administer and receive the Sacrament of Baptism. Equally noteworthy is the fact that the Sacrament is described as God's work and not man's work.

Identical language is used to describe the nature and institution of the Lord's Supper; the difference being, of course, the words pronounced and the visible sign, based on 1 Cor. xi. 23–25; Matt. xxvi. 26–28; Mark xiv. 22–24; Luke xxii. 19. What is primary with the Reformer—'the chief point'—is the Word and ordinance or command of God: 'Hie wöllen wir uns auch nicht in die Haar legen und fechten mit den Lästerern und Schändern† dieses Sakraments, sondern zum ersten lernen, da die Macht an liegt (wie auch von der Taufe), nämlich daß das fürnehmeste Stück sei Gottes Wort und Ordnung oder Befehl' (*Bek.*, p. 708. 33–39).

[1] In the *De captivitate Babylonica* (1520), Luther outlines three requisites of the Sacrament—the Word or divine command, the visible element, and the promise. And he goes on to say that though we find other signs and other evangelical commandments, they cannot be regarded as true Sacraments because one or other of the three requisites are missing. That is to say, we have the Word and the sign without the promise; or the Word and the promise without the sign, &c.: 'Sunt praeterea nonnulla alia, quae inter sacramenta videantur censeri posse, nempe omnia illa, quibus facta est promisio divina, qualia sunt Oratio, Verbum, Crux. . . . Siquidem omnia, quae scripta sint, aut praecepta aut promissa sunt: praecepta humiliant superbos exactionibus suis, promissa exaltant humiliatos remissionibus suis.

'Proprie tamen ea sacramenta vocari visum est, quae annexis signis promissa sunt. Caetera, quia signis alligata non sunt, nuda promissa sunt. Quo fit, ut si rigide loqui volumus, tantum duo sunt in Ecclesia dei sacramenta, Baptismus et panis, cum in his solis et institutum divinitus signum et promissionem remissionis

* Luther here is referring to the error of the *Schwärmerei* and the Anabaptists who were opposed to external rites and ceremonies, including the Sacraments, on the grounds that they were unnecessary to the inner man spiritually united to God through faith.

† The words *Lästerern und Schändern*—'traducers and blasphemers' (see *B.C.*, p. 210) probably refer to Karlstadt and Calvin, and their disciples, who questioned the real presence of Christ under the appearances of bread and wine.

mands¹ the Church to use it as a means of bestowing grace on her believing members.

To describe a Sacrament, therefore, Luther employs the Augustinian formula: '. . . accedat verbum² ad elementum et fit sacramentum'.³

peccatorum videamus. Nam poenitentiae sacramentum, quod ego his duobus accensui, signo visibili et divinitus instituto caret et aliud non esse dixi quam viam ac reditum ad baptismum' (*W.A.* vi. 571–2. 35–36, 1–17).

Bertram Lee Woolf, in his introduction to his translation of this work, says that the immediate urge causing Luther to write the *De captivitate Babylonica* 'was the fact that, about the middle of July 1520, he had received two documents of similar quality: one by Alvehd, an Augustinian friar of Leipzig, dealing with the question of communion in both kinds on the part of the laity; and the other an anonymous tract issuing from Cremona in Italy "revoking" Luther to the Holy See'. Woolf adds that this work 'still holds its place as the most important discussion of sacramental doctrine in the history of Protestantism' (*Reformation Writings of Martin Luther*, i. 204–5).

¹ The words *Gebot* and *Gepot* appear frequently throughout his description of the two Sacraments of Baptism and the Lord's Supper, and have the same force and function as a Decalogue commandment. We should observe, moreover, in the passage quoted below, p. 128, n. 2, how Luther relates the precepts and promises of the Sacraments to the despair-faith parallel. The precepts are meant to humble the proud and the promises to exalt the humble. Now we know from our preceding chapters that, for Luther, true humility belongs to those only who despair absolutely in their own righteousness and trust solely in Christ's righteousness.

² In this case *verbum* includes the promise.

³ See *Bek.*, p. 694. 29–30. The thirteenth-century Schoolmen also employed the Augustinian formula to define a Sacrament, but they added other formulas, such as 'Sacramentum [including the Word and the sign] producit id quod significat'; they too recognized the power of the Word and the divine ordinance as the principal cause of grace, but used words such as *producit* and *efficit* to stress the instrumental causality of the material sign. The Reformer, we know from the *Smalcald Articles*, saw in the Scholastic idea of instrumental causality an appeal to creatures and human works as means to salvation. He would have none of this; consistent with his interpretation of the Word and the command, he rejected both the Dominican and the Franciscan explanations of sacramental causality: '... halten wir's nicht mit Thoma* und den Predigermonchen [Dominicans], die des Worts (Gottes Einsetzung) vergessen und sagen, Gott habe eine geistliche Kraft ins Wasser gelegt, welche die Sunde durchs Wasser abwasche, auch nicht mit Scoto [Duns Scotus, see his *Sententiae*, 4, dist. 1, q. 2] und den Barfußenmonchen [Franciscans], die da lehren, daß die Taufe die Sunde abwasche aus Beistehen göttliches Willens, also daß diese Abwaschung geschicht allein durch Gottes Willen, garnicht durchs Wort oder Wasser' (*Bek.*, p. 450. 1–10).

From this quotation alone, we do not think that one can argue that Luther rejects totally and absolutely all idea of instrumental causality. Apparently what

* See *S.Th.*, IIIa, q. 62, a. 4: 'Et hoc modo vis spiritualis est in sacramentis, inquantum ordinantur a Deo ad effectum spiritualem.' Saint Thomas, however, contrary to what Luther says here, is not forgetful of the Word of God; indeed, it is by virtue of the Word and the divine ordinance that the Angelic Doctor understands the water to acquire a *vis spiritualis*.

According to his understanding of Scripture (see the last paragraph of Appendix III), only Baptism and the Lord's Supper meet the conditions of his definition of a Sacrament. These are the only two which he calls Sacraments in the *Large Catechism*. Penance or Repentance, to which he devotes a whole formulary[1] in the *Small Catechism*, he describes as a 'return and approach' to Baptism.[2] The other Sacraments, Marriage,[3] Holy Orders, Confirmation, and Extreme Unction, are not mentioned.[4]

Concerning the second question, the benefits of the Sacrament, we are not at all clear to what extent they are conferred on the recipient, or simply declared to be imputed. We should

he intends to exclude from the work of the Sacraments is any theory or practice that threatens to undermine or detract from the exclusive power of God's Word and ordinance. The theological explanations of the Dominicans and the Franciscans seem to him to be contrary to the manifest teachings of the Word. He does not, however, offer any explanation of his own. It is interesting and significant that for him the Word of God is not enough, it must be the Will of God as revealed by the external Word of Scripture and joined to the divinely established sign.

[1] The formulary is concerned mainly with the ritual of Confession. It states that penance embraces two parts only; confession of sins, felt to be in the heart, and the absolution given by the minister. The traditional division of penance into three parts—contrition, confession, and satisfaction—is unacceptable (see *De captivitate Babylonica*, the section on Penance). The formulary does not bother to link up Penance with the Sacrament of Baptism as does the *Large Catechism* (see n. 2, below). The 1531 edition of *Der deutsche Katechismus*, as mentioned earlier, contains a section on Confession, inserted between the Fourth and Fifth Parts.

[2] *B.C.*, p. 209, col. 2. See also *Bek.*, 'Und hie siehest Du, daß die Taufe beide mit ihrer Kraft und Deutunge begreift auch das dritte Sacrament, welches man genennet hat die Buße, als die eigentlich nicht anders ist denn die Taufe. Denn was heißet Buße anders, denn den Alten Menschen mit Ernst angreifen und in ein neues Leben treten? Darümb, wenn Du in der Buße lebst, so gehest Du in der Taufe, welche solch neues Leben nicht allein deutet sondern auch wirkt, anhebt und treibt; denn darin wird geben Gnade, Geist und Kraft, den alten Menschen zu unterdrücken, daß der neue erfurkomme und stark werde. Darümb bleibt die Taufe immerdar stehen ... Also ist die Buße nicht anders denn ein Wiedergang und Zutreten zur Taufe, daß man das widerholet und treibt, so man zuvor angefangen und doch davon gelassen hat' (pp. 705–6. 47–48, 1–26). We shall comment further on this important passage when we deal with the efficacy of the Sacraments below. See p. 119, for the English translation.

[3] Luther speaks of Marriage in the Decalogue section of the Catechism, but again not as a Sacrament but simply as a law of God and a necessity of nature. The subject comes up in his denunciation of monastic vows. Some editions of the *Small Catechism* contain a formulary on Marriage. This formulary, however, treats of the Sacrament as an ecclesiastical rite and not as a true Sacrament.

[4] Luther soon realized that the Sacraments of Marriage, Confirmation, Holy Orders, and Extreme Unction were incompatible with his understanding of evangelical faith and the Word (see Appendix III).

not expect to find a full reply to this problem in the Catechism; this book, dealing with elementary doctrine, does not develop, in any detail, the paradoxical and mysterious realities of personal sin and grace. Enough, however, emerges from the Fourth and Fifth Parts to state the following:

Baptism,[1] in its sign and power,[2] is continuous and ever-efficacious, an 'unrepeatable'[3] Sacrament,[4] a lifelong 'covenant'[5] or alliance which clothes the recipient, so to speak, 'in faith and its fruits',[6] and signifies and effects, basically, the dynamic inner tension of the Christian life—the death of the old Adam and the growth of the new: '. . . the operation of Baptism . . . is nothing else than putting to death the old Adam and after that the resurrection of the new man, both of which take place in us all our lives, so that a truly Christian life is nothing else than a daily Baptism once begun and ever continued'.[7] It is in this

---

[1] Using the language of Saint Paul [Tit. iii. 5], Luther calls Baptism a 'laver of Regeneration' ('Bad der Wiedergeburt'; see *Bek.*, p. 696. 14–16).

[2] For Luther, Baptism is not just a mere sign or symbol; it has the power and force of God's Word to effect salvation in men: ' "Wer da gläubt und getauft wird, der wird selig" [Mark xvi. 16]. Darümb fasse es aufs allereinfältigst also, daß dies der Taufe Kraft, Werk, Nutz, Frucht und Ende ist, daß sie selig mache. ... Selig werden aber weiß man wohl, daß nichts anders heißet, denn von Sunden, Tod, Teufel erlöset in Christus' 'Reich kommen und mit ihm ewig leben... Denn durchs Wort kriegt sie die Kraft, daß sie [die Taufe] ein "Bad der Wiedergeburt" ist ...' (*Bek.*, pp. 695–6. 39–47 and 1–16).

[3] We borrowed this word from Regin Prenter (see *More About Luther*, Iowa, 1958, vol. ii, p. 91).

[4] At the end of the Fourth Part on Baptism, Luther blames our disregard for the ever-efficacious and continuing work of Baptism on Saint Jerome's remark 'that repentance is the second plank by which we must swim forth and cross over after the ship is broken, on which we step and are carried across when we come into the Christian Church' (*B.C.*, p. 209, col. 2). Luther objects to this metaphor; he claims that the ship of Baptism is never wrecked. In Appendix IV we compare his views on this point with those of Saint Jerome.

[5] In a sermon on Baptism (1519) Luther introduces the important concept of covenant in order to explain the enduring effect and character of Christ's baptismal promise: 'Das hilfft dyr das hochwirdig sacrament der tauff, das sich gott daselbs mit dyr vorpindet und mit dyr eyns wird eyns gnedigen trostlichen bunds' (*W.A.* ii. 730. 20–22). Regin Prenter translates 'bunds' by 'covenant' (op. cit., pp. 90–91).

[6] 'Darümb soll ein iglicher die Taufe halten als sein täglich Kleid, darin er immerdar gehen soll, daß er sich allezeit in dem Glauben und seinen Fruchten finden lasse, daß er den alten Menschen dämpfe und im neuen erwachse' (*Bek.*, p. 707. 21–26).

[7] *B.C.*, p. 209, col. 1. In a sense, the death of the old Adam and the life of the new is the key-stone to Luther's Law-Gospel theology and despair-faith experience of salvation. This is the basic effect signified and produced by the Sacrament of Baptism (see p. 115, n. 2). Regin Prenter claims that this theology can be 'characterized as a theology of the Cross'. In order to understand Luther's teaching about

sense that Luther understands Baptism to incorporate us into the Christian Church[1] and to assure for us the 'Christian victory over death and the devil, forgiveness of sin, the grace of God and the entire Christ, and the Holy Ghost with His gifts'.[2]

Manifestly, this is the language of Saint Paul;[3] but for the Reformer, the expressions 'faith and its fruits', 'Baptism as a dress', 'forgiveness of sins', 'the grace of God', the 'gifts of the Holy Ghost', 'the death of the old Adam and the resurrection of the new' must be understood metaphorically and psychologically, not physically or ontologically. They are, as it were, included in the figure of Christ's cloak of merits which covers over our sins and prevents them from harming or damning us; but in no such way as to eradicate sin, to render the recipient of Baptism entitatively sinless; or to reinstate him into an entitative order of grace which prepares and disposes him to

the Word and the Sacrament, he says, 'it is necessary to relate his theology of the Word with his theology of the Cross'. Arguing from a passage taken from the *Freedom of a Christian Man*, which we ourselves have quoted in our First Chapter (see above, pp. 21–23) he explains 'that the radical distinction between law and gospel in their separateness and unity indicates that Christ is the centre of Scriptures. Through the law we are crucified as sinners in order to be united with the crucified Christ as our righteousness. Through the gospel we are raised as new creatures to live in fellowship with the risen Christ. . . . Thus the Scriptures in their totality make us conformable with Christ. Through them as law and gospel, His death and resurrection work our mortification and vivification, the death of the condemned sinner in us and the birth of the new and righteous man in his place' (op. cit., p. 70). Prenter's point here, on the theology of the Cross, is helpful in understanding Luther's description of the symbolism and effects of Baptism. We see how the Law and the Gospel of Scripture are essentially related to the Christian experience of dying to self and living with Christ in faith.

Prenter also argues from other important passages, such as the following taken from Luther's first lecture on the Psalms (1513), which agrees substantially with what he has just said: 'Unde notandum, quod lex vetus spiritualiter intellecta non est nisi crucifixio carnis . . . ideo non nisi Jhesum crucifixum prenunciat. Sed lex nova est salus et liberatio spiritus. Et sic veteri conveniunt omnia, que ad destructionem veteris hominis pertinent, nove autem omnia que ad constructionem novi hominis' (*W.A.* iv. 174. 17–18).

This passage, from Luther's early works, is another instance of the fact that long before the indulgence dispute, he had already formulated his basic Law-Gospel doctrine of salvation.

[1] 'Zum ersten aber nehmen wir uns die Taufe, dadurch wir erstlich in die Christenheit genommen werden' (*Bek.*, p. 691. 11–13).

[2] 'Darümb hat ein iglicher Christen sein Leben lang gnug zu lernen und zu uben an der Taufe; denn er hat immerdar zu schaffen, daß er festiglich gläube, was sie zusagt und bringet: Überwindung des Teufels und Tods, Vergebung der Sunde, Gottes Gnade, den ganzen Christum und heiligen Geist mit seinen Gaben' (*Bek.*, p. 699. 27–34).

[3] See, in particular, Rom. vi.

welcome the indwelling God.[1] The complete removal of sin and divinization of the soul belong to the rewards of the after life.[2] If, here below, we hope securely for the latter, it is solely because Christ's unique righteousness is imputed to us.

Thus, as far as the recipient is concerned, the Baptismal effects or benefits are felt as a consoling psychological transformation—an awakening of the Christian conscience of despair and faith—a new awareness that he has obtained God's unmerited favour and exclusive help in fulfilling the obligation to die to self and to live to Christ.

Luther's own description of these experienced benefits excludes the precise language of Scholastic theology, the clear distinctions and formal definitions of entitative and operative habits, actual and sanctifying grace, original and personal sin.[3] In his view, these distinctions threaten to substitute the false self-righteousness of men for the true imputed righteousness of Christ.[4] Between Heaven and Hell there are only ungrateful sinners and a merciful sinless God.

We cannot ignore these aspects of Luther's theology when reading his Catechism. They are absolutely essential to a fuller understanding of his description of the benefits of the Sacraments and their relation to the Law-Gospel work of the Word. Moreover, they help us to follow the next point, namely Luther's reason for rejecting Penance as a Sacrament distinct from Baptism.

Since Baptism does not remove sinfulness, our personal sins, distinct from original sin,[5] committed after Baptism, cannot be described as a falling out of a sinless state of grace. They are, rather, the visible manifestations and proof of our enduring sinfulness—of our wilful refusal of God's favour, our turning away from the new Adam to live with the old one. In these circumstances, Penance—confession, contrition, and satisfaction for

[1] See above, p. 28, n. 2.
[2] See p. 95, n. 1; also Appendix II.
[3] Luther, in point of fact, distinguishes between personal and original sin in his *Sermon on Two Kinds of Righteousness* (see above, p. 91, n. 1). But this personal sin is inseparable from his notion of enduring sinfulness; in this sense that the Christian, in sinning after Baptism, is not falling out of a state of sanctifying grace but merely allowing the old Adam—our nature, in no way made sinless by Baptismal graces—to take over.
[4] See his *post scriptum* to Melanchthon's letter, May 1531, *WAB*, vi. 99–100.
[5] See Appendix IV; also section B of chapter VI.

our sins—is necessarily called a *Widergang und Zutreten zur Taufe*. Thus Luther is perfectly consistent with the Law-Gospel dualism of his theology when he declares that the belief and practice of Penance is comprehended in Baptism:

... Here you see that Baptism, both in its power [*Kraft*] and signification [*Deutunge*], comprehends also the third Sacrament, which has been called repentance [*Buße* or Penance] as it is really [*eigentlich*] nothing else than Baptism. For what else is repentance [*Buße*] but an earnest attack upon the old man [*that his lusts be restrained*] and entering upon a new life? Therefore if you live in repentance you walk in Baptism, which not only signifies such a new life, but also produces, begins, and exercises it. For therein are given grace, the spirit, and power to suppress [*unterdrücken*] the old man, so that the new man may come forth and become strong.[1]

Now keeping in mind what we said in the previous chapters, we might add that this earnest attack—'den Alten Menschen mit Ernst angreifen'—springs exclusively from the work of the Word, from Christ moving the soul of the believer; the recipient of the Sacrament, on no account, can be considered, in his struggle against sin, the subject of any meritorious act or striving after personal grace: 'Thus we see plainly that there is here no work done by us but a treasure which He gives us, and which faith apprehends . . .'[2]

Similarly,[3] Luther describes the effects and benefits of the Lord's Supper. Christ's words[4] pronounced over the bread and wine signify and effect the real presence of His Body and Blood.[5]

[1] *B.C.*, p. 209, col. 2. For the German text see p. 115, n. 2.

[2] To the objection that Baptism is itself a work, Luther replies that this Sacrament is not our work but God's work demanding heartfelt faith; then he adds the words which we have quoted above in English 'Also siehest Du klar, daß da kein Werk ist, von uns getan, sondern ein Schatz, den er uns gibt und der Glaube ergreifet, so ...' (*Bek.*, p. 698. 22–30).

[3] 'Wie wir von der heiligen Taufe gehöret haben, müssen wir von dem andern Sakrament auch reden, nämlich die drei Stück: was es sei, was es nutze und wer es empfahen soll' (*Bek.*, pp. 707–8. 49–50, 1–3).

[4] 'Dominus noster Jesus Christus, in qua nocte tradebatur, accepit panem et gratias agens fregit et dixit: "Accipite et manducate. Hoc est corpus meum, quod pro vobis tradetur. Hoc facite in meam commemorationem." '

' Similiter et calicem, postquam coenavit, dicens: "Hic calix novum testamentum est in meo sanguine. Hoc facite, quotiescumque biberitis, in meam commemorationem" ' (see *Bek.*, p. 708. 16–30. See also 1 Cor. xi. 23–25; Matt. xxvi. 26–28; Mark xiv. 22–24; Luke xxii. 19–20.)

[5] Luther reiterates Saint Augustine's formula 'Accedat verbum ad elementum . . . etc.' (see *Bek.*, p. 709. 37–39) and says that as long as Christ's words remain with the bread and wine [the element] they are the body and blood of Christ (see

This Sacrament, properly received with evangelical faith,[1] 'strengthens the conscience',[2] bestows 'that treasure by which we obtain forgiveness of sins',[3] nourishes the soul and fortifies the new man,[4] regulates the new life so that 'it increase and progress',[5] and provides us with the grace of God and the Spirit with all His gifts, protection, shelter, and power against death and the devil and all misfortunes.[6] Also, we know, if not from the Fourth Part of the Catechism, at least from one of Luther's early sermons, that it 'signifies or effects' the *gemeynschafft aller heyligen*—our fellowship and incorporation with Christ and all His saints.[7]

B.C., p. 210, col. 2) 'Das Wort muß das Element zum Sakrament machen, wo nicht, so bleibt's ein lauter Element ...' (*Bek.*, p. 709. 42–44). Again further on: '... wenn Du das Wort davon tuest oder ohn Wort ansiehest, so hast Du nichts denn lauter Brot und Wein, wenn sie aber dabei bleiben, wie sie sollen und müssen, so ist's lauts derselbigen wahrhaftig Christus' Leib und Blut. Denn wie Christus' Mund redet und spricht, also ist es, als der nicht liegen noch triegen kann' (*Bek.*, p. 710. 16–23). We see clearly, from this passage, that Luther believes as much in the 'real presence' as Roman Catholics do; what he rejects, we shall see in the sixth chapter, is the sacrificial character of the Sacrament (i.e. the Mass) and the claim that the ordained priest effects the real presence of Christ in the elements by virtue of his sacerdotal character. These things, he misunderstands to be human works replacing God's Word and gifts (see chapter VI).

   [1] 'Nu ist je das ganze Evangelion und der Artikel des Glaubens: "Ich gläube eine heilige christliche Kirche, Vergebung der Sunde" etc. durch das Wort in dies Sakrament [Abendmahl] gesteckt und uns furgelegt' (*Bek.*, pp. 713–14. 46–48 and 1–3).

   [2] 'Aus dem Wort kannst Du Dein Gewissen stärken ...' (*Bek.*, p. 710. 2–3).

   [3] '... darümb gehen wir zum Sakrament [Abendmahl], daß wir da empfahen solchen Schatz, durch und in dem wir Vergebunge der Sunde überkommen' (*Bek.*, p. 711. 39–42). Luther is fond of using the word *Schatz* to describe the benefits of the Sacraments.

   [4] 'Darümb heißet es wohl ein Speise der Seelen, die den neuen Menschen nähret und stärkt' (*Bek.*, p. 712. 11–13).

   [5] 'Darümb ist es gegeben zur täglichen Weide und Futterung, daß sich der Glaube erhole und stärke, daß er in solchem Kampf nicht zurückfalle, sondern immer je stärker und stärker werde. Denn das neue Leben soll also getan sein, daß es stets zunehme und fortfahre' (*Bek.*, p. 712. 20–26).

   [6] 'Denn hie sollt Du im Sakrament empfahen aus Christus' Mund Vergebung der Sunde, welche bei sich hat und mit sich bringet Gottes Gnade und Geist mit alle seinen Gaben, Schutz, Schirm und Gewalt wider Tod und Teufel und alles Unglück' (*Bek.*, pp. 721–2. 46–48 and 1–4).

   [7] 'Die bedeutung odder das werck disses sacraments [The Lord's Supper] ist gemeynschafft aller heyligen ... Alsso ist diss sacrament yn brott und weyn empfahen nit anders dan eyn gewiß tzeychen empfahen disser gemeynschafft und eyn leybung mit Christo und allen heyligen ...' [*Ein Sermon von dem hochwürdigen Sakrament des heiligen wahren Leichnams Christi und von den Bruderschaften (1519)*, *W.A.* ii. 743. 7–8, 20). See also Regin Prenter, 'The Lord's Supper', in *More About Luther*, ii. 105.

Again the question arises: how are these benefits to be visualized with respect to the recipient himself? Granted, he receives Christ and enters into a new fellowship with Him, and obtains grace and forgiveness of sin; but how does all this affect him personally? Does he acquire any inner qualitative perfections of the soul which, as it were, divinize and prepare him to welcome and co-operate with the indwelling God? What is the special grace of this Sacrament as distinct from the permanent effects of Baptism and the special graces of Penance? Does the recipient, already in good faith, undergo, not just experience, a real intensification of personal grace and spiritual betterment in his daily struggling and striving for union with Christ?

In the Catechism, Luther does not ask these questions; they are not the purpose of that work; but bearing in mind the basic principles of his understanding of 'faith without works', we are unable to recognize the terms 'grace', 'gifts of the Holy Ghost', 'power', 'shelter', and 'perfection' as designating objective acquisitions of human nature. That is to say, we cannot conceive of these benefits as divinely imparted supernatural qualities really and personally possessed by the baptized sinner.

Perhaps Luther wishes this Sacrament, like Penance, to be comprehended in the work of Baptism. He does not say so in the Catechism,[1] but the following passage recalls to us the ever-efficacious dynamic symbolism of Baptism:

> For by Baptism we are first born anew; but (as we said before) there still remains besides, the old vicious nature of flesh and blood[2] in man, and there are so many hindrances and temptations of the devil and of the world. . . . Therefore it [the Lord's Supper] is given for a daily pasture and sustenance, that faith may refresh and strengthen itself so as not to fall back in such a battle, but become ever stronger and stronger. For the new life must be so regulated that it continually increase and progress.[3]

In this light, the Lord's Supper is more a pledge or a token[4] of grace than a means to it; like Penance, it promises and symbolizes what Christ has given and is continuously giving to the

[1] In the *De captivitate Babylonica*, Luther, while denying that there are 'seven Sacraments', says: '. . . quanquam, si usu scripturae loqui velim, non nisi unum sacramentum habeam et tria signa sacramentalia . . .' (*W.A.* vi. 501. 37–38).

[2] See p. 95, n. 1.

[3] *B.C.*, p. 211, col. 1.

[4] '. . . als ein gewiß Pfand und Zeichen ...' (*Bek.*, p. 712. 2).

baptized. If, besides the real presence in the bread and wine, there is an effect produced at all on the recipient, distinct from Baptism, it is expressed better in psychological than metaphysical language.

Each time the Christian receives the Lord's Supper, for instance, he is reminded of being aided anew by Christ in the battle of the Word against sinful self, the world, and the devil. In this sense, we can speak of the Sacrament as producing a special increase of grace: the recipient becomes more keenly aware of his evangelical relationship to Christ; he experiences an intensification of his faith, and an outpouring of his heart to the indwelling spirit; in this way, he obtains 'new power and refreshment'.[1] In other words, the Lord's Supper recalls to him and renews in him the promises and effects of Baptism. But enough on the 'benefits' of the Sacraments, now we shall consider how Luther answers the third question: who are the recipients of these Sacraments?

This aspect of his sacramentalism involves the dependence of Baptism and the Lord's Supper on the faith of the recipient. From his earlier sermons (between 1518-19)[2] and indeed from several passages in the *Large Catechism*[3] we gather that he regards these Sacraments as inefficacious and meaningless if not received with evangelical faith. Those who truly enjoy the effects and benefits are those who believe.[4]

Yet, in the same Catechism, he declares the effect of infant Baptism and the real presence of the Lord's Supper to be realized solely by virtue of the Word and the divine command, and not because of the minister's intentions or the qualifications of the recipient; in both instances, he is attacking the contrary teachings then rampant—the Anabaptists' rejection of the validity of infant Baptism and the denial of the real presence by Karlstadt and Zwingli.[5]

[1] '... daß er hie [The Lord's Supper] neue Kraft und Labsal hole ...' (*Bek.*, p. 712. 38–39).

[2] *Ein Sermon von dem Sakrament der Buße* (1519) (*W.A.* ii. 709). *Ein Sermon von dem heiligen hochwürdigen Sakrament der Taufe* (1519) *W.A.* ii. 724). *Ein Sermon von dem hochwürdigen Sakrament des heiligen wahren Leichnams Christi und von den Brüderschaften* (1519) (*W.A.* ii. 738). These three sermons taken together form the first complete exposition of Luther's doctrine of the sacraments published in German.

[3] See the following juxtaposition of texts; p. 123, nn. 1, 2, and 3.

[4] See p. 123, n. 1.

[5] See p. 133, n. 5.

The paradoxical contrast of his sayings about the necessity and non-necessity of faith in the Sacraments stands out in the following juxtaposition of texts. First of all on the necessity of faith:

... since we have learned the great benefit [*Nutz*] and power [*Kraft*] of Baptism, let us see further who is the person that receives what Baptism gives and profits. This is again most beautifully and clearly expressed in the words: *He that believeth and is baptized shall be saved.* That is faith alone makes the person worthy to receive profitably the saving [*heilsame*], divine water. For since these blessings are here presented [*furgetragen*] and promised [*verheißen*] in the words and with the water, they cannot be received in any other way than by believing them with the heart [*von Herzen gläuben*]. Without faith it profits nothing, notwithstanding it is in itself a divine superabundant treasure [*überschwänglicher Schatz*].[1]

Likewise for the Lord's Supper:

... Now we must also see who is the person that receives this power and benefit. That is answered briefly, as we said above of Baptism, and often elsewhere: whoever believes it has what the words declare and bring [*wie die Wort lauten und was sie bringen*].... For they are not spoken or proclaimed [*verkündigt*] to stone and wood.... And because He offers and promises forgiveness of sin it cannot be received otherwise than by faith [*... kann es nicht anders denn durch den Glauben empfangen werden*].[2]

Now secondly when faith is wanting:

Further, we say that we are not so much concerned [*daß uns nicht die größte Macht daran liegt*] to know whether the person baptized believes or not; for on that account Baptism does not become invalid [*unrecht*]; but everything depends [*liegt*] on the Word and Command of God ... Baptism is valid [*recht*], even though faith be wanting [*... obschön der Glaube nicht dazu kömmpt*]. For my faith does not make Baptism, but receives it. Now, Baptism does not become invalid even though it be wrongly received or employed; since it is not bound [*gebunden ist*] to our faith, but to the Word.[3]

And again for the Lord's Supper:

... the chief point is the Word and ordinance or command of God.... Just as the Ten Commandments, the Lord's Prayer, and

---

[1] *B.C.*, p. 207, col. 1; for the German text, see *Bek.*, p. 697. 27–42.
[2] *B.C.*, pp. 211–12; for the German text, see *Bek.*, p. 714. 19–30.
[3] *B.C.*, p. 208, col. 1; for the German text, see *Bek.*, p. 701. 30–47.

the Creed retain their nature and worth [*bleiben in ihrem Wesen und Wirden*], although you never keep, pray or believe them, so also does this venerable Sacrament remain undisturbed [*unverrückt*], so that nothing is detracted [*ihm nicht abgebrochen*] or taken from it, even though we employ and dispense it unworthily [*unwirdig brauchen und handeln*].[1]

And a few paragraphs on, he goes so far as to say:

Even though a knave [*ein Bube*] takes or distributes [*gibt*] the Sacrament, he receives [*nimmpt*] the true body and blood of Christ, just as truly as he who [receives or] administers it in the most worthy manner [*allerwirdigst*]. For it is not founded [*gegründet*] upon the holiness of men, but upon the Word of God.[2]

We think it would be unfair to Luther to accuse him, in this context, of self-contradiction. To argue, as he does, 'chiefly' in terms of the efficacy of the Word and command, is perfectly consistent with his evangelical theology. Besides, the conviction and anger with which he affirms his doctrine and denounces the 'blasphemers' and 'traducers'[3] of the Sacrament, make it quite plain that he does not wish to be misunderstood on this vital point. We should not attempt to hold him to negative and affirmative propositions of a purely dialectical order.

For all practical purposes, what he seems to be saying is this: the water joined to the Word constitutes the essence or nature of Baptism, regardless of the worth of the minister or the recipient; similarly, the bread and wine, joined to the Word, become the Body and Blood of Christ. In this sense, the two Sacraments are not regarded as mere signs or symbols but rather as having, *per essentiam*, the power of effecting what they signify. If a Sacrament fails to produce its effect on this or that recipient, it is not because God's Word or ordinance is deficient, but rather because the recipient does not receive it properly.[4] Since an infant cannot consciously oppose the work of the Gospel, there

---

[1] *B.C.*, p. 211, col. 1; for the German text, see *Bek.*, pp. 708–9. 37–48 and 1–2.

[2] *B.C.*, p. 211, col. 1; for the German text, see *Bek.*, p. 710. 39–45.

[3] See above, p. 113, n †.

[4] We make this statement with certain reservations. We know from the *De servo arbitrio* that, for Luther, no human obstacle can stop the effect of the divine Will. That is, if God so wills, His Sacrament can produce its effect despite the attitude of the recipient, and in such a way that man's freedom cannot oppose the power of the Word and the salutary work of grace. In this sense, we see no essential difference between infant Baptism and adult Baptism; the Sacrament remains exclusively the work of the Word.

is no reason why infant Baptism should be discontinued: 'We bring the child in the conviction and hope that it believes, and we pray that God may grant it faith; but we do not baptize it upon that, but solely upon the command of God . . .'[1] And likewise for the Lord's Supper, the words of Christ, pronounced over the bread and wine, effect the real presence of Christ even though the recipient be unworthy and will not profit by it.[2]

Catholic commentators on Luther's theology of the Sacraments sometimes describe his notion of the Sacrament as a pure symbol or sign.[3] But his view, in respect to infant Baptism and the real presence, is probably much closer to the Scholastic formula *ex opere operato*[4] than is generally thought. And we say this even though Luther himself attacked vehemently this Scholastic formula as he understood it.[5]

Where Luther differs fundamentally on this score from Roman Catholic theology is not on the question of whether a Sacrament produces an effect, but rather on *what* it effects in the recipient. And this difference, as with other catechetical matters, stems from his pessimistic picture of human nature and passively experienced imputed grace.

Luther's defence, here, of the primacy of the Word and command over the qualifications of the minister and the recipient, shows how he, despite apparent, perhaps unconscious, projections of his own convictions and sentiments into his interpretation of the Bible, teaches that our Christian faith is *objectively* centred on a divinely instituted fact. The validity of infant Baptism and the effect of the real presence depend on the divine ordinance—an objectively preached external reality which no amount of unworthiness or misuse, either on the part of the

[1] 'Also tuen wir nu auch mit der Kindertaufe; das Kind tragen wir erzu der Meinung und Hoffnung, daß es gläube, und bitten, daß ihm Gott den Glauben gebe, aber darauf täufen wir's nicht, sondern allein darauf, daß Gott befohlen hat' (*Bek.*, p. 702. 44–49).

[2] 'Denn wenngleich diesen Tag ein Jüde mit Schalkheit und bösem Fursatz erzukäme und wir ihn mit ganzem Ernst täufen, sollen wir nichts deste weniger sagen, daß die Taufe recht wäre. Denn da ist das Wasser sampt Gottes Wort, ob er sie gleich nicht empfähet, wie er soll, gleich als die unwirdig zum Sakrament gehen, das rechte Sakrament empfahen, ob sie gleich nicht gläuben' (*Bek.*, pp. 701–2. 47–49 and 1–7).

[3] See B. Leeming, *Principles of Sacramental Theology*, p. 14.

[4] See Appendix V, where we discuss, at some length, Luther's understanding of the formula *ex opere operato*.

[5] Ibid.

minister or the recipient, can change.[1] In support of this view, he even cites the Scholastic dictum: 'Abusus non tollit sed confirmat substantiam'.[2] Thus we see that the Reformer, however much he may be responsible for subjectivism in religion, is not, on this fundamental point, a subjectivist.

His objectivity, in this respect, throws some light on his statements in the *De captivitate Babylonica* to the effect that we receive what we believe to be given in the Sacrament regardless of what the minister does or does not do, even though he acts through dissimulation or in open mockery.[3] The Council of Trent was very disconcerted over such statements; the fathers of the Council thought that Luther rejected the principle that the minister must 'intend to do at least what the Church does'.[4] From his Catechism remarks, however, it seems that, basically, he is trying to maintain the objective value of the Sacrament and keep the power of God's Word and command totally independent of human works. In Luther's mind, perhaps, this position is not meant to exclude, absolutely speaking, the intention to do at least what the Church does.

Concerning the sacerdotal role of the minister and the sacrificial and expiatory character of the Lord's Supper, Luther does not mention them in his Catechism.[5]

Finally, we should conclude our analysis of the Fourth and Fifth Parts of the Catechism by explaining further how Luther presents the Sacraments as precepts as well as promises: to administer and receive the Sacraments is as much a Christian duty and obligation as belief in the articles of the Creed, the Lord's Prayer, and obedience to the Ten Commandments.

No man has spun the Ten Commandments, the Creed and the Lord's Prayer out of his head, but they are revealed and given by God Himself, so also I can boast that Baptism is no human trifle, but

---

[1] Against the *neuen Geister* (see Chapter VI, p. 133, n. 5) Luther defends the external character of the Word and the Sacrament: 'Nu sind sie so toll, daß sie vonander scheiden den Glauben und das Ding, daran der Glaube haftet und gebunden ist, ob es gleich äußerlich ist. Ja, es soll und muß äußerlich sein, daß man's mit Sinnen fassen und begreifen und dadurch ins Herz bringen könne, wie denn das ganze Evangelion ein äußerliche mündliche Predigt ist. Summa, was Gott in uns tuet und wirket, will er durch solch äußerliche Ordnung wirken' (*Bek.*, p. 697. 1–10).

[2] *Bek.*, p. 703. 26–27.

[3] See Leeming, op. cit., pp. 450–2.

[4] Ibid., pp. 446, 474, 482–5.   [5] See above, p. 119, n. 5.

instituted by God Himself, moreover, that it is solemnly and strictly
commanded, that we must be baptized or we cannot be saved. . . .[1]

Also, in connexion with the partaking of the Lord's Supper, he
says that we must 'render satisfaction and obedience to this
commandment'.[2] And the fact that it is God's commandment
should be sufficient incentive for keeping it without mere compulsion or human commandments.[3]

Moreover, comparable to the Decalogue precepts, these New
Testament commandments are accompanied by the divine sanctions, the threats and promises,[4] which show us how important
and pleasing they are to God. And our obedience to them is a
higher, holier, and nobler work than the most difficult works of
monks and nuns.[5] These arguments are identical to those which
Luther develops in the Decalogue section of the Catechism (see
above, Chapter IV).

Again, in connexion with the precept[6] to partake, from time

[1] *B.C.*, p. 205, col. 1; for the German text, see *Bek.*, p. 692. 1–9.

[2] 'Willt Du aber ein Christen sein, so mußt Du je zuweilen diesem Gepot
genugtuen und gehorchen' (*Bek.*, p. 718. 1–3).

[3] Luther wishes to exclude from the spontaneity of the Christian life the compulsion and fear of human commandments or Papal canons which, in his mind,
force people to receive the sacraments without inclination, love or respect for
God's commandments. Thus he writes: 'Und zwar, weil wir uns so frembde dazu
stellen, spüret man wohl, was wir fur Christen in dem Bapstumb gewesen sind,
als die aus lautern Zwang und Furcht menschlichs Gepots sind hingangen ohn
Lust und Liebe und Christus' Gepot nie angesehen. Wir aber zwingen noch
dringen niemand, darf's uns auch niemand zu Dienst oder Gefallen tuen. Das soll
Dich aber reizen und selbs zwingen, daß er's haben will und ihm gefället. Menschen soll man sich wider zum Glauben noch irgend einem guten Werk nötigen
lassen' (*Bek.*, p. 718. 8–21).

[4] First of all the promise: 'Zum andern ist über das Gepot auch eine Ver-
heißunge, wie auch oben gehöret, die uns aufs allerstärkiste reizen und treiben
soll. Denn da stehen die freundliche, liebliche Wort: ..."Das ist mein Blut fur
Euch vergossen zur Vergebunge der Sunden" ' (*Bek.*, p. 720. 42–48). The idea of
the accompanying threat, he develops further on: 'Das ist wohl wahr, daß, die es
verachten und unchristlich leben, nehmen's ihn zu Schaden und Verdammnis'
(ibid., p. 721. 36–38).

[5] '... es viel höher ist denn kein Werk, von einem Menschen oder Heiligen
getan [He is speaking of Baptism]. Denn was kann man fur Werk größer machen
denn Gottes Werk' (*Bek.*, p. 693. 3–6)? He continues on to explain how much
finer and nobler Baptism is to all the splendid works of the Carthusians.

[6] We should note how Luther draws an analogy between God's Gospel commandment to administer the Sacraments and the Fourth Commandment of the
Decalogue: 'Darümb lehren wir allezeit, man solle die Sakrament und alle äußerlich Ding, so Gott ordnet und einsetzet, nicht ansehen nach der groben äußer-
lichen Larven, wie man die Schalen von der Nuß siehet, sondern wie Gottes Wort
darein geschlossen ist. Denn also reden wir auch von Vater und Mutterstand und

to time, of the Lord's Supper, he states the functional role of the
commandment as a mirror of sinful self: 'This commandment
ought ever to move you to examine yourself and to think: see
what a Christian I am'.[1]

In addition, our attitude and response to the Sacrament as
commandment depends, psychologically, on our moral distress,
our consciously acknowledged sinfulness—what we have been
calling all along the act of despairing in self. It is for this that
the commandment has been given:

> Thus you have, on the part of God, both the command [*Gebot*]
> and the promise [*Verheißung*] of the Lord Jesus Christ. Besides this, on
> your part, your own distress which is about your neck and because
> of which this command [*Gebieten*], invitation [*Locken*] and promise
> [*Verheißen*] are given [*geschicht*], ought to impel you [to receive the
> Lord's Supper]. For He Himself says: 'They that be whole need not a
> physician, but they that be sick' [Matt. ix. 12]; that is those who be
> weary [*müheselig*] and heavy-laden [*beschweret*] with their sins, with
> the fear of death, temptations of the flesh [*Anfechtung des Fleischs*] and
> of the devil. If, therefore, you are heavy-laden and feel your weak-
> ness, then go joyfully to this Sacrament and obtain refreshment, con-
> solation and strength [*und laße Dich erquicken, trösten und stärken*].[2]

In this passage, once again, we see the psychological pattern of
moving from a state of moral distress to one of consolation.
Indeed, the implication is that the more intensely we experience
our distress, the more we feel the need for the Sacrament, and
thus the more efficacious it becomes. Our distress and despair,
as well as God's commandment, prepares and 'impels' us to
embrace Christ's Sacrament. The Sacrament, however, unlike
the Decalogue precepts, contains the grace and the means, as
we have just seen, of fulfilling the Law—the Old Testament and
New Testament Commandments.

Here, then, we have the essentials of Luther's sacramenta-

---

weltlicher Oberkeit ...' (*Bek.*, 694. 37–44). He says further that if we are obedient
to our father it is because of God's commandment which is the chain of gold about
his neck and the crown upon his head; 'Das Gepot [the Fourth Commandment]
... ist die gülden Ketten, so er am Hals trägt, ja die Krone auf seinem Häupt, die
mir anzeigt, wie und warümb man dies Fleisch und Blut ehren soll' (*Bek.*, p. 695.
4–8).
[1] 'Denn solch Gepot sollt' Dich je bewegen, in Dich selbs zu schlagen und zu
denken: Siehe, was bin ich fur ein Christen? Wäre ich's, so würde ich mich je ein
wenig sehnen nach dem, das mein Herr befohlen hat zu tuen' (*Bek.*, p. 718. 3–8).
[2] *B.C.*, p. 214, col. 1. For the German text, see *Bek.*, p. 722. 8–20.

lism. Like the previous parts, they are founded on his basic Law-Gospel position—man, with or without grace, can do nothing meritorious;[1] he has nothing to give to God but his sinfulness; and God, by His Word, accomplishes all things, and bestows on men all that is pleasing in His sight.

It is the Word of God that institutes and commands the Sacrament, effects the benefits of the Sacraments, and gives 'profitable' faith to the recipient of the Sacraments. The Sacraments, moreover, are precepts as well as promises, not unlike the Decalogue precepts. And the whole sacramental economy symbolizes, signifies, and produces the Law-Gospel dualism of personal salvation—the act of despairing in self and trusting in God—with all that it implies concerning the force and function of the Law, the passive experience of faith and grace, and the imputative character of righteousness.

Our study of the last two parts of the Catechism, therefore, far from being a digression from our subject proper, contributes further evidence to our contention that the Law-Gospel relation of the Christian life must be described, not defined, exclusively according to the Word commanding and fulfilling the justification, redemption, and sanctification of sinners, and inasmuch as it is part of man's personal experience of self and of God.

Throughout our treatment of the Catechism, we have tended to dampen the personal tone and emotional content of Luther's language. Yet it rings out in every word and line, and underlines the importance of his own religious experience or *crise de conscience* in the formulation and development of his Law-Gospel doctrine of faith without works. Before summing up our findings, we should complete our picture of Luther's confessional writings by a study of the *Smalcald Articles*.

---

[1] 'All the rest are works and fruits which are produced afterwards spontaneously. These do not reform a man's character; rather, they are the things a man does after he has been regenerated by faith in God's faithfulness' (*Pagan Servitude* (De captivitate Babylonica), in *Reformation Writings of Martin Luther*, i. 284).

VI

THE *SMALCALD ARTICLES*

A. *Historical setting and plan*

THE *Smalcald Articles* are meant, by Luther, to be as much of a confessional testimony of fundamental doctrine as his Catechisms.[1] Yet, because of the historical setting, they are not planned in the same manner[2] or for the same immediate purpose.

Pope Paul III, through his Bull, *Ad dominici gregis*, summoned a general council which was supposed to be held in Mantua, on 23 May 1537.[3] This council was to bring about, among other things, 'the utter extirpation of the poisonous, pestilential Lutheran heresy'.[4] The papal Legate, Peter-Paul Vergerio, in a personal interview with Luther, in Wittenberg, invited the latter to attend the proposed council.

The Elector, John Frederick, Duke of Saxony, favoured attending the council, but he thought it necessary to prepare for it with proper confessional documents. He therefore requested the Reformer to draw up a series of articles which could serve as a basis for discussion at the council sessions. The Elector wanted Luther to single out those issues where concessions were out of the question, and those where conciliation or compromise might be possible.[5]

Luther set about the task in the last days of 1536 and finished[6]

[1] In his preface to these articles, Luther writes: 'So hab ich gleichwohl diese Artikel indes wollen durch offentlichen Druck an den Tag geben, ob ich ja ehe sterben sollt, denn ein Concilium würde ... damit die, so nach mir leben und bleiben werden, mein Zeugnis und Bekenntnis haben vorzuwenden über das Bekenntnis, das ich zuvor hab lassen ausgehen ...' (Luther is referring here to his work *Von Abendmahl Christi Bekenntnis*, 1528, the Third Part of which also appeared separately as the *Bekenntnis der Artikel des Glaubens*; see *Bek.*, p. 409. 14–23).

[2] The first eight articles of Part III are planned, like the Catechism (see below, p. 134), according to the Law-Gospel relation.

[3] The council was postponed until 1545 and met in Trent.

[4] W. D. Allbeck, op. cit., p. 187.

[5] One finds very little, if anything, in the *Smalcald Articles* that can be considered a compromise or a concession.

[6] The original document was prepared in German. Luther had finished Parts I and II and article 3 of Part III before he became ill, 18 Dec. The rest, apparently,

a brief series of articles which André Jundt claims rightly, are divided as follows:

(i)   Articles which are not disputed.[1]
(ii) Articles about which discussion is inadmissible.[2]
(iii) Articles[3] concerning which it is possible to enter into negotiations with the most reasonable and religious of the Romans, not by way of making concessions but in order to enlighten them on the doctrines of the Reformation.[4]

At the request of the Elector, these articles were submitted by Luther to his Wittenberg colleagues[5] who, after some discussion and modification, approved them.[6] Later, February 8, 1537, the Elector, hoping to strengthen the Smalcald League of Lutheran princes and theologians, then assembled at Smalcald to discuss the political and religious significance of the proposed Mantua council, tried to get the members to accept Luther's articles. It was believed, however, unnecessary to bring these articles up for discussion since they already had the *Confession of Augsburg* and the *Wittenberg Concord*.[7] These articles were not officially

he dictated to two persons since the original manuscript shows two hand writings (see Allbeck, op. cit., p. 189).

[1] At the end of the First Part, Luther says: 'Diese Artikel [four in number, see below] sind in keinem Zank noch Streit, weil wir zu beiden Teilen dieselbigen [gläuben und] bekennen' (*Bek.*, p. 415. 1–3).

[2] Concerning the first or chief article of Part II, Luther writes: 'Von diesem Artikel kann man nichts weichen oder nachgeben' (*Bek.*, p. 415. 21–22); likewise for the other three articles which follow.

[3] In his introduction to the Third Part, Luther simply remarks on the possibility of discussing these articles with *gelehrten, vernunftigen* (Bek., p. 433. 5–7). However, the first eight articles are as much an essential part of his evangelical doctrine as the chief article of Part II. He is as adamant and uncompromising about these articles as about the preceding ones (see below).

[4] See *L.S.* ii. 9.

[5] John Agricola, George Spalatin, Nicholas von Amsdorf, together with Melanchthon, Bugenhagen, Jonas, and Cruciger (see Allbeck, op. cit., p. 189).

[6] A copy of the modified document, drawn up by Spalatin, was signed by them and submitted to the Elector on 3 Jan. 1537 (see Allbeck, op. cit., p. 189).

[7] 'The *Wittenberg Concord* of 1536 was a statement of Lutheran agreement, especially on the Lord's Supper. It was an attempt to preserve unity between Lutherans of Northern Germany and those in the south under Zwinglian influence' (ibid.). Another reason for not wishing to consider Luther's articles was the fear of disunity and disagreement over his position on the real presence in the Lord's Supper. The Reformer refused, persistently, to give in on this point and reaffirmed his belief in the real presence in article 6, Part III, of the *Smalcald Articles*.

sanctioned by the Smalcald Assembly and the members agreed, after mature deliberation, to decline Paul III's invitation.

But just before the Assembly broke up, Bugenhagen, a pastor and professor at the Wittenberg theological faculty, presented the articles to a private reunion of theologians, and asked his colleagues to sign them. Forty-three theologians, acting as private individuals, and not officially, did so immediately, others followed later.

Although these articles were never officially sanctioned by the Smalcald Assembly, they are none the less called after it. They soon received wide acceptance, and were preferred to Melanchthon's irenic *variata* edition of the *Augsburg Confession* (1531), and were gradually recognized as a confessional writing, being included in the book of doctrine of Brunswick (1563), and eventually in *The Book of Concord*.

Luther himself, perhaps wrongly informed about the Smalcald proceedings, always considered his articles as officially sanctioned by the assembled princes and theologians.[1] It is as such that he offers them in his preface to the first printing of the articles in 1538.[2]

This brief historical survey helps us to see how the *Smalcald Articles* differ from the *Large Catechism*. They do not constitute an instruction booklet for children, but rather a list, with partial explanations and defence, not untainted by Luther's characteristic polemical spirit,[3] of controversial issues for theologians.

Luther always takes a strong stand in his affirmation of fundamental doctrine; and in his attacks on the Roman Church, he is never able to speak with tongue in cheek. But in this instance

---

[1] On this score Allbeck says the following: 'It is something of a puzzle why Luther wrote in the second paragraph of his preface to the articles that they were "accepted and unanimously confessed" (see following note). Two possible answers have been proposed. One suggestion is that Luther's illness, which kept him away from the sessions and in ignorance of Melanchthon's manipulations, prevented him from knowing the facts fully. The other suggestion is that since only a few theologians withheld their signatures, the dissent could be disregarded . . .' (Allbeck, op. cit., pp. 190–1).

[2] 'Demnach hab ich diese Artikel zusammenbracht und unserm Teil überantwortet. Die sind auch von den Unsern angenommen und einträchtiglich bekennet ...' (*Bek.*, p. 408. 10–12).

[3] Luther was very ill in December 1536, when working on his *Smalcald Articles*. The irritation caused by his illness may have intensified the vehemence of his attacks on what he regarded as Roman abuses; we are thinking, in particular, of his attacks on the Holy Sacrifice of the Mass (see Part II, article 2, in *Bek.*, p. 416).

the changed historical situation affords him the greatest opportunity to speak out vehemently against what he regards as the
tyranny of the Papacy and reliance on good works. Since he
first began his open revolt, and likewise since the appearance of
the *Augsburg Confession* (1530), his doctrine has met with wide-
spread success; Lutheranism is firmly entrenched in many parts
of Germany and has the support of numerous princes and theologians. There is now no call, in preparing for a council with the
Roman churchmen, to issue an irenic moderate document such
as Melanchthon's *variata* edition of the *Augsburg Confession*.[1]

At the same time, Luther sees no reason why he should give
in to his adversaries in the Protestant camp; against their
various objections, he remains immovable. Against Zwingli,
Calvin, and the Sacramentarians, he continues to teach the real
presence in the Lord's Supper;[2] against the Anabaptists, he
reaffirms the necessity of infant baptism;[3] against the Antinomians, he explains the evangelical uses of the Law and the
necessity of good works as the fruits of justification,[4] and against
the *Enthusiasten* or *Geistern*,[5] he defends the objectivity and indispensable character of the outer or oral Word.[6] All in all, we are

[1] 'Melanchthon was bitterly attacked by ultra-Lutherans for his conciliatory
attitude towards Roman Catholics and Evangelicals who did not believe that
Luther was infallible. . . . Melanchthon was only thirty-three when he prepared
the seventeen articles of the *Augsburg Confession*. He designed it as a spacious canopy
to shelter several parties with honour' (A. L. Drummond, *German Protestantism
since Luther*, pp. 17–18).

[2] See *S.A.*, Part III, art. 6.   [3] Ibid., art. 5.

[4] Ibid., arts. 2, 3, and 13.

[5] Although Luther, in the above instances, holds firm to doctrinal positions
unacceptable to the Sacramentarians, the Anabaptists, the Antinomians as well
as the *Enthusiasten*, he only mentions the latter by name in his articles. However,
as Mr. Watson explains, in the Preface to his English translation of Luther's *Commentary on Galatians*, the term 'Enthusiasten' is employed by the Reformer to
designate all groups claiming a spiritual superiority with regard to the Reformation
movement. 'Those whom Luther called Enthusiasts . . . were a very heterogeneous
crowd and by no means a united body. Most of them, it is true, belonged to the
left wing of the Reformation movement; but they were divided into numerous
sects and parties, which differed from each other as well as from Luther. . . . They
included revolutionary radicals like Münzer and those responsible for the passions
of the Peasants' Revolt, or for the excesses, ten years later, of Anabaptist Münster.
But they also included world-renouncing puritans like Carlstadt, and men of
a mystical-rational turn of mind like Schwenkfeld and Franck; and even the
Zwinglians could in certain respects be numbered among them. In view of their
obvious diversity, they had some ground for complaint when Luther lumped them
all together and dismissed them as "Schwärmer" ' (*C.G.*, p. 6).

[6] '... mündlich, äußerlich Wort ...' (see *S.A.*, Part III, art. 8).

dealing with a 'clear-cut'[1] Lutheran profession of faith on fundamental doctrine.

What these *Smalcald Articles* reveal to us, on the Law-Gospel relation, is best understood within the context of the whole. So let us begin with an outline of the contents.

The First Part, in four articles,[2] is merely a reaffirmation of the Credo, expressed in Luther's own words, already adequately expounded in the Catechisms; the Second Part is a series of four articles,[3] affirming or denying teachings and practices which he judges to be in accord with or opposed to his evangelical doctrine. Thus it begins with an urgent declaration that the chief article (*der erste und Häuptartikel*) is '... Jesus Christus, unser Gott und Herr, sei umb unser Sunde willen gestorben und umb unser Gerechtigkeit willen auferstanden ...' (Rom. iv. 26).[4] Then he proceeds to point out the following as definitely opposed to this chief article: the celebration of the Mass as a Sacrifice,[5] the intercession of saints,[6] the misuse of cloisters and chapters, and the teaching that the Pope, and not Christ, is the head of all Christendom. These are all means, in his view, of substituting the false righteousness of works for the true righteousness of Christ.

The Third Part embodies fifteen articles,[7] the first eight of which restates Luther's basic evangelical principles. They are arranged, like the Catechism articles, along the Law-Gospel,

---

[1] The *Smalcald Articles*, says Mr. Allbeck, 'are a bold clear-cut testimony of the Lutheran position in sharp distinction from that of the Roman Church. They are polemic, and incisive, carrying the battle to the enemy' (op. cit., p. 191).

[2] These are the articles of faith not disputed.

[3] These are the articles about which discussion is inadmissible.

[4] *Bek.*, p. 415. 7–9. Luther also quotes from John i. 29 and Isa. liii. 6.

[5] Luther's attack on the Mass is extremely harsh: '... die Messe im Bapsttum muß der großeste und schrecklichste Greuel sein ...' (*Bek.*, p. 416. 9–10). What he denounces so vehemently is what he thinks is a human practice or exercise based on a false concept of merit.

[6] The section on the invocation of Saints was not in the original manuscript, but appears in his printed edition (see Allbeck, op. cit., p. 197).

[7] Mr. Allbeck says that 'the fifteen articles are not in the order in which systematic theology would arrange them. They suggest the order of salvation from sin to fellowship' (ibid., p. 198). We would like to say that they do more than suggest it but that this is the order. Luther usually follows this order in his confessional writings. We have already seen it in his Catechisms, his treatise on the *Liberty of a Christian Man*, his *Sermon on Good Works*, and numerous other sermons. The order or plan according to which he arranges his treatment of positive fundamental doctrine is the dynamic experience of despair and faith.

or despair-faith, pattern of personal salvation. Article 1 asserts that man is so corrupted by original sin that he is powerless to fulfil the Law; articles 2 and 3 enlarge the problem, discussing the office of the Law, showing how it restrains sinners, reveals to them their enduring wickedness and prepares them for repentance and the transforming work of the Gospel. The latter part of article 3, and the following five articles, describe how the Gospel transforms the sinner, aids and counsels him, re-assures and consoles him, justifies and produces good works in him through the Word, by which the forgiveness of sin is preached,[1] through Baptism,[2] through the Holy Sacrament of the Altar,[3] through the powers of the keys,[4] and also through the mutual conversation and consolation of brethren.[5]

The remaining articles (9–15), except for article 13, consider more the negative implications of this Law-Gospel doctrine, condemning and rejecting such Roman practices as major excommunication,[6] Holy Orders,[7] clerical celibacy, monastic vows, reliance on good works, human authority, ordinances, and traditions as necessary means to salvation. To us, they appear as an additional enumeration of abuses opposed to the chief article of faith and the written Word. Logically speaking, they would have fitted just as well into the list of negations of the Second Part.[8] However, Luther, it appears, has separated

---

[1] *S.A.*, Part III, art. 4.

[2] Ibid., art. 5.   [3] Ibid., art. 6.   [4] Ibid., arts. 7 and 8.

[5] '. . . per mutuum colloquium et consolationem fratrum' (*Bek.*, p. 449. 12–13).

[6] Luther wanted excommunication to be merely exclusion from the Sacraments. This is what Canon Law would call minor excommunication as distinct from major excommunication, which, in the Middle Ages, deprived a Christian of all privileges, including Christian burial. It also meant that the excommunicant could be turned over to the civil authorities for punishment. Luther did not want 'to mingle secular punishments with ecclesiastical punishment' (*B.C.*, art. 9, p. 147).

[7] Luther teaches that the Church ought not to be without ministers: 'So muß ... die Kirche nicht ohn Diener bleiben' (*S.A.*, p. 458. 6–7). However, he refuses to acknowledge the need for bishops to ordain or confirm them in their office. They do not become ministers by virtue of the Bishop's consecration but in so far as they are chosen and ordained by the community of believers to preach the Word (see *An den christlichen Adel* ..., 'Die erste Maur', *W.A.* vi). For sake of unity, but not out of necessity, he is willing to let the bishops call and ordain ministers to the work of the Church: 'So mochte[n] man das umb der Liebe und Einigkeit willen, doch nicht aus Not [das] lassen gegeben sein, daß sie uns und unsere Prediger ordinierten und konfirmierten ...' (*Bek.*, p. 457. 8–10).

[8] Johannes Stier has referred to article 12 and those that follow as 'marginal' (*Luthers Glaube und Theologie in den Schmalkaldischen Artikeln*, Gütersloh, 1937, p. 54).

these articles so as to be treated 'mit gelehrten vernunftigen oder unter uns selbs' (i.e. himself or his disciples).[1]

In any event, the gist of the articles, in their essential content and purpose, is a reavowal and defence of the pure Word of God and the right use of the Sacraments.[2] Like the Catechism, it is always a question of what God has revealed, commanded, ordained, promised, and accomplished, in and through Holy Scripture, as opposed to what men have taught, commanded, ordained, promised, and accomplished through their own sinful efforts and reliance on the Law without the Gospel.

It is not the Pope, or the bishops, or the councils, or monastic observances, or fraternities, or masses, or ceremonies, or inner zeal and enthusiasm, or human works of any kind,[3] but solely the Word of God and the Sacraments, preached and believed in, which constitute the true Christian Church[4] and render its members righteous before God. 'Darumb sollen und müßen wir darauf beharren daß Gott nicht will mit uns Menschen handlen denn durch sein äußerlich Wort und Sakrament.'[5]

Within this general framework, and mindful of the primary elements involved, we wish now to examine the central articles[6] of the Third Part, on Sin, the Law, Repentance, and Confession. These articles reaffirm and make more explicit the Law-Gospel doctrine which we observed in the *Large Catechism*.

---

[1] *Bek.*, p. 433. 7–8.

[2] '... denn unser Kirchen sind nu durch Gottes Gnaden mit dem reinen Wort und rechtem Brauch der Sakrament ... erleucht und beschickt' (*Bek.*, p. 411. 20–24).

[3] '... welchs alles [the Roman Mass and all abuses attached to it] nicht zu leiden ist [so] und auch nicht allein ohn Not, ungepoten, sondern zuwider ist dem ersten Artikel; denn Christus' Verdienst nicht durch unser Werk oder Pfenning, sondern durch den Glauben aus Gnaden erlanget wird ohn alles Geld und Verdienst, nicht durchs Bapsts Gewalt, sondern durch die Predigt oder Gottes Wort furgetragen' (*Bek.*, p. 424. 3–9). Here Luther is speaking only of the Roman Mass and abuses stemming from it; but these words apply equally well to the 'Roman abuses' which he singles out in the subsequent articles.

[4] See *S.A.*, Part III, art. 12.

[5] *Bek.*, pp. 455–6. 1–3.

[6] In our preceding chapters we dealt, at length, with the transforming work of the Word and the Sacraments; also, indirectly with Luther's attacks on Roman abuses, inasmuch as they enlightened us on the Law-Gospel relation. On these matters, we quoted amply from the *Smalcald Articles*, in our reference notes, to clarify and substantiate his catechetical exposition of the main points. They tallied with the doctrine of the *Large Catechism*. It would therefore be superfluous here to undertake an analysis of each single article. We are limiting ourselves to those articles which show best the Law-Gospel relation.

B. *Man's sinfulness*

Relying, as always, on Saint Paul, Rom. v. 11,[1] he restates his basic position on original sin—what he calls *Erbsunde* or *Häuptsunde*, originating from Adam's first disobedience.[2] The fruits of this sin, he tells us, are all the evil deeds which are forbidden in the Ten Commandments;[3] and it is so deep a corruption of nature—'so gar tief bose Verderbung der Natur'—that no reason can understand it, but must be believed from the revelation of Scriptures.[4] He therefore concludes that it is nothing but error and blindness to teach, as the *Sophisten*[5] do, that the natural powers of man have remained entire and incorrupt, that human nature has a right reason and good will, that man is free to do good and avoid evil; and conversely, that by his natural powers he can keep God's Commandments, and love God above all else, that if man does his best, God certainly grants him grace, that if one has no wicked intention to commit sin, though he may not have a sincere intention to do good, it suffices to receive the Sacrament efficaciously, and finally that the Holy Ghost with His grace is not necessary, according to Scriptures, to perform a good work.[6]

[1] See also n. 4, below.   [2] *Bek.*, pp. 433–5.

[3] *Bek.*, p. 434. 1–2: 'Solcher Sunden Fruchte sind darnach die bosen Werke, so in den zehen Geboten verboten sind ...' Notice here how the knowledge of sinfulness or original sin is related to the Ten Commandments, see below.

[4] Luther also cites: Ps. li. 5; Rom. v. 12; Exod. xxxiii. 3; Gen. xxxvii.

[5] The Nominalist Scholastics.

[6] 'Darumb sind das eitel Irrtum und Blindheit wider diesen Artikel, das die Schultheologen gelehrt haben:

'1. Nämlich daß nach dem ... Erbfall Adae des Menschen naturlichen Kräfte [vires naturales] sind ganz und unverderbt blieben. Und [daß] der Mensch habe von Natur eine rechte Vernunft und guten Willen, wie die Philosophi solchs lehren.

'2. Item daß der Mensch habe einen freien Willen, Guts zu tun und Boses zu lassen und widerumb Guts zu lassen und Boses zu tun.

'3. Item daß der Mensch muge [Gottes Gebot] aus naturlichen Kräften [die] alle Gebot Gottes tun und halten.

'4. Item er muge aus naturlichen Kräften Gott lieben uber alles und seinen Nächsten als sich selbs.

'5. Item wenn ein Mensch tut, soviel an ihm ist, so gibt ihm Gott gewißlich seine Gnade.

'6. Item wenn er zum Sakrament will gehen, ist nicht not ein guter Fursatz, Guts zu tun, sondern sei gnug, daß et nicht einen bosen Fursatz, Sunde zu tun, habe, so gar gut ist die Natur und das Sakrament so kräftig.

'7. Es sei nicht in der Schrift gegrundet, daß zum guten Werk vonnotten sei der heilige Geist mit seiner Gnaden' (*Bek.*, pp. 434–5).

Compare these theses with Biel's propositions quoted above in Chapter II, section A, p. 34.

Here, Luther's pessimism concerning man's moral capacity (*coram Deo*) to do good works without grace is absolute and unmitigated. In no way does it differ from his description of *peccatum originale* in his early lectures on Romans (1515–16), which we quoted above (see Chapter II, section A).

Thus twenty-one years afterwards, Luther is still teaching the same thing on fundamental doctrine. His polemics with the 'Papists', the *Schwärmerei*, and *Rottengeister*, the Zwickau and celestial prophets, the Anabaptists and the Antinomians, and his famous quarrel with Erasmus on free will, have not caused him to deviate one iota from his initial Protestant position.

Moreover, there is evidence, from the very Scholastic assertions which he is condemning, such as 'Wenn ein Mensch tut, soviel an ihm ist, so gibt ihm Gott gewißlich seine Gnade', that he is affirming his doctrine within a Pelagian Nominalist context.[1] That is to say, as we have endeavoured to explain in our second chapter,[2] he is arguing not entirely from the written Word, but also from his own experience and reaction to Pelagian practices which were, to some extent, fostered by such assertions.[3] During his own monastic days, he had tried to realize the perfect love of God and to do all that was in him possible, yet he never, for one moment, felt himself to be without one or other of the sins condemned by the Ten Commandments.[4] In this *contexte expérientiel*[5] he could very well conclude that his nature, by itself, was powerless to obtain grace and to

[1] See Gabriel Biel's Sentences listed above, p. 137, n. 6.

[2] See Chapter II, section A, pp. 32–45; especially p. 34, n. 2.

[3] On reading Biel's sentences, listed above, one is ever conscious of great stress being placed on man's moral capacity to do good unaided by grace. Now a theoretical or academic over-emphasis on this side of human nature could, in practice, encourage a semi-Pelagian, if not a downright Pelagian, approach to God. We can understand, therefore, how Luther, on the basis of a real inner experience and deep awareness of his own sinfulness, should react violently to such Nominalist assertions and reject them *en bloc*.

[4] See Luther's Autobiographical Fragment, above, Chapter I, p. 13. Also: 'I tried to live according to the Rule with all diligence, and I used to be contrite. . . . The more I tried to remedy an uncertain, weak and afflicted conscience with the traditions of men, the more each day found it more uncertain, weaker, more troubled' (*W.A.* xl (ii). 15; see G. Rupp, op. cit., p. 104).

[5] 'One thing is more and more clear from recent research: the inner personal experience of Luther, and his scholarly, theological and above all, exegetical discoveries cannot be separated' (H. Boehmer, *Der junge Junge Luther*, p. 362; see Rupp, op. cit., p. 102).

love God, and in this respect be described as totally corrupt, vitiated by Adam's fall from grace.

Indeed it is precisely because the *Sophisten* or Schoolmen, he says farther on, have not 'perceived' or recognized real sin that they teach incorrectly concerning repentance.[1] That is to say, they have not experienced the torments of a 'bruised conscience',[2] the anguish of the damned. He adds, moreover, that if their teachings are right, then Christ has died in vain since there is nothing for which Christ should have died, unless it be the body alone, the soul being considered perfectly healthy and without sin.[3]

Luther's position about the sinfulness of human nature, in so far as it is the authentic reaction of an afflicted conscience to semi-Pelagian and Pelagian practices, is by no means incompatible with Catholic interpretations of Holy Scripture, in particular Saint Paul's Epistle to the Romans. But the Reformer's 'inner personal experience',[4] in our opinion, carried him on a few steps farther: he experiences, in himself, such a corruption of nature, that he refuses to concede to man even the minimum moral goodness or power of corresponding *freely*[5] to God's promptings and blessings; thus he insists and defends, against Erasmus, an absolute notion of passive justification.[6] Likewise, he experiences the enduring quality of his own sinfulness; despite the reception of faith and grace, he continues to sin, but not in the Catholic sense of falling from a 'state of grace', but rather of falling back on self in the dynamic struggle of the new spiritual man with the old carnal man.[7] The transformation

[1] 'Unmuglich ist's gewest, daß sie [Sophisten] sollten recht von der Buße lehren, weil sie die rechten Sunde nicht erkenneten ...' (*Bek.*, p. 438. 8–10). On reading these lines, we should remember that, for Luther, the true theologian is one who knows and teaches from living and experiencing and not from reading, thinking and speculating: '. . . . vivendo, immo moriendo et damnando fit theologus, non intelligendo legendo aut speculando' (*W.A.* v. 163. 28).

[2] See G. Rupp, op. cit., Chapter V.

[3] '. . . so ist Christus vergeblich gestorben, weil kein Schaden noch Sunde im Menschen ist . . . dafur, er sterben mußte, oder wäre allein fur dem Leib, nicht fur die Seele auch gestorben, weil die Seele gesund und allein der Leib des Todes ist' (*Bek.*, p. 435. 12–16).   [4] See above, p. 138, n. 4.

[5] This negation, we feel, is unequivocally developed in his treatise, *De servo arbitrio*.

[6] In the *Smalcald Articles* Luther speaks of *passiva contritio* as contrary to *activa contritio*. In the context (see below, p. 143) they appear to be synonymous with passive and active justice.

[7] See above, Chapter V, pp. 91–95; also p. 92, n. 1.

wrought by grace remains, at best, psychological, depicted in terms of the *Anfechtung*;[1] he rejects any entitative description of the transforming work of the Word; man's sin endures deep rootedly until death. Thus the necessity of a kind of forensic or imputative righteousness.[2] But we have discussed these points in our previous chapters.

Jumping ahead to the section of article 3 on the false repentance of the Papists, and to article 8 on confession, we come across another point on sin, clearly advocated by Luther, and of equal relevance to the Law-Gospel doctrine. It is Luther's awareness of the totality of man's sinfulness as the ever-present immediate object of repentance and grace.

The true penitent takes all his sins, original or actual,[3] irrespective of their kind[4] or number, and throws them into a heap so to speak, to be condemned by the Law and pardoned

[1] '*Anfechtung* is that unremitting spiritual conflict which never ends until death, the final *Anfechtung* for which all previous temptation is a preparation. This battle comes home to the Christian in his conscience, in that ultimate and inescapable separateness of each human soul' (see G. Rupp, op. cit., p. 105). When we say that the transformation is depicted in terms of the *Anfechtung*, we mean that the sinner becomes conscious of his faith and God's blessings, of being favoured by God, when he suddenly realizes that he is engaged in battle with Christ against himself, the world and the devil. It is in this sense that he is transformed, and in this transformation Christ's righteousness is imputed to him.

[2] In the *S.A.*, Part III, art. 13, Luther shows again how we acquire a new and clean heart through faith, and how faith, renewal, and forgiveness is followed by good works. But this account cannot be interpreted to mean that we are entirely purified or cleansed from sin. For, he adds, though sin in the flesh has not altogether been removed or become dead, God will not, for Christ's sake punish or remember it. And what is imperfect or sinful, in our good works, produced by faith, God will not account it as sin or defect: 'Obwohl die Sunde im Fleisch noch nicht gar weg oder tot ist, so will er sie doch nicht rechnen noch wissen Und auf solchen Glauben, Verneuerung und Vergebung der Sunde folgen denn gute Werk, und, was an denselben auch noch sundlich oder Mangel ist, soll nicht fur Sunde oder Mangel gerechnet werden eben umb desselben Christi willen, sondern der Mensch soll ganz, beide nach der Person und seinen Werken, gerecht und heilig heißen und sein aus lauter Gnade und Barmherzigkeit in Christo uber uns ausgeschutt und ausgebreit [*effusa, expansa et amplificata*]' (*Bek.*, p. 460. 11–19). Here, Luther does not use the words 'forensic' or 'imputed' righteousness, but what he actually says, and apparently intends, amounts to a description of this kind of righteousness. In faith, we experience a renewal of the soul, we sense a newness or purity of heart, we perform good works; but the newness and purity of the heart and the goodness of our works exist, not by virtue of any real intrinsic change or worth in us, but only because Christ sheds and spreads over us and our deeds His perfect righteousness.

[3] *wirklichen Sunde* or *actualia peccata*; see *Bek.*, p. 438. 14–15.

[4] In this context, Luther has no use for the traditional distinction between mortal and venial sin.

by the Gospel as by a single stroke.[1] Thus on Gospel repentance he writes:

> This repentance is not piecemeal ... and beggarly ... like that which does penance for actual sins, nor is it uncertain like that. For it does not debate what is or is not sin, but hurls everything on a heap, and says: All in us is nothing but sin ... what is the use of ... investigating, dividing, or distinguishing a long time? For this reason, too, this contrition is not ... uncertain. For there is nothing left with which to pay for sin, but there is only a sure despairing concerning all that we are, think, speak, or do ... (*B.C.*, p. 145).[2]

Through this true repentance, the conscience is spared the torment of counting and distinguishing hidden and innumerable sins,[3] and saved from the temptation of relying on the Papists' works of active contrition, confession, and satisfaction.[4] Certitude of complete forgiveness results from an unconditional surrender to Christ crucified and resurrected for the totality of our sinfulness.[5]

This all-embracing sense of sin underlies Luther's sacramental theology and relates it to the Law-Gospel pattern of salvation, such as we saw in our previous chapter.[6] Baptism is meant not so much to remove original sin at its roots but to engage the Christian, with Christ, or the new Adam, in a life-long battle or

---

[1] See below, section C, on the Law-Gospel passage.

[2] For the German text, see *Bek.*, pp. 446-7. 19–24, 1–3.

[3] '... the enumeration of sins ought to be free to everyone, as to what he wishes to enumerate or not to enumerate' (*B.C.*, p. 146).

[4] 'Und zu solcher Buße setzten sie [Papisten] drei Teil, Reu, Beicht, Gnugtun mit solcher Vertrostung und Zusage: wo der Mensch recht reuet, beichtet, gnugtät, so hätte er damit Vergebung verdienet und die Sunde fur Gott bezahlet, weiseten so die Leute in der Buße auf Zuversicht eigener Werk ...'
Hie war kein Christus und nichts vom Glauben gedacht, sondern man hoffete, mit eigenen Werken die Sunde fur Gott [Coram deo] zu uberwinden und zu tilgen' (*S.A.*, p. 439. 7–9). Notice again, in this instance, how Luther is attacking what appears to him to be a Pelagian emphasis on the penitential acts of contrition, confession, and satisfaction. For similar reasons, he scorns the Scholastic attempt to substitute sufficient 'attrition' for perfect contrition (see *Bek.*, pp. 439–40. 17–19, 1–4).

[5] This unconditional surrender to Christ is plainly understood in Luther's similar remarks about true Confession: 'Desgleichen kann die Beicht auch nicht falsch, ungewiß oder stucklich sein; denn wer bekennet, daß alles eitel Sunde mit ihm sei, der begreift alle Sunde, läßt keine außen und vergisset auch keine. Also kann die Gnugtuung auch nicht ungewiß sein; denn sie ist nicht unser ungewisse, sundliche Werk, sondern das Leiden und Blut des unschuldigen "Lämmlin" Gottes, das der Welt Sunde trägt' (*Bek.*, p. 447. 4–10).

[6] For our treatment of Luther's sacramental theology and the Law-Gospel pattern of salvation, see above, Chapter V, section C.

Anfechtung against all sin; and confession is merely a going back
to this baptismal declaration of war—a 'Wiedergang und Zutreten zur Taufe'; likewise the Lord's Supper regulates and inten-
sifies this struggle, promising and symbolizing what Christ has
given and is continually giving to the baptized. For Luther,
then, the Sacraments are correlated means by which God continues and produces in us the inner dynamic struggle of the new
Adam against the old Adam.[1]

So far we have been considering three relevant aspects of
Luther's convictions about man's sinfulness; the extent to which
it has rendered man morally impotent, the enduring quality of
this moral impotence, and the totality of sinful man, both in
himself and all his acts, as the immediate object of the Law and
of grace. It remains now to show that the Christian awareness
of these aspects of sinfulness is not the result of human knowledge or personal effort but the fruit of God's gratuitous Word
preached and believed in.[2] This brings us back to article 2 on
the office or function of the Law, *Ampt oder Kraft des Gesetzs*,[3] and
the first part of article 3 on true or Gospel repentance.

C. *The related work of the Law and the Gospel*

Here we find the following, perhaps most succinct and
explicit, description of the Law-Gospel relation:

[1] This dynamic dualistic struggle of the Christian man, fighting alongside of
and with the help of God, appears also in the *S.A.*, in Luther's descriptions of
Christian or Gospel repentance: 'Und diese Buße währet bei den Christen bis in
den Tod; denn sie beißt sich mit der ubrigen Sunde im Fleisch durchs ganze
Leben, wie S. Paulus Ro., 7: 19, zeuget, daß er kämpfe mit dem Gesetz seiner
Glieder etc., und das nicht durch eigen Kräfte, sondern durch die Gabe des
heiligen Geists, welche folget auf die Vergebung der Sunden. Dieselbige Gabe
reiniget und feget täglich die ubrige Sunden aus und erbeitet, den Menschen
recht rein und heilig zu machen' (*Bek.*, p. 447. 20–27).
We must be careful not to misunderstand the final words of this passage, explaining how the gift of the Holy Ghost 'cleanses and sweeps out the remaining sins, and
works so as to render man truly pure and holy'. We have seen elsewhere that, for
Luther, our sinfulness remains until death regardless of how pure or holy God's
gifts can be said to render us (see Chapters II and V). The Reformer's sense of
acquired holiness or sanctification is best described as a psychological transformation rather than as an entitative or physical perfection inhering in man. In his
theology of grace and salvation there is no room, at least in this world, for entitative
and operative habits.
[2] We recall what Luther said above: 'Solche Erbsunde ist so gar ein tief bose
Verderbung der Natur, daß sie kein Vernunft nicht kennet, sondern muß aus der
Schrift Offenbarung gegläubt werden ...' (*Bek.*, p. 434. 8–11).
[3] *Bek.*, p. 436. 5–6.

We hold that the Law was given by God first, to restrain sin by threats and the dread of punishment, and by the promise and offer of grace and benefit. But all of this miscarried on account of the wickedness which sin has wrought in man. For thereby a part were rendered worse, those namely who were hostile to the Law because it forbids what they like to do, and enjoins what they do not like to do. Therefore, wherever they can escape . . . punishment they . . . do more against the Law than before. These, then, are the rude and wicked . . . men, who do evil wherever they have the opportunity.

But the chief office or force of the Law is that it reveals original sin with all its fruits, and shows man how very low his nature has fallen, and has become . . . utterly corrupted; as the Law must tell man that he has no God nor regards . . . God, and worships other gods, a matter which before and without the Law he would not have believed. In this way he becomes terrified, is humbled, desponds, despairs, and anxiously desires aid, but sees no escape; he begins to be an enemy of . . . God, and to murmur, etc. This is what Paul says, Rom. iv. 15: 'The Law worketh wrath' and Rom. v. 20: 'Sin is increased by the Law.'

This office . . . the New Testament retains and urges, as Saint Paul, Rom. i. 18, does, saying: 'The wrath of God is revealed from heaven against all ungodliness and unrighteousness of men.' Again, iii. 19: 'All the world is guilty before God. No man is righteous before Him.' And Christ says, John xvi. 8: 'The Holy Ghost will reprove the world of sin.'

This then, is the thunderbolt of God by which He strikes in a heap . . . both manifest sinners and false saints . . . and suffers no one to be in the right . . . but drives them all together to terror and despair. This is the hammer, as Jeremiah says, xxiii. 29: 'Is not my Word like a hammer that breaketh the rock in pieces?' This is not *activa contritio* or manufactured repentance, but *passiva contritio* . . . true sorrow of heart, suffering and sensation of death.

This then is what it means to begin true repentance; and here man must hear such a sentence as this: You are all of no account, whether you be manifest sinners or saints. . . .

But to this office the New Testament immediately adds the consolatory promise of grace through the Gospel, which must be believed, as Christ declares, Mark i. 15: 'Repent and believe the Gospel', i.e. become different and do otherwise . . .

But whenever the Law alone, without the Gospel being added, exercises this its office, there is . . . death and hell, and man must despair, like Saul and Judas; as Saint Paul says: 'Through sin the

Law killeth' (Rom. vii. 10). On the other hand, the Gospel brings
consolation and remission, not only in one way, but through the
Word and the Sacraments . . . (*B.C.*, pp. 142–3).[1]

In the opening paragraph, we observe that Luther maintains
the first function of the Law; it confirms what we said in our
fourth chapter (see sections C and D). There we pointed out
that the Law's role and sanctions were best seen in a 'split
perspective'; that is to say, applied as punishment and restraint
to the wicked, the unregenerate; or evangelically to the Christian. Because of this perspective, however, we must not envisage
two kinds of Law or two separate uses of the Law; it is one and
the same Law, God's Commandments, which effects both roles,
either to condemn or to save.

In the latter instance—'the chief office or force of the Law'—
we are dealing with the threefold evangelical function of the
Law—what Mr. Whale has aptly summed up in three metaphors: the Law as mirror, as hammer, and as mask.[2] As mirror,
it reveals to the Christian the extent of his sinfulness. This point
is manifest in paragraphs 1 and 2 of the above-quoted passage.
Like a hammer, it crushes him into despair and near blasphemy,
forcing him to acknowledge the totality of his sinfulness, and the
utter hopelessness of his case before God; in this way the
hammer of the Law makes him renounce self-reliance on works and
abandon himself completely to the work of the Gospel. This
second point is equally manifest in paragraphs 3 and 4. But this

[1] For the German text of this passage see *Bek.*, pp. 435–8. 18–27, &c.

[2] 'Luther answers by saying three things about the Law. He uses the three
metaphors of the mirror, the hammer, and the mask to describe its successive
functions.

'First the Law is mirror. It shows us ourselves, and the mysterious nature and
operation of sin. It reveals our impotence and our secret unwillingness to do the
will of God. . . . In short, the Law discloses our self-centred alienation from God
even in our very quest for God. And the result, among other things, is despair.

'For, in the second place, the Law is a hammer. It breaks us down, at last
reducing us to despair. Just as grace may be defined as love in action, so wrath is
law in action; the Law is more than a mirror; it is the hammer of God actively at
work upon us, that wrath of God which is revealed against all unrighteousness. . . .

'. . . the Law has a third function; and here Luther begins to expound its
evangelical import. The Law is a mask, since the sinner's despair is part of God's
beneficent intention. For it is only when we despair that he does his "proper work"
of redemption in us; only when we say "Nothing in my hand I bring", can he
come to us as sheer grace. . . . Under the imagery of a mask, then, Luther faces the
old paradoxical problem of wrath and love, of law and Gospel—in God himself'
(see J. S. Whale, op. cit., pp. 37–38).

preparation itself, remains, in a paradoxical sense, unrecognizable, hidden from the consciousness of the despairing soul, until Christ works into it the gift of faith. Thus we have the Law as a mask, disguising behind its crushing effects—despair and anguish —'God's beneficent intention'. The subsequent paragraphs of the quoted passage bear this out.

But what is crucial in this passage is Luther's stress on personal experience. The words he employs re-echo the intense language of his autobiographical fragment of 1545;[1] first in connexion with the work of the Law: 'terrified', 'desponds', 'despairs', 'anxiously desires aid, but sees no escape', 'he begins to be an enemy of God and to murmur', 'true sorrow of heart, suffering and sensation of death';[2] secondly, in connexion with the work of the Gospel: 'consolatory promise', 'the Gospel brings consolation . . .'[3] These expressions do more than describe the soul-shaking experience of sinfulness and forgiveness; they exhort Christ's disciples to abandon themselves to that experience, inasmuch as it is God's will and produced in them through His Word.

The vital, dynamic, personal experience of despairing in self and trusting in God is inseparable from the dual work of the Word—the Word of God as Law, condemning sinful man, and the Word of God as Gospel or grace, redeeming and declaring him righteous. Thus, in the *Smalcald Articles*, published eight years after the appearance of the Catechisms, we find the same unchanging fundamental Law-Gospel doctrine of Martin Luther.

[1] See above, Chapter I.
[2] '... wird er erschreckt, gedemutigt, verzagt ... verzweifelt, wollte gern, daß ihm geholfen wurde, und weiß nicht, wo aus fäht an, Gotte feind zu werden und murren ...' (*Bek.*, p. 436. 10–15). And 'das recht Herzeleid, Leiden und Fuhlen des Todes' (ibid., p. 437. 3–4).
[3] '... trostliche Verheißung', 'Trost und Vergebung' (ibid.).

CONCLUSION

THREE things seem to emerge conclusively from our study. Firstly, Luther's confessional writings expound fundamental doctrine according to a Law-Gospel plan of salvation, showing how God alone, to the exclusion of human merit and works, establishes, enforces, and fulfils all His precepts and promises—His Decalogue precepts and promises and His Gospel precepts and promises. Secondly, this totality of God's work, produced by the fullness of His Word—the Word as Law and the Word as Gospel—cannot be grasped, appreciated, and believed in apart from what it primarily effects in the daily life of the Christian—namely, the tense dynamic personal experience of sinfulness and grace; that is to say, apart from an *erlebnismäßig* crisis of despair in self followed by the consoling reassurances of faith; apart from a crisis in which the sinner becomes permanently conscious of his moral impotence before the Law, his purely passive role in the spiritual struggle against sin and the transforming effects of faith, and the external or imputed character of his righteousness before God. Thirdly, this Law-Gospel experience, both in its cause and scope, is not a mere aspect of Luther's theology but the very heart and core of his basic convictions.

Within the psychological, one might say existentialist, framework of this vital despair-faith experience, Luther's picture of God and man, of sin and grace, of Law and Gospel, is biblical, soteriological, and personal; it is not based on formal definitions, Nominalist possibilities, or abstract essences; one will commit a serious error if one tries to reduce his position to a dialectic of Scholastic syllogisms. Indeed, it is only within the despair-faith framework—the daily struggle of the Christian man 'simul peccator, simul penitens, simul justus'—that we are able to comprehend the various labels and paradoxes often attributed to his theology.

If we speak of his paradoxical dualism—the carnal and spiritual man—immediately we think of the Law condemning the whole man as sinful, and the Gospel, or Christ's cloak of merits, covering the whole man as graced. If we point to an apparent contradiction in his rejection of the works of the Law and his retention of the works of the Gospel, we hear him saying that he is rejecting the false works of self-righteousness but retaining the true works produced in us through our faith in Christ's righteousness. Again, if we find that his description of moral despair caused by the Law is anthropocentric, we cannot help observing that his faith in the work of the Gospel, paradoxically, makes it theocentric. Though the movement of salvation is downwards from God to man, and all of God's precepts and promises are focused on man's sinfulness to condemn and pardon it, Luther's perspective is none the less upwards; he means to show, by the judgement of the Law, how all our goodness, our redemption and sanctification depend solely on the work of the Blessed Trinity. Likewise, if we wish to understand the paradox of his theology of the cross, we are obliged to adopt this same Law-Gospel view: the condemnation of the Law, as it were, crucifies the Christian with Christ, so that he is completely dead to self, and all his self-righteousness buried in the tomb of despair; but simultaneously the consoling promise of the Gospel instils into him the new life of faith and the imputed righteousness of his Redeemer, raising him with Christ from the tomb. And finally, if we criticize the subjectivism of his personal experience, we can expect him to answer: this experience is itself the effect and fruit of God's objective external Word.

BIBLIOGRAPHY

Bibles Used

La Sainte Bible, traduite en français sous la direction de l'École Biblique de Jérusalem. Les Editions du Cerf, Paris, 1956.

The Holy Bible, Revised Standard Version, Thomas Nelson & Sons, New York, 1953.

The Holy Bible, Douay Version, William Clowes & Sons, London, 1956.

Primary Sources

D. MARTIN LUTHER. *Werke*, kritische Gesamtausgabe, Hermann Böhlau, Weimar, 1883–.

—— *Vorlesung über den Römerbrief*, ed. J. Ficker, in two parts, 'Die Glossen' and 'Die Scholien', Leipzig, 1908.

—— *Vorlesung über den Hebräerbrief*, ed. J. Ficker, Leipzig, 1929.

—— *Vorlesung über den Galaterbrief*, ed. H. von Schubert, Abhandlungen der Heidelberger Akademie der Wissenschaften, *Phil.-hist. Klasse*, vol. v, 1929.

—— *Die Schmalkaldischen Artikel*, vom Jahre 1537, nach D. Martin Luthers Autograph in der Universitäts-Bibliothek zu Heidelberg zur 400jährigen Geburtstagsfeier Luthers, hersg. von Karl Zangemeister, mit 47 Seiten in Lichtdruck, Heidelberg, 1886. The author consulted this manuscript in the summer of 1958, during a visit to Heidelberg.

—— *Deudsch Catechismus*, Wittemberg, Georg Rhaw, 1529, erste Ausgabe d. großen Katechismus (in der Stadtbibliothek in Worms)—*W.A.* xxx (i), pp. 57–123.

—— *Ein Sendbrief von Dolmetschen und Furbitte der Heiligen*, ed. Amburger-Stuart, London, 1940.

—— *Die Bekenntnisschriften der evangelisch-lutherischen Kirche*, herausgegeben im Gedenkjahr der Augsburgischen Konfession, 1930, 2. verbesserte Auflage, Göttingen, 1952.

—— *Der deutsche Katechismus*, in *Die Bekenntnisschriften ...*, pp. 545–733.

—— *Die Schmalkaldischen Artikel*, in *Die Bekenntnisschriften ...*, pp. 405–68.

Dokumente zu Luthers Entwicklung (bis 1519), ed. O. Scheel, Zweite Auflage, Tübingen, 1929.

Translations

D. MARTIN LUTHER. *Works*, in six volumes, ed. Jacobs, Philadelphia, 1943.

—— *Works*, American edition in fifty-five volumes (still in progress), Philadelphia, 1957–.

—— *Reformation Writings*, in two volumes, trans. by Bertram Lee Woolf, London, 1952.

—— *Propos de table*, French translations of the *Tischreden*, by Louis Sauzin, Paris, 1932.

—— *The Table Talk of Luther*, trans. by W. Hazlitt, London, 1902.

—— *Primary Works*, trans. by H. Wace and C. A. Buchheim, London, 1896.

D. MARTIN LUTHER. *Letters of Spiritual Counsel*, ed. and trans. by Tappert, Library of Christian Classics, vol. xviii, London, 1955.
—— *On the Bondage of the Will*, trans. by Packer and Johnston, London, 1957.
—— *Traité du serf arbitre*, trans. by Denis de Rougemont, Paris, 1936.
—— *Letters of Martin Luther*, trans. by Margaret A. Currie, London, 1908.
—— *Thirty-four Sermons* (on the Law-Gospel theme), trans. by W. Gace. Publd. by T. Paine, London 1649 [in the British Museum Library, 695, a. 11].
—— *A Commentary on Saint Paul's Epistle to the Galatians*, a revised and complete translation based on the 'Middleton edition' of the English version of 1575, by Philip S. Watson, London, 1956.
—— *Les Livres symboliques de l'église luthérienne*, French translation of the confessional writings in two volumes (incomplete), by André Jundt, Paris, 1947.
—— *Book of Concord*, English translation prepared by F. Bente and W. H. Dau, based on the original German and Latin texts respectively, and on the existing English translation, chiefly on those incorporated in Dr. Jacobs's *Book of Concord*, Saint Louis, 1957.
—— *Les Grands Écrits réformateurs* ('A la noblesse chrétienne de la nation allemande', 'La liberté du chrétien'), Collection bilingue, tr. par Maurice Gravier, Paris, 1955.

Secondary Sources

ALAND, KURT. *Hilfsbuch zum Lutherstudium*, Gütersloh, 1956.
ALBRECHT, OTTO. 'Wichtige Einleitungen zu den beiden Katechismen', in *W.A.* xxx (i), pp. 426–91.
ALLBECK, WILLARD D. *Studies in the Lutheran Confessions*, Philadelphia, 1952.
ALTHAUS, PAUL. *Paulus und Luther über den Menschen*, Gütersloh, 1951.
—— *Die christliche Wahrheit*, chapters 22 and 23 deal with 'Die Bekenntnisse' and 'Die Konfessionen', Berlin, 1958.
AQUINAS, THOMAS. *Summa theologiae*, ed. Piana, in five volumes, Ottawa, 1941.
—— *Opuscula Omnia*, ed. P. Mandonnet, in five volumes, Paris, 1927.
—— *Scriptum super libros sententiarum Magistri Petri Lombardi*, ed. by R. P. Mandonnet, in three volumes, Paris, 1929.
ARNOLD, F. X. *Zur Frage des Naturrechts bei M. Luther*, Munich, 1937.
AUGUSTINE, SAINT. *De spiritu et littera*, ed. William Bright, Oxford, 1914.
AULÉN, GUSTAF. *Christus Victor*, trans. by A. G. Hebert, London, 1931.
BADCOCK, F. J. *The History of the Creeds*, London, 2nd ed. 1938.
BAINTON, ROLAND. *Here I Stand*, New York, 1950.
—— *The Reformation of the Sixteenth Century*, London, 1953.
—— *Bibliography of the Continental Reformation*, materials available in English, 1935.
BARCLAY, ALEX. *The Protestant Doctrine of the Lord's Supper . . .* (Luther, Zwingli, and Calvin), Glasgow, 1927.
BAUDRY, L. *Guillaume d'Occam*, Tome 1, Études de philosophie médiévale, Paris, 1950.

BEYER, H. *Luther und das Recht* (Die Lehre Luthers, Heft 4), Munich, 1935.
BIEL, GABRIEL. *Quaestiones de justificatione* (Opuscula et textus historiam ecclesiae eiusque vitam atque doctrinam illustrantia), series scholastica, Fasc. 4, ed. Carolus Feckes, Münster i. W., 1929.
—— *Lectura super canone Missae*, Reutlingen, 1488.
—— *Epithomata et collectorium . . . circa quattuor sententiarum libros*, Tübingen, 1488.
BIZER, ERNST. *Ex auditu, Eine Untersuchung über die Entdeckung der Gerechtigkeit Gottes durch Martin Luther*, Neukirchen Kreis, Moers, 1958.
BOEHMER, HEINRICH. *Luther and the Reformation in the Light of Modern Research*, trans. by E. S. Potter, London, 1930.
—— *Der junge Luther*, ed. H. Bornkamm, 4th ed., Stuttgart, 1951; Eng.tr., *Road to the Reformation*, trans. by Doberstein and Tappert, Philadelphia, 1946.
BOOTH, EDWIN. *Martin Luther, the Oak of Saxony*, New York, 1933.
BORNKAMM, HEINRICH. 'Justitia Dei in der Scholastik und bei Luther', *Archiv für Reformationsgeschichte*, vol. xxxix, 1942.
BRAUN, WILHELM. *Die Bedeutung der Concupiscenz in Luthers Leben und Lehre*, Berlin, 1908.
BRING, RAGNAR. 'Gesetz und Evangelium und der dritte Gebrauch des Gesetzes in der Lutherischen Theologie', in *Zur Theologie Luthers*, vol. i, Helsinki, 1943.
BRUNNER, E. *Das Gebot und die Ordnungen*, Tübingen, 1933.
BÜHLER, P. *Die Anfechtung bei Luther*, Zürich, 1942.
CADIER, J. 'Saint Augustin et la Réforme', in *Recherches augustiniennes*, vol. iv, Paris, 1958.
CARLSON, EDGAR. *The Reinterpretation of Luther*, Philadelphia, 1948.
CLARK, JAMES M. *The Great German Mystics*, Oxford, 1949.
CLAYTON, J. *Luther and his Work*, Wisconsin, 1937.
COCHLAEUS, JOHANN. *Commentaria de actis et scriptis Martini Lutheri . . .*, Mainz, 1549.
COHRS, FERDINAND. *Die evangelischen Katechismusversuche vor Luthers Enchiridion*, Berlin, 1900.
CONGAR, YVES. *Vraie et fausse réforme dans l'Église*, Paris, 1950.
CRANZ, E. 'An Essay on the Development of Luther's Thought on Justice, Law, and Society', *Harvard Theological Review*, extra number, vol. xix, Cambridge, 1959.
CRISTIANI, L. 'The Reformation on the Continent', in *European Civilization*, ed. W. Eyre, vol. iv, New York, 1936.
—— *Luther tel qu'il fut*, Paris, 1955.
DEGERING, HERMANN. *Luthers Randbemerkungen zu Gabriel Biels Collectorium in quattuor libros Sententiarum und zu dessen Sacri canonis missae expositio*, Lyons, 1514, Weimar, 1933.
DENIFLE, HEINRICH. *Luther und Luthertum*, 2nd ed., in three volumes, Mainz, 1904 and 1906; French trans. by Paquier, 3 vols., Paris, 1913–16.
DIEM, HERMANN. 'Luthers Lehre von den zwei Reichen', *Evangelische Theologie*, vol. v, Munich, 1938.
—— 'Evangelium und Gesetz oder Gesetz und Evangelium?', *Evang. Theol.*, 1936.

DILLENBERGER, JOHN. 'Luther Studies, 1956–1959', in *Church History*, vol. xxx, New York, March 1961, pp. 61–87.

DRUMMOND, A. L. *German Protestantism since Luther*, London, 1951.

ELERT, WERNER. *Morphologie des Luthertums*, in two volumes, Munich, 1931–2.

—— *Zwischen Gnade und Ungnade* (Abhandlungen des Themas Gesetz und Evangelium), Munich, 1948.

—— 'Eine theologische Fälschung zur Lehre von tertius usus legis', *Zeitschrift für Religions- und Geistesgeschichte*, vol. 1, 1948, pp. 168–70.

ERHARDT, EUGÈNE. *La Notion du droit naturel chez Luther*, Paris, 1901.

ERIKSON, ERIK H. *Young Man Luther*, London, 1958.

FEBVRE, LUCIEN. *Martin Luther, un destin*, Paris, 1928; trans. into English by Roberts Tapley, London, 1930.

FIFE, ROBERT H. *The Revolt of Martin Luther*, New York, 1957.

FORELL, GEORGE W. *Faith Active in Love*, New York, 1948.

FUNCK-BRENTANO, J. C. *Luther*, trans. by E. F. Buckley, London, 1939.

GERDES, HAYO. *Luthers Streit mit den Schwärmern um das Verständnis des Gesetzes Mose*, Göttingen, 1955.

GILMORE, M. P. *The World of Humanism*, New York, 1952.

GILSON, ÉTIENNE. *The Spirit of Medieval Philosophy*, London, 1936.

—— *Introduction à l'étude de saint Augustin*, Paris, 1949.

GRANT, A. J. *A History of Europe from 1494–1610*, 4th ed., London, 1948.

GRIMM, HAROLD J. *The Reformation Era, 1500–1650*, New York, 1954.

GRISAR, HARTMANN, *Martin Luthers Leben und sein Werk*, Freiburg, 1911; trans. by E. M. Lamond, in six volumes, 1913–17.

GUERICKE, N. E. F. *Allgemeine christliche Symbolik*, Leipzig, 1861.

HÄGGLUND, BENGT W. 'Theologie und Philosophie bei Luther und in der occamistischen Tradition', *Acta Universitatis Lundensis*, N.F., Band 51, Lund, 1955, pp. 1–108.

HAMEL, ADOLF. *Der junge Luther und Augustin*, 2 vols., Gütersloh, 1934–5.

HARNACK, THEODOSIUS. *Luthers Theologie*, 2 vols., Munich, 1927.

HAZLITT, W. *The Table Talk of Martin Luther*, London, 1902.

HEINTZE, G. *Luthers Predigt von Gesetz und Evangelium* (Forschungen zur Geschichte und Lehre des Protestantismus, Zehnte Reihe, Band 11), Munich, 1958.

HERMANN, R. *Luthers These, Gerecht und Sünder zugleich*, Gütersloh, 1930.

HILDEBRANDT, F. *Melanchthon, Alien or Ally*, Cambridge, 1946.

HILL, CHARLES. *The Loci Communes of Philip Melanchthon*, Boston, 1944.

HIRSCH, E. *Initium theologiae Lutheri*, Tübingen, 1920.

HOF, OTTO. *Luthers Lehre von Gesetz und Evangelium* (Ev.-luth. Kirchenzeitung), Heft 9–11, 1949.

HOLL, KARL. *Gesammelte Aufsätze zur Kirchengeschichte*, 3 vols., Tübingen, 1927, esp. vol. i: 'Luther' (orig. ed., 1921).

HUGHES, PHILIP. *A Popular History of the Reformation*, London, 1957.

—— *History of the Church*, vol. iii, London, 1947.

HUMBERT-CLAUDE, H. *Érasme et Luther, leur polémique sur le libre arbitre*, Paris, 1909.

HUSFELDT, PAUL. *Studien zum Problem des Gesetzes in der Theologie Luthers*, Kiel, 1939.

HYMA, ALBERT. *The Christian Renaissance*, New York, 1925.
—— *Luther's Historical Development from Erfurt to Augsburg*, New York, 1928.
JEAN DE LA CROIX, *Les Œuvres spirituelles*, traduit par le R. P. Cyprien, revu par le R. P. Lucien Marie, Paris, 1949.
JOEST, WILHELM. *Gesetz und Freiheit, das Problem des tertius usus legis bei Luther und die neutestamentliche Parainese*, Göttingen, 1951.
KIERKEGAARD, S. *The Journals*, 1834–54, ed. and trans. by Alexander Dru, Fontana Books, Glasgow, 1958.
KATTENBUSCH, F. *Deus absconditus bei Luther*, Tübingen, 1920.
KÖBERLE, A. *Rechtfertigung und Heiligung*, Leipzig, 1930.
KOLDE, THEODOR. *Historische Einleitung in die symbolischen Bücher der evangelisch-lutherischen Kirche*, Gütersloh, 1907.
KÖLLNER, EDUARD. *Symbolik der lutherischen Kirche*, Hamburg, 1837.
KOOIMAN, W. J. *By Faith Alone*, trans. by Bertram L. Woolf, London, 1954.
KÖSTLIN, JULIUS. *The Life of Luther*, London, 1898.
KRAMM, H. H. *The Theology of Martin Luther*, London, 1947.
LAU, FRANZ. *Luthers Lehre von den beiden Reichen* (Luthertum, Heft 8), Berlin, 1953.
—— *Äußerliche Ordnung und weltliche Dinge in Luthers Theologie* (Studien zur systematischen Theologie, Heft 12), Göttingen, 1933.
LEEMING, B. *Principles of Sacramental Theology*, London, 1955.
LINDBECK, G. 'Nominalism and the Problem of Meaning as illustrated by Pierre d'Ailly, or Predestination and Justification', in *Harvard Theological Review*, vol. lii, January, 1959, pp. 43–60.
LINDSAY, T. M. *A History of the Reformation*, 2 vols., Edinburgh, 1906.
LOEWENICH, W. VON. *Luthers Theologia Crucis*, Munich, 1933.
LORTZ, JOSEPH. *Reformation in Deutschland*, 2 vols., Freiburg, 1947.
MACKINNON, JAMES. *Martin Luther and the Reformation*, 4 vols., London, 1925–30.
MCGIFFERT, A. C. *Martin Luther, the Man and His Work*, New York, 1919.
MCNEILL, J. T. 'Natural Law in the Thought of Luther', in *Church History*, vol. x, 1941, pp. 211–27.
MARITAIN, J. *Three Reformers*, Eng. tr. London, 1928.
MELANCHTHON, P. *Historia de vita et actis reverendi viri D. Martini Lutheri*, bona fide conscripta a Philippo Melanchthon, Wittenberg, 1549.
MEYER, JOHANNES. *Historischer Kommentar zu Luthers kleinem Katechismus*, Gütersloh, 1929.
MICHELET. *Mémoires de Luther*, Paris, 1837.
MÜLLER, H. M. 'Das christliche Liebesgebot und die lex naturae', *Zeitschrift für Theologie und Kirche*, N.F., vol. ix, 1928, pp. 61–83.
—— *Erfahrung und Glaube bei Luther*, Leipzig, 1929.
MURRAY, R. H. *Erasmus and Luther*, London, 1920.
NEVE, J. L. *Introduction to the Symbolic Books of the Lutheran Church*, Columbus, 1926.
—— *A History of Christian Thought*, 2 vols., Philadelphia, 1946.
NÜRNBERGER, RICHARD. 'Die *lex naturae* als Problem der *vita Christiana* bei Luther', *Archiv für Religionsgeschichte*, vol. xxxvii, 1940, pp. 1–12.

Nygren, Anders. *Agape and Eros*, vol. i, tr. by A. G. Hebert, London, 1932; vol. ii, tr. by P. S. Watson, London, 1939.

Paquier, J. Article 'Luther' in *Dictionnaire de théologie catholique*, tome ix, Paris, 1926.

Pascal, R. *Social Basis of the German Reformation*, London, 1933.

Pauck, Wilhelm. *The Heritage of the Reformation*, Boston, 1950.

—— The Historiography of the German Reformation, in *Church History*, vol. ix, 1940, pp. 305–40.

Pelikan, J. J. 'Luther and the Liturgy', in *More About Luther*, vol. ii, Decorah, Iowa, 1958.

Peter of Poitiers. De theologicis sententiis, in J. P. Migne, *P.L.*, vol. ccxi, cols. 789–1280.

Pinomaa, L. B. *Der existenzielle Charakter der Theologie Luthers* (Annales Academiae Scientiarum ..., Series B, I), Helsinki, 1940.

Prenter, Regin. 'Luther on the Word and Sacrament', in *More About Luther*, vol. ii, Decorah, Iowa, 1958.

—— *Spiritus Creator*, trans. by John M. Jensen, Philadelphia, 1953.

Preuss, Hermann. 'The Christian and the Church,' in *More about Luther*, vol. ii, Decorah, Iowa, 1958.

Proceedings of the Lutheran World Federation Assembly, Lund, Sweden, 30 June–6 July 1947, United Luth. Pub. House, Philadelphia, 1948.

Quanbeck, Warren. 'Luther's Early Exegesis', in *Luther Today* (Martin Luther Lectures), vol. i, Decorah, Iowa, 1957.

Reiter, J. Paul. *Martin Luthers Umwelt, Charakter und Psychose*, 2 vols., Copenhagen, 1937 and 1941.

Reu, A. V. *Thirty-five Years of Luther Research*, Chicago, 1917.

—— *D. Martin Luther's Small Catechism*, Chicago, 1929.

Richard, J. W. *The Confessional History of the Lutheran Church*, Philadelphia, 1909.

Rupp, Gordon. *The Righteousness of God*, London, 1953.

Saarnivaara, U. *Luther Discovers the Gospel*, St. Louis, 1951.

Schaff, Philip. *The Creeds of Christendom*, 3 vols., New York, 1899.

Schlink, Edmund. *Theologie der lutherischen Bekenntnisschriften*, Munich, 1946.

Schmauk, T. E. *The Confessional Principle and the Confessions of the Lutheran Church*, Philadelphia, 1911.

Schottenloher, K. *Bibliographie zur deutschen Geschichte im Zeitalter der Glaubensspaltung*, 6 vols., Leipzig, 1933–40, works consecrated to Luther and his work are found in vol. i, pp. 458–629.

Schultz, Robert. *Gesetz und Evangelium in der lutherischen Theologie des 19. Jahrhunderts*, Berlin, 1958.

Schwiebert, E. C. *Luther and His Times*, St. Louis, 1951.

Scotus, John Duns. *Opus Oxoniense*, Lyons, 1639.

—— *Reportata Parisiensia*, Lyons, 1639.

Seeberg, Erich. *Luthers Theologie in ihren Grundzügen*, Stuttgart, 1950.

—— *Luthers Theologie*, Band 2, 'Christus, Wirklichkeit und Urbild', Stuttgart, 1937.

——, R. *Text-Book of the History of Doctrines*, trans. by C. E. Hay, Philadelphia, 1905.

SEHLING, E. *Die evangelischen Kirchenordnungen des XVI. Jahrhunderts*, Leipzig, 1902.

SIRALA, A. *Gottes Gebot bei Martin Luther*, Helsinki, 1956.

SMITH, P. *Luther's Table Talk*, Columbia, 1907.

—— *Life and Letters of Martin Luther*, Columbia, 1911.

—— *Luther's Correspondence*, 2 vols., Philadelphia, 1913–18.

SOMMERLATH, E. *Gesetz und Evangelium* (Luthertum, Heft 17), Berlin, 1955.

STIER, JOHANNES. *Luthers Glaube und Theologie in den Schmalkaldischen Artikeln*, Gütersloh, 1937.

STROHL, HENRI. *L'Évolution religieuse de Luther*, Strasbourg, 1922.

—— *L'Épanouissment de la pensée religieuse de Luther*, Strasbourg, 1924.

—— *La Pensée de la Réforme*, Paris, 1951.

—— *Luther, sa vie et sa pensée*, Strasbourg, 1953.

THIEL, R. *Luther*, trans. by Gustaf Wienke, Philadelphia, 1955.

—— 'Der Gott der Katechismen', *Zeitschrift für Theologie und Kirche*, 1929, pp. 183.

TOBAC, EDOUARD. *Le Problème de la justification dans saint Paul*, Louvain, 1908.

ULBRICH, HEINRICH. *Urkunden und Aktenstücke zur Geschichte von Martin Luthers Schmalkaldischen Artikeln*, 1536–74, Berlin, 1957.

VIGNAUX, PAUL. 'Sur Luther et Occam' in *Wilhelm Ockham* (Franziskanische Studien), Münster, 1950.

—— *Luther commentateur des Sentences*, Paris, 1935.

VOGELSANG, ERICH. *Der angefochtene Christus bei Luther*, Berlin, 1932.

WATSON, P. S. *Let God be God*, London, 1947.

WEIJENBORG, R. 'La Charité dans la première théologie de Luther', *R.H.E.*, vol. xlv, p. 304, 1950.

WHALE, J. S. *The Protestant Tradition*, Cambridge, 1955.

WARD, A. W., and other editors. 'The Reformation', in *Cambridge Modern History*, vol. ii, 1904.

WOLF, ERNST. 'Gesetz und Evangelium in Luthers Auseinandersetzung mit den Schwärmern', *Evangelische Theologie*, Munich, vol. v, 1938, pp. 96–109.

—— 'Naturrecht und Gerechtigkeit', *Evangelische Theologie*, Munich, vol. vii, 1947–8, pp. 233–53.

WOOD, A. S. 'The Theology of Luther's Lectures on Romans', in *Scottish Journal of Theology*, Edinburgh, vol. iii, 1950, pp. 1–18 and 113–26.

APPENDIXES

APPENDIX I

Merit *de condigno* and *de congruo*

THE scholastic distinction between grace merited *de condigno* and *de congruo* was known to Luther. Probably, he first came across the terms in his readings of Biel's Commentary on the Sentences. One of his most remarkable statements on the distinction is to be found in his *Commentary on Galatians*: 'Wherefore the wicked and pernicious opinion of the Papists is utterly to be condemned, which attributes the merit of grace and remission of sins to the work wrought. For they say that a good work before grace is able to obtain grace of congruence (which they call *meritum de congruo* because it is meet that God should reward such work). But when grace is obtained, the work following deserveth everlasting life of due debt and worthiness (which they call *meritum de condigno*): as for example: if a man being in deadly sin, without grace, do a good work of his own good natural inclination—that is, if he say or hear a mass, or give alms and such like—this man of congruence deserveth grace. When he hath thus obtained grace; he doth now a work which of worthiness deserves everlasting life. For the first, God is no debtor; but because He is just and good, it behoveth Him to approve such a good work, though it be done in deadly sin, and to give grace for such service. But when grace is obtained, God is become debtor, and is constrained of right and duty to give eternal life. For now it is not only a work of free will, done according to the substance, but also done in grace, which maketh a man acceptable unto God [*gratia gratificante*], that is to say, in charity [*dilectione*]'.

'This is the divinity of the Anti-Christian kingdom. . . . For if I being in deadly sin, can do any little work which is not only acceptable in God's sight of itself and according to the substance, but is able to deserve grace of congruence, and when I have received grace, I may do works according to grace, that is to say, according to charity, and get of right and duty eternal life; what need have I now of the grace of God, forgiveness of sins, of the promise, and of the death and victory of Christ? Christ is now to me unprofitable and his benefit of none effect; for I have free will and power to do good works, whereby I deserve grace and congruence, and afterwards by the worthiness of my work, eternal life.'

'Such monstrous and horrible blasphemies should have been set forth to the Turks and Jews, and not to the Church of Christ' (*C.G.* ii, 16. 129–30; see also *W.A.* xl (i), 220–21. 17–29, 9–10).

Here, in no uncertain terms, we have Luther condemning what he considers to be the Schoolmen's teaching on merit *de congruo* and *de condigno*. In this context, his indignation seems perfectly justified; since any theology claiming or declaring that sinful man can merit grace without and before the intervention of God's mercy and will, is not only vain and foolish but downright blasphemous—it is most contrary to the manifest teachings of the written and oral Word of God.

Moreover, even presupposing that God has bestowed on a sinner the grace of true repentance and forgiveness, and also transformed him through the power of the Word and the Sacraments, it still does not follow that he can stand before God, with his good works and personal sanctification, as a self-righteous creditor. However much the creature is transformed by grace or untouched by sin, the distance between him and God remains infinite, and he can never dare say that his own efforts and works, by themselves, unaided by Christ's merits, are sufficient to pay the debt of sin or to win the divine favour. The saint simply says to God: 'I have tried to do my best with your help, I am sorry I could not do more, but even for this limited effort you have promised and offered to reward me, I await your judgement and mercy.' To the extent to which Luther understands *meritum de condigno* as teaching the contrary, he is equally justified in refuting and rejecting it.

But notwithstanding, there is another, more carefully defined sense in which these terms are used by certain theologians. Saint Thomas, for one, when employing these terms, explains them as follows: 'Dicendum quod opus meritorium hominis dupliciter considerari potest: uno modo, secundum quod procedit ex libero arbitrio; alio modo, secundum quod procedit ex gratia Spiritus Sancti. Si consideretur secundum substantiam operis, et secundum quod procedit ex libero arbitrio, sic non potest ibi esse condignitas propter maximam inaequalitatem.[1] Sed est ibi congruitas propter quandam aequalitatem proportionis: videtur enim congruum ut homini operanti secundum suam virtutem, Deus recompenset secundum excellentiam suae virtutis.[2] —Si autem loquamur de opere

---

[1] That is to say, there can be no merit condignly, according to a strict rule of justice of debtor to creditor, of due service and due payment.

[2] Here, for Saint Thomas, it is not a question of meriting first graces *de congruo*; on the contrary, in the fifth article of the same question, he argues that man can merit *primam gratiam* in no sense whatever (see below). On no account, therefore, is Saint Thomas suggesting, in this article, that the merit of a man's good deeds is not preceded, accompanied, and followed by God's graces. He is simply showing how a certain congruity exists between a man doing what he can and God rewarding it; but the matter of meriting graces *de congruo* is discussed farther on. One can only hope to grasp the full meaning of Saint Thomas's teaching on merit by read-

meritorio secundum quod procedit ex gratia Spiritus Sancti, sic est meritorium vitae aeternae ex condigno. Sic enim valor meriti attenditur secundum virtutem Spiritus Sancti moventis nos in vitam aeternam, secundum illud Ioann. 4, 14, "fiet in eo fons aquae salientis in vitam aeternam". Attenditur etiam pretium operis secundum dignitatem gratiae, per quam homo consors factus divinae naturae adoptatur in filium Dei, cui debetur hereditas ex ipso iure adoptionis, secundum illud *Rom.* 8: 17, "Si filii et heredes" '(*S. Th.*, Ia IIae, q. 114, a. 3, c.).

When it is a question of one person meriting grace for another, Saint Thomas answers as follows in article 6 of the same question: 'Primo quidem, ex vi motionis divinae; et sic meretur aliquis ex condigno.[1] Alio modo habet rationem meriti, secundum quod procedit ex libero arbitrio, inquantum voluntarie aliquid facimus. Et ex hac parte est meritum congrui: quia congruum est ut, dum homo bene utitur sua virtute,[2] Deus secundum superexcellentem virtutem excellentius operetur.[3] Ex quo patet quod merito condigni nullus potest mereri alteri primam gratiam nisi solus Christus.[4] Quia u- nusquisque nostrum movetur a Deo per donum gratiae ut ipse ad vitam aeternam perveniat; et ideo meritum condigni ultra hanc motionem non se extendit. Sed anima Christi mota est a Deo per gratiam non solum ut ipse perveniret ad gloriam vitae aeternae, sed etiam ut alios in eam adduceret, inquantum est caput Ecclesiae et Auctor salutis humanae, secundum illud *ad Hebr.*, 2, 10: "Qui multos filios in gloriam adduxerat, Auctorem salutis. . . ." Sed merito congrui potest aliquis alteri mereri primam gratiam. Quia enim homo in gratia constitutus implet Dei voluntatem congruum est secundum amicitiae proportionem[5] ut Deus impleat hominis voluntatem in salva- tione alterius; licet quandoque possit habere impedimentum ex parte illius cuius aliquis sanctus iustificationem desiderat' (ibid. a. 6, c.).

ing the whole of his treatise on Grace (see in particular articles 5 and 6 of the same question).

[1] That is to say, by virtue of being an adopted son of God, which adoption is owing uniquely and entirely to Christ's merits.

[2] That is to say, what God has given him both in the order of nature and of grace, as well as the power to merit *de congruo*.

[3] In other words, God, by His most excellent power, uses what He has created and according as He has created to accomplish yet greater things; not indeed because He has need of the creature but because He so wills to act thus.

[4] Here, Saint Thomas, as much as Luther, gives the lie to the false doctrines of indulgence disseminated by ill-informed or ignorant preachers during the fifteenth and sixteenth centuries. It certainly allows for no defence of Tetzel's exaggerations, or for the ridiculous rhyme: 'When the coin in the coffer rings, the soul from Purgatory springs' (see Bainton, *Luther, Here I Stand*, p. 83).

[5] Note carefully here, *meritum de congruo* is according to God's Will and in keeping with His friendship for us: *secundum amicitiae proportionem*.

The fundamental idea behind the Angelic Doctor's teaching on merit is, as J. Rivière puts it, that it presupposes 'une proportion entre l'œuvre humaine et la récompense divine' (see *D.T.C.*, 'Mérite,' x. 700). But this proportion being itself produced by the work of grace. If our good deeds are, in any sense, meritorious before God, it is not so much that God has become, of necessity, our debtor, but rather because He Himself wishes His own decree to be fulfilled: 'Quia actio nostra non habet rationem meriti nisi ex praesuppositione divinae ordinationis, non sequitur quod Deus efficiatur simpliciter debitor nobis, sed sibi ipsi, in quantum debitum est ut sua ordinatio impleatur' (*S. Th.*, Ia IIae, q. 114, a. 1, ad tertium). This divine ordination must not, however, be confused with the nominalist *De potentia ordinata*. Saint Thomas does not separate God's Will from the activity of the divine Mind (see below).

While these passages do not give us a complete picture of Saint Thomas's teachings on merit, any more than our study presents a complete picture of Luther's Law-Gospel doctrine, they none the less outline a theology of merit that bears no resemblance to the erroneous doctrines of merit which the Reformer attacks and refutes in his *Commentary on Galatians*.

But irrespective of Saint Thomas's careful wording, his theology of merit still remains incompatible with Luther's pessimism; for, unlike the Reformer, he admits of man's freewill as a secondary subordinate and providential cause of merit; and also understands grace to transform us really and physically and not merely imputatively or forensically.

The Nominalist position on merit has its beginnings in the Scotist distinction between the substance of a moral act, which rests upon us, and its meritorius character which depends on God's good pleasure (see J. Rivière, 'Mérite' in *D.T.C.* x. 701): 'In actu meritorio . . . duo considerare oportet: videlicet illud quod praecedit rationem meritorii, et in hoc gradu includitur et intentio actus et substantia actus et rectitudo moralis. Ultra hoc considero et ipsam rationem meritorii, quod est esse acceptum a divina voluntate in ordine ad praemium, vel acceptabile esse sive dignum acceptari' (see next ref.). In this sense, the human work or deed can only be a *dispositio*, the efficaciousness of which is guaranteed by the order or plan of divine Providence: 'Completio in ratione meriti non est in potestate mea nisi dispositive, tamen sic dispositive quod ex dispositione divina semper sequitur illud completivum ad agere meum, sicut semper sequitur animatio ad organizationem factam a causa naturali' (Duns Scotus, *Opus Oxon.*, in Bk. 1, dist. 17, q. 3, nn. 24–25, edit. de Lyon, 1639, t. 5(b), pp. 964–5). Thus it follows that the divine acceptance is an essential element in the *ratio meritorii*.

Underlying these views, of course, is the well-known Scotist distinction between God's absolute power and His decreed or ordained power; that is to say, between what He could or might have done, *de potentia absoluta* and what He did in fact do, *de potentia ordinata*. We find in the Subtle Doctor's writings passages such as: 'Dico quod Deus de potentia absoluta bene potuisset acceptare naturam beatificabilem acceptione spirituali praedicta existentem in puris naturalibus et similiter actum ejus, ad quem esset inclinatio ejus mere naturalis, potuisset acceptare ut meritorium' (ibid., n. 29, p. 968). In other words, God, if He had so desired, could have willed to accept and recognize morally good deeds of a purely natural order as meritorious of eternal salvation. If, in fact, God requires that our works be supernaturalized by grace, and rendered, in a certain *de condigno* sense proportional to our celestial rewards, it is uniquely because He has decreed it, *de potentia ordinata* (see John Duns Scotus, *Reportata Parisiensia*, ed. de Lyon, 1639, Bk. 1, dist. 17, g. 2, t. 10, n. 10, p. 97; see also J. Rivière, op. cit., c. 702).

According to Rivière, we can trace the Scotist manner of reasoning throughout the main representatives of the nominalist school: 'Ces positions sont restées, dans la suite, celles de toute l'école nominaliste, . . . chez Ockham, en particulier, l'affirmation de la liberté divine est poussée à son extrême limite. Sans doute, il admet, qu'il n'y a pas d'acte méritoire "sine gratia creata"; mais c'est uniquement *de potentia ordinata*, c'est-à-dire "propter leges voluntarie et contingenter a Deo ordinatas". Rien donc ne s'oppose à ce que cet ordre pût être changé . . .' (ibid.).

The Nominalist theology of merit, when studied in its proper context, is not necessarily incompatible with the traditional teachings of Holy Mother the Church. But granting this point, it remains that in emphasis and tendency the nominalist position threatens, at least in the obvious movement of its logic, to undermine the objective and intrinsic value of human acts as such, whether these acts be envisaged in the order of nature or of grace. So much stress is placed on the divine Will that one finds it hard to speak of the substantial merit of an act in any *de condigno* sense. That is to say, a human act is rendered substantially meritorious not because of a certain due proportion existing between the work done and the reward received but uniquely because God looks with favour upon the act, *de potentia ordinata*. In the context of this theological voluntarism, Saint Thomas's idea of merit *de condigno* becomes meaningless.

We may add, moreover, that this Scotist manner of reasoning, in terms of what God might or could have done, is quite foreign to Saint Thomas's theology. He never separates the operations of the divine Will from the activity of the divine Intelligence, so that everything willed by God can, indeed must, be seen under the aspect of being and goodness—that is to say, as intelligible and desirable. This holds true for the human act, as well as for anything else created by God, and with all that it includes by way of merit and grace; man's good deed, aided or unaided by grace, has its *ratio entis*, its formal cause, and consequently a due proportion and objective value before the divine Intelligence; what God wills and causes is never without intrinsic worth, objective being and intelligibility.

Paradoxically, the idea of merit *de congruo*, in the Nominalist School, particularly with Gabriel Biel, becomes so accentuated that man seems capable of meriting almost everything that pertains to his salvation, provided, of course, that it is previously understood as God's Will. As Rivière states: 'En effet, la part de la préparation humaine à la grâce est ici de plus en plus large, et l'école nominaliste se montre à ce point généreuse pour la nature qu'on a pu se demander si elle ne compromettait pas la nécessité d'un secours divin surnaturel' (op. cit., c. 704). Biel, for instance, affirms the following: 'Anima obicis remotione ac bono motu in Deum ex arbitrii libertate elicito primam gratiam mereri potest de congruo' (*Collectorium ... circa quattuor Sententiarum libros*, in Bk. 2 of the Sentences dist. 27, a. 2, concl. 4; cf. also in Bk. 4 of the Sent. dist. 14, q. 2, a. 1, n. 2). And even though he admits that medicinal grace is not absent in this case, one feels that he is laying too much stress on the power of nature to merit God's blessings. Compare this position to Saint Thomas: to the question, 'Utrum homo posset sibi mereri primam gratiam', he replies: 'Sed contra est quod ratio gratiae repugnat mercedi operum, secundum illud Rom. 4, 4: "Ei qui operatur, merces non imputatur secundum gratiam, sec secundum debitum." Sed illud meretur homo quod imputatur secundum debitum quasi merces operum eius. Ergo primam gratiam non potest homo mereri" (*S. Th.*, Ia IIae, q. 114, a.5. sed contra).

He explains further, in the *Corpus*: "Respondeo: Dicendum quod donum gratiae considerari potest dupliciter. Uno modo, secundum rationem gratuiti doni. Et sic manifestum est quod omne meritum repugnat gratiae, qui, ut ad Rom. 11, 6, Apostolus dicit "Si ex operibus, iam non ex gratia". Alio modo potest considerari secundum naturam ipsius rei quae donatur. Et sic etiam non potest cadere sub merito non habentis gratiam; tum quia excedit proportionem naturae, tum etiam quia ante gratiam in statu peccati homo habet impedimentum promerendi gratiam, scilicet ipsum peccatum. Postquam autem iam aliquis habet gratiam, non potest gratia iam habita sub merito cadere; quia merces est terminus operis, gratia vero est principium cuiuslibet boni operis in nobis, ... si vero aliud donum gratuitum aliquis mereatur virtute gratiae praecedentis, iam non erit prima. Unde manifestum est quod nullus potest sibi mereri primam gratiam' (ibid., c.).

The clarity and precision of Saint Thomas's statements here are in perfect harmony with the traditional teachings of the Church and show no dangerous tendency towards Pelagianism on the one hand or despondent pessimism on the other, and his manner of reasoning and thinking is quite different and distinct from the Nominalist School.

To return to Luther: it would be wrong to say that he was formally a nominalist (see Chapter II, p. 42, n. 1); he reacted as vehemently against Biel's conception of merit *de congruo* as he did against Tetzel's doubtfully orthodox sermons on indulgences. Yet we think that his biblical interpretation of imputative and passive righteousness is more readily formulated in a Nominalist context of theology where one stresses more the divine Will than the divine Intelligence; also where forensic justice is at least a possibility, *de potentia absoluta*. In Saint Thomas's view, a man's justice and justification—what God wills and causes—must bear a certain resemblance and due proportion to the divine idea of human righteousness. A righteousness or justification of rational creatures that is strictly or purely forensic and divorced absolutely from all formal and 'exemplar' causality makes no sense in the Angelic Doctor's theology.

APPENDIX II

Intrinsic Sanctification

'DENN wider Du noch ich künnten immer mehr [je] etwas von Christo wissen noch an ihn gläuben und zum Herrn kriegen, wo es nicht durch die Predigt des Evangelii von dem heiligen Geist würde angetragen [angeboten] und uns in Bosam [Busen] geschenkt. Das Werk is geschehen und ausgericht; denn Christus hat uns den Schatz erworben und gewonnen. . . . Aber wenn das Werk verborgen bliebe daß niemand wüßte, so wäre es ümbsonst und verloren . . . . Darümb ist das Heiligen nicht anders, denn zu HERREN Christo bringen, solch Gut zu empfahen, dazu wir von uns selbs nicht kommen künnten' (*Bek.*, p. 654. 22–42).

It is interesting to compare this passage with similar ones in the *Catechism of the Council of Trent*. This latter work says the following when explaining how belief in the Holy Ghost, according to Acts xix. 2, is necessary to the faithful: *In quo ergo baptizati estis?* (Saint Paul inquiring, on hearing that certain Ephesians had not heard of the Holy Ghost) 'Quibus verbis significavit, distinctam huius articuli notitiam fidelibus maxime necessariam esse, ex qua eum praecipue fructum capiunt; quod, quum attente cogitant, se, quidquid habent, Spiritus sancti munere et beneficio consequutos esse, tum vero de seipsis modestius et humilius sentire, et in Dei praesidio omnem spem ponere incipiunt; qui primus homini christiano gradus ad summam sapientiam et felicitatem esse debet' (ch. 9, para. 1).

And several paragraphs on: 'Quare ex eo consequitur, ut Spiritus sanctus *donum* appelletur: nam doni vocabulo significatur id, quod benigne et gratuito, nulla spe remunerationis proposita, donatur. Ac proinde quaecumque bona et beneficia a Deo in nos collata sunt (quid [1 Cor. iv. 7] autem habemus, quod a Deo, ut inquit Apostolus, non acceperimus?) ea nobis Spiritus sancti concessu et munere data esse, pio et grato animo agnoscere debemus' (ibid., para. 7).

Though Christ is not here mentioned explicitly as the gift of the Holy Ghost, and though also the Third Person of the Blessed Trinity is called the 'Vivificans' (ibid., para. 5) or 'Giver of Life' rather than 'Sanctificator', the special role of the Holy Ghost, both in our acceptance of Christ and our Sanctification, is manifestly implied. The similarity of meaning of the above passages to Luther's statements is undeniable.

However, the word 'Sanctification', in the Catholic tradition, comprises much more than a mere statement about the fact that the

Holy Ghost is necessary for our faith in Christ and our holiness. It brings to mind, also, the question of how the recipient of grace is physically and inwardly, and not merely forensically or imputatively, transformed—divinized so to speak—by God's work; and how, also, he is made capable of meriting an increase in grace and personal perfection; how, in brief, grace and nature are so related causally as to produce Christian goodness.

From the time of Saint Augustine to our own day, saints and theologians have been intrigued and concerned about these questions (see Henri Rondet, S.J., *Gratia Christi* (Essai d'histoire du dogme. . ., Paris, 1948). Saint Thomas and the doctors of the thirteenth century were particularly preoccupied with the problem of defining grace and distinguishing between its many forms—between God Himself as grace (the gift of Himself) and what He causes to be given to the creature extrinsic to Himself, or created grace; and then again between actual grace (God's operation on creatures) and habitual or sanctifying grace (a spiritual quality which, by virtue of God's mercy and creative action, inheres, in a certain permanent way, in the soul of the just man constituting the basis of his spiritual life, what Saint Thomas calls an 'entitative habitus'); and between the various operative virtues or stable dispositions of the baptized soul infused by God —such as faith, hope, and charity, not to mention the Beatitudes and the special gifts of the Holy Ghost.

In *Der deutsche Katechismus*, Luther does not discuss these questions; indeed, they are beyond the scope of such a work. But he does make one point clear: the essential or main gift of the Holy Ghost—which includes all the other benefits and blessings—is Christ Himself, given and received through the influence and mysterious workings of the Third Person of the Blessed Trinity. But the fact that God is truly and really given to man raises, obviously, thorny metaphysical and difficult theological questions concerning the way in which He offers Himself and is received by each Christian personally.

Luther himself seems to be concerned with these problems only inasmuch as they are involved in his more psychological and soteriological problem—'how to find a gracious God', or how to find certitude of personal salvation?

His interpretation of Holy Scripture, influenced by nominalism, German mysticism, and Saint Augustine, points to the 'righteousness of God by which He justifies the sinner'. But this interpretation implies, as we have seen in our first chapter, imputative and passive righteousness on the part of the recipient creature.

There does not appear to be any room for infused created grace, given to and physically possessed by the subject of justification and sanctification; nor again is there a place for merit and free will on the part of the sinner. The work of the Holy Ghost is simply to move us to accept Christ passively and to acknowledge His righteousness as imputed to us. This is our sanctification, which increases and becomes more intense according as the Holy Ghost moves us to God and away from ourselves;[1] our only work and role is to be passive.

The very movement, in us, of receiving and acknowledging Christ, and even of bettering our lives, by means of His help, cannot be regarded, in any positive sense, as a meritorious secondary cause of God's favour—as a divine work which includes effects and expects the *free* gift of ourselves to God.

What we are trying to say is that, for Luther, the possession and use of God's grace excludes the meritorious participation of nature and free will. The just man, though his sins be forgiven and remitted, and his relationship to God transformed by faith, remains, somehow, sinful, incapable of executing a meritorious act, be it simply the free acceptance of and correspondence with imparted graces. These things are borne out by the Reformer's *De servo arbitrio* and also by his *Post Scriptum* to Melanchthon's letter, May 1531 (see above, Chapter II, section C). We should not push these problems and notions aside when reading Luther's Catechism.

---

[1] 'So bleibt der heilige Geist bei der heiligen Gemeine oder Christenheit bis auf den jüngsten Tag, dadurch er uns holet, und brauchet sie dazu, das Wort zu führen und treiben, dadurch er die Heiligung machet und mehret, daß sie täglich zunehme und stark werden im Glauben und seinen Früchten, so er schaffet' (*Bek.*, pp. 657–8. 42–47, 1–2).

APPENDIX III

Luther's Scriptural Arguments for the Sacraments

IN the beginning, Luther believed in the traditional Catholic teaching on the efficacy and necessity of the Seven Sacraments as divinely instituted means of sanctification. But he was not long in realizing that the Sacraments of Marriage, Confirmation, Holy Orders, and Extreme Unction were incompatible with his under- standing of evangelical faith and the Word. As early as 1519, he said, in a letter to Spalatin, 18 December, that 'no one need expect treatises from him on the other Sacraments [i.e. the ones listed above], since he cannot acknowledge them as such' (see J. Schindel, in *Ph.*, ii. 7). In the same year, previous to the letter, he had already written four treatises on Baptism, the Lord's Supper, Penance, and the Ban.

Luther's principal[1] arguments for or against the existence of a Sacrament, as we know from his treatise, *De captivitate Babylonica*, are based on Holy Scripture. He finds no authority for what he regards as the fictitious character of Holy Orders: 'Huic ... tam debili fundamento [Dionysius (Areopagiticus)] nixi caracteres effinxerunt, quos huic suo sacramento tribuerent, qui imprimerentur ordinatis indelebiles. Unde, quaeso, tales cogitationes? qua autoritate [from the context, it is clear that Luther, here, is asking for scriptural authority], qua ratione stabiliuntur' (*W.A.* vi. 562. 30–33)? He would undoubtedly ask the same question in connexion with the indelible character of Baptism and Confirmation; Penance has the Word and the promise but is lacking in any external sign: 'Nam poenitentiae sacramentum, quod ego his duobus accensui, signo visibili et divinitus instituto caret et aliud non esse dixi quam viam ac reditum ad baptismum' (*W.A.* vi. 572. 15–17). The divine inspiration of Saint James's Epistle, containing certain passages which seem to command the administration of Extreme Unction as a Sacrament, according to Luther's own definition, he considers doubt- ful.[2] And he argues, that even if it were divinely inspired, it would

---

[1] Sometimes the Reformer argues from the authority of the Fathers and the statements of the councils, and sometimes he employs the opinions of the philo- sophers to illustrate a point. But these authorities are acceptable to him only inasmuch as they conform to and support his fundamental understanding of the Gospel as Faith without works.

[2] Commenting on Luther's remark about Saint James's Epistle in the *De capti- vitate Babylonica*, Bertram Lee Woolf writes in a footnote: 'This remark [see Latin quotation above beginning with "Omitto"], which is in accord with modern scholarship, does not occur in the introduction which Luther wrote to the epistle

still not prove Extreme Unction to be a Sacrament, properly speaking, because 'no apostle was licensed to institute a Sacrament on his own authority, or to give a divine promise with an accompanying sign'. In the Latin context, the argument reads as follows, beginning with the bit on Saint James's Epistle: 'Ego autem dico: si uspiam delyratum est, hoc loco praecipue delyratum est [i.e. that Extreme Unction be a Sacrament after Saint James's Epistle]. Omitto enim, quod hanc Epistolam non esse Apostoli Iacobi nec apostolico spiritu dignam multi valde probabiliter asserant, licet consuetudine autoritatem, cuiuscunque sit, obtinuerit. Tamen si etiam esset Apostoli Iacobi, dicerem, non licere Apostolum sua autoritate sacramentum instituere, id est, divinam promissionem cum adiuncto signo dare. Hoc enim ad Christum solum pertinebat' (*W.A.* vi. 568. 8–14). Similarly, Luther argues that there is no scriptural warrant for treating Marriage and Confirmation as Sacraments (ibid., *De Matrimonio*, and *De Confirmatione*).

Catholic theologians do not agree with Luther's scriptural arguments against accepting the other five Sacraments. His arguments appear more convincing within the context of his evangelical dualism and pessimistic doctrine of original sin, such as we have described in the previous chapters. If human nature is morally depraved and the Christian's righteousness solely the work of God to the exclusion of personal effort and merit, then it is perfectly logical and consistent, for instance, to reject Marriage and Penance as Sacraments.

To regard Marriage as a Sacrament would be to recognize a human state and human works as means to grace and salvation; and Penance, understood as a co-operative meritorious work of contrition and satisfaction, would run counter to the Reformer's doctrine of faith without works. Moreover, the sacramental *caracteres* of Baptism, Confirmation, and Holy Orders, conceived of as inherent qualities, imprinted on the recipient's soul, would not fit in well with his imputative and psychological description of grace, not to mention the

in his translation of the New Testament, first published in 1522 (cf. *D.B.* vii. 383). The famous judgment about the "epistle of straw", usually quoted in a truncated form, occurs only in the Introduction to the New Testament as a whole, and was withdrawn after the first edition. This general introduction, however, nowhere denies James's authorship' (cf. *D.B.*, vol. vi, pp. i–ii) (*Reformation Writings*, n. 2, vol. 1, p. 320). We would like to add that in his Preface to the Epistles of Saint James and Saint Jude, 1545 (1522), while not denying explicitly the divine inspiration of Saint James's Epistle, Luther most certainly claims that it is opposed to Saint Paul and 'all the rest of Scripture' because it 'ascribes righteousness to works . . .' (see *Ph.* vi. 478). The implication is that the Epistle of Saint James is worthless when discussing the fundamental message of the Gospel, namely, faith without works. For the same reason, Luther probably considers it of little value when discussing the institution of a Sacrament.

special graces and entitative perfections which all the Sacraments confer upon the recipient to aid him to act freely and co-operatively with the Three Persons of the Blessed Trinity in the acquisition of personal sanctity.

We point out these factors because it seems that Luther's treatment of the Sacraments depends, to some extent, on his experience and view of sinful man as well as on his study of the Word. His understanding of Saint Paul's doctrine of faith without works cannot be separated from the moral pessimism of his radical teaching on original sin. Indeed, he questions any authority, even scriptural authority, when it suggests or confirms the value and goodness of meritorious human works in God's economy of salvation. In his preface to the epistles of Saint James and Saint Jude, he justifies his preferences for certain Books of the New Testament, in particular Saint Paul and Saint John, precisely on the grounds that they are a more perfect expression of the doctrine of faith without works. And Saint James's Epistle, in comparison with the other New Testament writings, he calls an 'epistle of straw'. This, in our opinion, indicates a bias on Luther's part which comes from within himself and not from the written Word. It is not enough to say that his experience of sinful man and his doctrine of original sin are themselves the true teachings of God's Word; that has to be proved. For our part, we cannot agree that Luther's doctrine of original sin emerges conclusively and persuasively from an objective exegesis of Sacred Scripture.

APPENDIX IV

Saint Jerome's Metaphor, the 'Shipwreck of Baptism'

AT the end of the Fourth Part on Baptism, in the Catechism, Luther warns us against falling into the opinion that our Baptism is something past, which we can no longer use after we have sinned again (see *B.C.*, p. 209, col. 2). The reason for this opinion, he claims, is due to looking upon Baptism merely according to the completion of the external act (ibid.); which, he adds, arose from the fact that Saint Jerome wrote: 'Die Buße sei die andere Tafel; damit wir müssen ausschwimmen und überkommen, nachdem das Schiff gebrochen ist';[1] in which Ship [Baptism], Luther paraphrases, 'wir treten und überfahren, wenn wir in die Christenheit kommen' (see *Bek.*, p. 706. 39–44). In his view, the statement is not correct: Damit ist nu der Brauch der Taufe weggenommen, daß sie uns nicht mehr nützen kann. Darümb ists nicht recht geredt, denn das Schiff zubricht nicht, weil es (wie gesagt) Gottes Ordnung und nicht unser Ding ist. Aber das geschicht wohl daß wir gleiten und erausfallen, fället aber imand eraus, der sehe, daß er wieder hinzuschwimme und sich dran halte, bis er wieder hineinkomme und darin gehe, wie vorhin angefangen' (*Bek.*, pp. 706. 45–707. 1–10).

It is possible that some of Luther's teachers, in the Augustinian cloisters of Erfurt and Wittenberg, misinterpreted and misused Saint Jerome's metaphor. And this could very well have led Luther to think that they were trying to present Penance—the *secunda tabula* —as a substitute for Baptism. Yet on reading the references to Saint Jerome, on the matter of the *secunda tabula*, mentioned below (see n. 1), we find two things to consider: firstly, it is hard to ascertain whether Saint Jerome is, in these instances, speaking of virtuous acts of Penance or the actual Sacrament of Penance. Most probably, he is referring to the primitive Church's practice of administering the Sacrament of Penance once in a lifetime, to penitents who have committed grievous sins after Baptism (see *Handbuch der Dogmengeschichte*, Band 4, Faszikel 3: 'Buße und Letzte Ölung', von Prof. Dr. Bernhard Poschmann, 'Unwiederholbarkeit und lebenslängliche

---

[1] Hieronymus, Ep. 130 ad Demetriadem de servanda virginitate, *M.P.L.*, xxii. 1115: 'illa [Penance] quasi secunda post naufragium miseris tabula sit'; see also Ep. 122 ad Rusticum and Ep. 147 ad Sabinianum lapsum, xxii. 1046; also Comment. in Ies., cap. 3, 8–9, xxiv. 65. These references are given by the editors of *Bek.* (see p. 706, note 9). Luther is here paraphrasing Saint Jerome's remarks about the *secunda tabula post naufragium*.

Verpflichtung der Buße', Herder, Freiburg i. Br., 1951, p. 54).
Secondly, his metaphor is not meant to suggest that mortal sin, subsequent to Baptism, is a total shipwreck; at least not in the sense in
which Luther seems to be accusing him. That is to say, as implying
that Baptism ceases to have any permanent effects, or that the *secunda
tabula* is altogether unrelated to the initial gift of faith signified and
imparted by Baptism. Saint Jerome was most likely employing a
common image of classical antiquity which he found ready at hand
and apt to illustrate his point; namely that mortal sins, after Baptism, could, by virtue of Christ's merits, be forgiven and remitted
through Penance. We find, for instance, under the word *tabula* in
Lewis and Short's *Latin Dictionary*, the following uses: 'si tabulam de
naufragio stultus arripuerit' (Cic., off. 3. 23. 89; cf. Att. 4. 18. 3); and
tabula navis (Juve. 14. 289).

On the other hand, Luther's metaphor of the unsinkable ship, or
rather, 'unbreakable'[1] ship, is not without its own merits when
illustrating the permanent effects of Baptism. However, his insistence
on the ever efficacious and continuous effects of Baptism arises, not
from a reaction to Saint Jerome's metaphor, but fundamentally from
his own Law-Gospel understanding of what a Sacrament signifies
and effects.

Explaining, as we have seen (see above, Chapter II), the forgiveness of sin declaratively, passively and psychologically, to the exclusion of free will on the part of the recipient, and equating human
nature itself with sin, he cannot draw clear distinctions between the
remission of original and personal sin,[2] venial and mortal sin,[3] actual
and sanctifying grace, and between the psychological and ontological effects of grace; he can only envisage, in the sign and effect of
Baptism, a dualistic, personalized, perpetual struggle of Christ's
imputed Righteousness against sinful self. In this view there is no
need to see Penance as anything more than a reaffirmation of one's
faith in Christ crucified and resurrected; indeed, it is impossible to
regard it, in sign and effect, as a Sacrament distinct from Baptism.
That is to say, as signifying and effecting specifically, to use the
words of Saint Thomas, the remission of subsequent mortal sins
which impede the effects of Baptism: '. . . baptismus operatur in

---

[1] '... das Schiff zubricht nicht ...' (*Bek.*, p. 707. 3).
[2] Luther, in point of fact, distinguishes between personal and original sin in his
Sermon on the Two kinds of Righteousness (see above, Chapter V, p. 91, n. 1). But this
personal sin is inseparable from his notion of enduring sinfulness; in this sense that
the Christian, in sinning after Baptism, is not falling out of a state of sanctifying
grace but merely allowing the old Adam—our nature, in no way made sinless by
Baptismal graces—to take over.
[3] See chapter VI, section C.

virtute passionis Christi . . . et ideo sicut peccata sequentia virtutem passionis Christi non auferunt, ita etiam non auferunt baptismum, ut necesse sit ipsum iterari; sed poenitentia superveniente tollitur peccatum, quod impediebat effectum baptismi' (S. Th., IIIa, q. 66, q. 9, ad primum).

A Lutheran today will agree with much of what Saint Thomas here enunciated. But the strict sense in which Saint Thomas understands the hindrance of mortal sins is foreign to the Reformer's dualistic way of thinking. Since, for him, the sinfulness of our 'Adamic' nature remains, even after Baptism, and irrespective of God's favour, which merely covers over and disregards our sins, he can say that we are never without sin, that it is never really absent from the Christian life, here below. So that between committing personal sins and afterwards repenting of them there is a kind of flux and reflux between two opposed psychological states—between an awareness of our own unrighteousness, affirmed by us in our disobedience, and a soul-shaking awareness of Christ's imputed righteousness, affirmed in our faith. In so far as the latter awareness endures and dominates the former, and produces good works in us—the fulfilment of the Law—it is exclusively signified and effected by the Word and the sign of Baptism. We have developed this point at length to show, more precisely, what Luther means when he says '... bleibt die Taufe immerdar stehen' (Bek., p. 706. 13) and that Penance [die Buße] is 'ein Wiedergang und Zutreten zur Taufe' (Bek., p. 706. 23-24).

APPENDIX V

Ex opere operato

THE chief texts in which Luther criticizes what he considers to be the Scholastic teachings on the principle *ex opere operato*, are found in the following works: *Eyn sermon von dem neuen Testament, das ist von der heyligen Messe* (1519), *W.A.*, ii. 371. 6–14; *De captivitate Babylonica* (1520), *W.A.* vi. 518. 24–33; and *Eyn sermon von dem hochwirdigen sacrament des heyligen waren leychmans Christi.* . . . *W.A.* ii. 751–2. All of these texts deal with the principle in so far as it applies to the Mass and the Blessed Sacrament.

A careful analysis of these texts reveals that Luther is opposed to this principle, or rather formula, *ex opere operato*, because he thinks that it is being used to teach false doctrines about the efficacy of the Sacrament, and to encourage simoniacal abuses. In his opinion, it teaches falsely that the mere repetition and multiplication of masses are pleasing to God, in themselves, independently of the spiritual needs and faith of the members of the Christian community; as if the Sacrament had been instituted for God and not for sinful men. Also that the fruits of the Sacrament are bestowed on the recipient irrespective of any change of heart or act of evangelical faith: 'Es seynd yhr vill, die disses wechsels der lieb und des glaubens ungeachtet sich darauff vorlassen, daß die meß odder das sacrament sey, als sie sagen, opus gratum opere operati, das ist, eyn solch werck das von ym selb gott wollgefellet, ob schon die nit gefallen, die es thun. Darauß sie dan schließen, daß dennoch gutt sey vill meß haben, wie unwirdiglich sie gehalten (werden, den der schad sey der, die sie unwirdig halten) oder prauchen. Ich laß eynem yden seynen syn, aber solch fabelen gefallen mir nit. Dan also zu reden tzo ist keyn creatur noch werk, das nit von yhm selbs got wol gefalle ... Was frucht kommet davon, tzo man brot, weyn, golt und alles gut ubel braucht, wie wol sie an yhn selbs got wohlgefallen? Ja vordamnis folget darnach. Also auch hie: yhe edler das sacrament ist, yhe größer schaden aus seynem mißprauch kommet ubir die gantzen gemeyn, dan es is nit umb seynet willen eyngesetzt, daß es gott gefalle, ssondern umb unsser willen, daß wir seyn recht brauchen, den glauben dran uben, und durch dasselb gott gefellig werden' (*W.A.* ii. 751. 18–33; see also the other references mentioned above).

Notwithstanding possible misuses and misinterpretations of the Schoolmen's language, *ex opere operato* and *ex opere operantis*, we think it necessary to point out that this terminology was invented precisely to avoid erroneous conceptions of the Sacrament's efficacy, such as Luther is here denouncing, and to defend the primacy of God's Word and ordinance over the qualifications of the minister or the recipient; in other words, to show how the efficacy and value of the Sacrament, administered by an unworthy priest or received by an unworthy recipient, springs, not from human agents, but from the divine institution and power. The terminology was not meant, in any sense, to separate the proper use of the Sacraments from the faith of the recipient. Basically what it teaches—this terminology—is this: Christ is offered in the Sacrament *ex opere operato*; i.e. when it is administered according to the intention of the Church; but the effect on the recipient depends on his faith and contrition for sins, his disposition to accept what is offered and signified in the Sacrament. That is to say, the recipient does not enjoy the fruits of the Sacrament *ex opere operato* but rather *ex opere operantis*, inasmuch as he, aided by grace, accepts and cooperates freely and sincerely, in true faith, with God's offer.

In 1205 Peter de Poitiers applied the distinction *opus operans* and *opus operatum* to Baptism (see *De theologicis sententiis*, Bk. 1, dist. 1, q. 16, and Bk. 5, dist. 6, in *M.P.L.*, vol. ccxi, cols. 863 and 1235), the minister's act of performing Baptism was the *opus operans* and the thing done, Baptism itself, was the *opus operatum*. Saint Thomas distinguished between the Sacrament itself and the use of the Sacrament. The Sacrament itself was the *opus operatum*, and the use and performing of the Sacrament was the *opus operans* (*In Sent.*, d. 1, q. 1, a. 5, *Responsio ad primam quaestionem*). Even Gabriel Biel (1495 d.) applied the term *opus operatum* to the Sacrament itself, and the term *operans* to the use of the Sacrament on the part both of the minister and the recipient (see op. cit., in Bk. 4 of the Sentences, dist. 1, q. 4).

Is this not precisely the same distinction that Luther himself is making, in more rhetorical language, in the Catechism, when he argues for the validity of Infant Baptism and the effect of the real presence, irrespective of the minister's worth or the recipient's qualifications? Apparently, he is not unaware of this meaning in the use of the Scholastic terminology, for, in the continuation of the passage, which we have just quoted above, he writes: 'Es [the Sacrament of the Lord's Supper] wirckt nichts uberall, wen es alleyn opus operatum ist, dan schaden, es muß opus operantis werden. Gleych wie brott und weyn wirckt nichts dan schaden, tzo man seyn nit braucht, sie gefallen gott an yhn selb, wie hoch si mugen. Also ist's nit gnug, daß das sacrament gemacht werde (das ist opus operatum), es muß auch praucht werden ym glauben (das ist opus operantis) (*W.A.* ii. 751–2).

Luther, however, adds that we should take heed and beware of such 'dangerous glosses' lest our minds be turned away from the power of the Sacrament and our faith perish: 'Und ist zubesorgen, das mit solchen ferlichen glossen des sacraments crafft und tugent von unss gewand werden, un der glaub gantz unter gehe durch falsche sycherheit des gemachten sacramentis' (*W.A.* ii. 751–2). Where Luther deviates seriously from the Catholic tradition is on the matter of the Mass as a Sacrifice.

INDEX

All Luther's important published works mentioned are listed under the heading
Luther's Writings